THE FRONTIER OF BRIEF PSYCHOTHERAPY

An Example of the Convergence of Research and Clinical Practice

David H. Malan
Tavistock Clinic

Overwhelming evidence in support of the extensive practice of brief psychotherapy is presented in this definitive study of the controversial form of treatment and its practical applications. Clinical in orientation, this work contains detailed case studies of eighteen patients treated with brief psychotherapy.

The Frontier of Brief Psychotherapy refutes the outdated practice of confining the use of brief psychotherapy to crisis situations using superficial techniques, and the belief that its results can only be very limited. This volume describes in detail principles of brief psychotherapy; selection of candidates for brief psychotherapy; therapeutic techniques; and psychodynamic assessment of outcome.

ALTERNATIVES TO MENTAL HOSPITAL TREATMENT

ALTERNATIVES TO
MENTAL HOSPITAL
TREATMENT

Edited by
Leonard I. Stein
University of Wisconsin Medical School
Madison, Wisconsin

and

Mary Ann Test
Mendota Mental Health Institute
Madison, Wisconsin

PLENUM PRESS • NEW YORK AND LONDON

Library of Congress Cataloging in Publication Data

Conference on Alternatives to Mental Hospital Treatment, Madison, Wis., 1975.
    Alternatives to mental hospital treatment.

    Includes index.
    1. Mentally ill—Rehabilitation—Congresses. 2. Community mental health services—Congresses. I. Stein, Leonard I. II. Test, Mary Ann. III. Title. [DNLM: 1. Community mental health services—Congresses. WM30 C741a 1975]
RC439.5.C66 1975   362.2'2   77-17576
ISBN 0-306-31120-8

Proceedings of a Conference on Alternatives to Mental Hospital
Treatment held in Madison, Wisconsin, October, 1975

© 1978 Plenum Press, New York
A Division of Plenum Publishing Corporation
227 West 17th Street, New York, N.Y. 10011

Preface

    This book addresses itself to the treatment of the patient with chronically disabling psychiatric illness, a condition that, until recently, has been "treated" by hospitalization lasting years and often a lifetime. In the past two decades, however, the trend has been to shorten markedly hospital stay and to continue treatment in the community through aftercare. During these same two decades the environments within hospitals have changed dramatically. Relative to 20 years ago, the psychiatric wards in public hospitals are clean and often aesthetically pleasing. Minimum standards have been explicated for the physical plant and the professional staff. And indeed, the acute manifestations of psychosis are rapidly and effectively treated. Then why alternatives? First, let us clarify by being more specific regarding the alternative. Although hospital stays have been shortened, the hospital still remains the <u>primary locus</u> for the treatment of the chronically disabled psychiatric patient. It is precisely this function of the hospital which must be eliminated and in its place viable alternatives developed.

    The treatment of chronic illness, whether it be arthritis, diabetes, or schizophrenia, focuses upon helping patients normalize their lives to the greatest degree possible and to raise optimally their level of functioning. The hospital is useful in treating severe exacerbations of the above illnesses but is unable to play a meaningful role in keeping the patient <u>functioning</u> and stable outside of the hospital after the acute episode is over. Thus, for instance, the primary management of arthritis and diabetes takes place in the community through careful and continuous monitoring and treatment. Unfortunately, for the psychiatric patient, the development of models for community treatment lag far behind the advances made in improving psychiatric hospitals. Community treatment of the chronic psychiatric patient is in its infancy in explicating conceptual models and developing and evaluating treatment programs based on those models. The field has not progressed anywhere near the point where standards can even be thought about. What does exist is meager - e.g., isolated programs, usually with insufficient staff and resources to handle a large patient population. In other words, what exists is a fragmented nonsystem which by default has forced the psychiatric hospital into being the primary locus of care for the chronically disabled psychiatric patient - a role it is unable to fulfill. In order to help the chronically disabled psychiatric patient stabilize his illness and live as normal a life as possible, the primary locus of care must be shifted from the hospital to the community. This book is dedicated to advancing the development of that alternative.

Leonard I. Stein, M.D.
Mary Ann Test, Ph.D.

Contents

III. Examples of Systems of Alternatives to Mental Hospital Treatment

IV. The British Experience

V. Planning and Implementing Models for Change

Part I

THE RATIONALE FOR CREATING

ALTERNATIVES TO MENTAL

HOSPITAL TREATMENT

THE CLINICAL RATIONALE FOR COMMUNITY TREATMENT:

A REVIEW OF THE LITERATURE

Mary Ann Test* and Leonard I. Stein**

*Mendota Mental Health Institute, Madison, Wisconsin

**University of Wisconsin, Madison, Wisconsin

There are a number of factors which have influenced the movement to treat the chronically disabled psychiatric patient in the
community rather than in the hospital. These include legal issues
primarily revolving around protection of civil rights, economic
motives directed towards reducing or shifting costs, mental health
principles intrinsic to the community psychiatry movement, and
clinical evidence supported by research and observation. This
chapter is devoted to reviewing the latter influence on the community treatment of the chronically disabled psychiatric patient.
It will present both the evidence relating to the debilitating
effects of long-term institutional treatment as well as those
attempts to remedy this problem. The latter include efforts to
improve inhospital treatment, attempts at shortening hospital stay,
and finally, the movement toward community treatment of the chronically disabled patient and its early results.

DEBILITATING EFFECTS OF INSTITUTIONS

Much disenchantment with mental institutions has occurred
since World War II following extensive documentation (both descriptive and empirical) of the possible debilitating effects of institutions. Problems in this area appear to be of two kinds:
(1) long stay in an institution appears to lead to development of
an "institutional syndrome" whereby the patient acquires characteristics markedly unadaptive for future community living; (2) mere
admission to a mental institution appears to stigmatize the patient
in such a fashion that his own and the attitudes of others about
him change; this alteration in attitude affects not only his opportunity for successful community adjustment, but his chances for a

3

disposition other than rehospitalization upon the recurrence of serious problems.

The "institutional syndrome" has been adeptly described by Barton (1966), Goffman (1961), Gruenberg (1967), Hansell and Benson (1971), and others and may be characterized by apathy, lack of initiative, loss of interest, apparent inability to plan for the future, and lack of individuality. It is generally theorized that this pattern of behavior develops as an interaction between a pre-morbid inadequate lifestyle, the disease process, and factors operating within an institution that both limit an individual's contact with the outside world and take over life management functions to the extent that an individual's own personality functions atrophy. Additionally, observation has led to the theory that patients soon become active participants in this process, and that they develop skillful techniques for maintaining their dependent, "non-responsible," patient status (Ludwig and Farrelly, 1966; Ludwig and Farrelly, 1967; Towbin, 1969).

Empirical evidence for the existence of an institutional syndrome related to long stay in institutions comes from a number of sources. Wing (1962), for instance, surveyed the attitudes and behaviors of male schizophrenics with over two years stay in a hospital and found the longer the stay, the more unfavorable the patient's attitude towards discharge. Honigfeld and Gillis (1967), meanwhile, documented the hypothesis that time in the hospital is linearly related to the development of a "social breakdown syndrome" (see Gruenberg, 1967) even when other variables are partialed out of the relationship. Paul (1969) in a comprehensive review of research on the chronic patient, cites a number of studies showing that the longer a person remains in the hospital, the poorer his chances of release. He points to other research indicating that this finding is a result of an interaction between patient and environmental variables.

The fact that not only long term hospitalization, but any psychiatric hospitalization, may have adverse effects has been made clear by Langsley and Kaplan (1968) in a survey of studies demonstrating the effects of hospitalization and the label "mentally ill" on the attitudes and expectancies of the patient himself and on the reactions of family and community members to him. Additionally, Mendel and Rapport (1969), in a study investigating determinants of the decision for psychiatric hospitalization, document the effects of previous hospitalization on clinicians' attitudes about an individual. These researchers found that a history of previous hospitalization heavily influenced the decision to hospitalize, independent of the severity of the individual's current illness. Mendel and Rapport state: "This observation is further evidence for the conclusion that to hospitalize a patient is a major decision which forever after changes the attitude of both the patient and those who care for them." (page 327).

RESULTS OF IN-HOSPITAL ATTEMPTS TO AMELIORATE
THE DEBILITATING EFFECTS OF INSTITUTIONS

In the past two decades, response to the above-described problems created by long stay in institutions has been intense and has proceeded in several directions. Among these have been attempts at making treatment in hospitals more humane and/or more intense and effective.

Research evaluating the effect of more humane, pleasant hospital environments has revealed that while such treatment does appear to correlate positively with in-hospital adjustment, it is unrelated to release rates or post-hospital adjustment. Wing and Brown (1961), for instance, surveyed three mental hospitals in Britian which differed from one another in the degree of social and humane treatment offered. Measures of patients' symptomatology led to the conclusion that there was less clinical disturbance in the hospitals with more advanced social treatment. Linn (1970) extended this area of research, however, by surveying institutions along many hospital and treatment variables and then asking which variables correlated favorably with treatment outcome (defined here as rapid release). He found that the cluster of variables related to humane treatment (e.g., hospital atmosphere, good facilities, humanistic policies toward patients) was unrelated to release rates.

Meanwhile, efforts at making in-hospital treatment more intensive and effective have led to the design of ingenious and skillful programs ranging from highly psychodynamic approaches to those stressing the teaching of coping skills for community living. Research evaluating the outcome of these efforts, however, reveals disappointing results. After surveying the literature in this area, Paul (1969) concluded that while intensive treatment programs are frequently effective in improving within-hospital adjustment and increasing and accelerating release rates, it appears that within-hospital adjustment is only slightly related to post-hospital adjustment and is essentially uncorrelated with length of community stay. Sanders, et al., (1967) and Fairweather (1964) present two of the better studies demonstrating this point.

Sanders et al., compared three milieu programs, varying in the degree of social interaction required, with a control treatment consisting of the usual hospital program. The subjects in the experimental groups evidenced greater in-hospital improvement in socialization than did the controls. In addition, the discharge rate was highest for that experimental group demanding the most social interaction (78% vs. 58% in the control group). However, when rehospitalizations during the study and follow-up periods were taken into account, the net relapse rates over the four year period varied from 27% to 38% and did not differ significantly between groups. Fairweather (1964), meanwhile, combined a milieu and learning theory approach in an experimental program focused on resocialization and instrumental role performance. Problem-solving patient groups were established, and a step system in which responsibilities, passes and funds were contingent upon appropriate behavior was implemented. A traditional ward program served as a control. The results indicated that significant differences were obtained in favor of improved within-hospital performance for the experimental program, and that the experimental program resulted in earlier release rates. Again, however, by the time of a six month post release follow-up, rehospitalizations were such to indicate that no differences in net relapses existed between the experimental and control groups.

Although much more could be said in regards to in-hospital programs (for an excellent and more extensive review, see Anthony et al, 1972), even after this brief review it can be concluded that thus far they have failed to provide effective treatment for a substantial segment of the severely disturbed population. Much of the remainder of this literature review will deal with attempts at finding effective treatment for the mental hospital patient that have moved away from the hospital and toward the community as the site of treatment.

RESULTS OF ATTEMPTS AT SHORTENING HOSPITAL STAY

One attempt at eliminating the debilitating effects of institutions and of providing more effective treatment of the severely disturbed while moving away from hospitals and toward the community is a recent emphasis on short term hospitalization. Research comparing the effectiveness of short term vs. longer term hospital treatment varies considerably in the quality of control groups used, but results are in a consistent direction and will be summarized following brief discussion of several of the studies.

Caffey et al. (1968) randomly assigned patients from a Veterans Administration Hospital population of newly admitted male schizophrenics to three treatment conditions. Condition A involved "normal hospital care" with usual aftercare; condition B consisted of brief intensive care with special aftercare; and condition C was normal hospital care with special aftercare. The mean times spent in the hospital by patients in these three groups were 80, 29 and 86 days, respectively. Follow-up of patients for a period of one year after discharge indicated remission rates of 36%, 32%, and

24%, differences not statistically significant. Differences between groups on time out of the hospital before readmission also were not statistically significant. Caffey et al. conclude from these findings that short term treatment is efficacious relative to long term treatment because, while readmission rates remain similar, total time in the community is longer for Group B patients because of the brevity of their initial treatment.

Gove and Lubach (1969) admitted all patients from one geographic area serviced by Northern State Hospital of Washington to an experimental program involving three days of intensive treatment aimed at alleviating severe anxiety and disorganization, followed by several weeks in a "readjustment area" designed to prepare the patient for resumption of responsible functioning in the community. Patients from the same geographic area who had been admitted to the hospital the previous year served as controls. The length of in-patient hospitalization for the C Group was 2 1/2 times longer than that of the E Group (80 vs. 33 days). Patients from both groups were followed for a year after their entrance date to the hospital. Results indicated that there was no significant difference in re-admission rates between C and E Groups (22% vs. 25% respectively), even though the E patients had left the hospital, on the average, 47.1 days earlier and accordingly had a greater opportunity to be rehospitalized. Moreover, when rehospitalization did occur, its duration was significantly longer for the C patients than the E patients. While these results again point favorably toward the merit of short vs. longer stay hospitalization, it should be pointed out that the C Group proceeded the E Group in time and hence differences between groups might be accounted for by any of the number of other variables (subject, staff, or treatment) differing from one year to the next.

Weisman et al. (1969), in the emergency treatment unit (ETU) at the Connecticut Mental Health Center, experimented with a model of three day hospitalization plus thirty days of outpatient treatment, and compared outcome of this program with that of other private or university-affiliated hospitals using longer-term care to treat similar patient populations. Although such a control is far from adequate, results at a one year follow-up date revealed that of the patients treated on ETU, 63% had not been rehospitalized or transferred after their three day treatment, and that overall re-hospitalization rates were not strikingly different from the control hospitals examined. In reports of programs lacking entirely in control procedures, Mendel (1968) and Rhine and Mayerson (1971) also comment favorably on the feasibility and merits of their attempts at short-term hospitalization. Additionally, Mendel (1966), in a retrospective cross sectional study of patients discharged from Los Angeles County Hospital after spending varying periods of time there, reports that (a) the rate of return of patients with only a short term stay is no higher than that of longer term stay; and (b) the longer the patient remained in the hospital during his index hospitalization, the longer he tended to stay in if he required rehospitalization.

In contrast to the above studies, which looked primarily at readmission rates, Glick et al (1976a, 1976b) utilized a wide variety of outcome measures in their study of short vs. long-term hospitalization. In addition to readmission data they compared symptomatology, family functioning, work functioning and involvement with leisure time and social activities. The study was carefully performed utilizing research diagnostic criteria and random assignment. Short stay was defined as 21 to 28 days and long stay 90 to 120 days. The inpatient unit utilized was the Clinical Research Ward of the Langley Porter Institute. They found that although there were no statistically significant differences between groups in readmission or level of community adjustment, the schizophrenic sub-sample of subjects did show results favoring long-term hospitalization on the Health Sickness Rating Scale and on the overall severity item of the Psychiatric Evaluation Form. Unfortunately, however, the two groups had an imbalance in socio-economic status and level of education favoring the long hospitalization group. Long hospitalization schizophrenics, in addition, obtained significantly more aftercare than subjects in the short hospitalization group. The authors caution that these confounding factors may be responsible for the differences found. No significant differences between groups were found in the non-schizophrenic sub-sample.

The most recent study comparing short versus long hospitalization was carried out by Herz et al. (1977). They report the results of a two-year follow-up controlled study of 175 newly admitted inpatients who had lived with their families prior to admission. Three conditions were compared, brief hospitalization (average of 11 days) with and without transitional day care, and standard hospitalization (average of 60 days); all patients were offered outpatient aftercare. As in every study of this kind they found no significant differences between groups in readmission rates. In contrast to Glick's study, however, Herz found that whatever differences did occur between groups in levels of psychopathology and in adequacy of role functioning favored the brief hospitalization group. In addition they found that the use of day care reduced the number of inpatient days.

In a summary of results of the research cited above, the most consistently found outcome of short term vs. longer term hospitalization is that readmission rates for the former were no higher than those of the latter. This finding not only casts serious doubt on the notion that long term hospitalization is necessary for effective treatment of the severely disturbed, but points to an advantage of short term hospitalization in that the patients spend more total time out of the institution. That short term treatment is not the panacea for the severely disturbed, however, is evident from the finding that readmission rates, while no higher than those of long term treatment, are still high. Specifically, a national rate has been cited as between 35 and 38% (Silverstein, 1968), and although there has been a decrease every year since 1955 in the actual number of patients in public mental hospitals, there has been a steady increase in the number of readmissions (Kanno and Glasscote, 1966). Indeed, the failure of short term hospitalization to resolve the readmission problem while placing much emphasis on rapid discharge has led this orientation often to be called the "revolving door approach."

STUDIES ATTEMPTING TO TREAT WITHOUT USING THE HOSPITAL

An extreme effort at avoiding the debilitating effects of hospitalization by moving to the community as the site of treatment has been the attempt of some to use no hospitalization for even the severely disturbed. A pioneer, though unresearched, effort in this area was by Greenblatt, et al., (1963), who treated patients on the waiting list to the Massachusetts Mental Health Center outside of the hospital and found that a substantial number of these individuals required no hospitalization. Recently, three well designed studies by other researchers have been carried out comparing the effectiveness of no hospitalization plus "home treatment" with inpatient treatment, using populations of patients who have traditionally been treated within institutions. These studies are reviewed below.

Pasamanick, Scarpitti, and Dinitz (1967) compared home treatment vs. hospital treatment of newly admitted schizophrenics to Louisville State Hospital. Patients for the study were non-suicidal or homicidal, and had a family or relative willing to provide supervision at home. Individuals meeting these criteria were randomly assigned to one of three groups: home on drugs (N=57), home on placebo (N=41), or hospital care (control group; N=54). Home treatment consisted of visits to the patient and family by a public health nurse, who left off medication or placebo and discussed any problems encountered by the family unit. All patients were followed for a period of time ranging from well over six months at the least to a maximum of 30 months, with home care patients receiving decreasing amounts of input during this period. The major findings of interest here involve comparison of the home care drug patients with the hospital controls. Concerning readmission rates, 46% of the controls were rehospitalized after discharge during the study period, relative to only 23% of the home care patients (whose hospitalization after failure to remain

in the community in fact represented their initial hospitalization
during the study period). Regarding psychiatric functioning
(measured primarily by a standard rating scale), the mental status
of patients in both groups improved significantly, though there was
no difference in the amount of improvement between the two groups.
The authors add that despite much initial improvement in symptomatology and role functioning for patients in both groups, the outcome level of adjustment for many of the patients remained quite
low. Additionally, in a five year follow-up study after treatment
ceased (Davis et al, 1974), it was found that the differences between home treatment and hospital treatment disappeared over time
with many patients from both groups requiring hospitalization.
The overall results of this study allow the conclusion that it is
possible to treat severely disturbed patients without hospitalization, but suggest that assertive support in the community may need
to be on-going rather than time-limited in order to maintain the
gains of home treatment.

A second well controlled study of no hospitalization was performed by Langsley and others (see Langsley and Kaplan, 1968;
Langsley et al., 1969; Langsley et al., 1971) at the Colorado
Psychopathic Hospital (CPH). The population of patients in this
study appeared somewhat healthier than in the Pasamanick research,
and the treatment approach followed a crisis intervention model.
Patients to CPH who met criteria designating them as requiring
immediate hospitalization and who lived in a family within an
hour's travel from CPH were randomly assigned to either the experimental (E) Group (Family Crisis Therapy) or the control (C) Group
(admission to CPH, a university-affiliated psychiatric hospital).
The goals of Family Crisis Therapy were to reintegrate the patient
and to teach the family ways of handling crises without hospitalization. Treatment consisted of a mean number of 4.2 office visits,
1.3 home visits, 5.4 phone calls, and 1.2 collateral contacts with
social agencies. The mean time from "admission" to termination of
this home treatment was 24.2 days. The C group, meanwhile, spent
an average of 28.6 days in the hospital receiving whatever treatment was deemed appropriate. Results of the study revealed that:
(a) no one assigned to the E condition required hospitalization
during the treatment period (N=150); (b) during a six month follow-
up period after discharge, a significantly smaller proportion of
the E than C group were readmitted (13% vs. 29%); (c) those E
patients that were readmitted spent a significantly shorter time in
the hospital than readmitted C group patients; (d) both groups
showed significant improvement in measures of recompensation and
readjustment at the end of treatment, although differences in the
amount of improvement between groups did not reach significance;
(e) at a follow-up point 18 months after discharge differences between the proportion of patients readmitted in each group was reduced, but remained in favor of the FCT group; (f) cost of the FCT
condition was estimated to be 1/6 that of hospital treatment.

Another controlled investigation of no hospitalization was carried out at the Ft. Logan Mental Health Center in Denver in an effort to determine whether endurance of effect of family unit treatment in the community was greater than that of identified patient treatment in the hospital (Rittenhouse, 1970). The population for the study consisted of all individuals from a given geographic area who were accepted for inpatient admission to Ft. Logan and who had a family which agreed to become involved in family unit treatment. Patients meeting these criteria were randomly assigned to the experimental (E) or control (C) group. Control patients were admitted to Ft. Logan and received in-hospital treatment involving a therapeutic community orientation. Experimental Ss remained in the home and staff went to that site and implemented family unit therapy along a model outlined by Satir (1964). All patients were followed after discharge at points of 3 months, 6 months, and 12 months. Results during the follow-up period indicated that symptomatology of patients in both groups increased with time after discharge, but for the most part, differences between home treatment and hospital groups were not significant. Readmission rates for the E group were significantly lower at the three month follow-up point, however, and patients in this group reported functioning significantly better in all tested aspects of the work area than did controls. Readmission rates at the six month and 12 month follow-up points did not differ significantly, but remained in a direction favorable to the home treatment group. Rittenhouse accounts for the success of the home treatment group by the explanation that these individuals have learned to look for help in their immediate environments of family and work instead of to the hospital.

A summary of the above research reveals no hospitalization plus home treatment to be an encouraging trend in the treatment of the severely disturbed. The following points may be made in its favor: (a) it is clearly possible to treat severely disturbed individuals without hospitalization; (b) decrease in symptomatology is as great with this modality of treatment as with in-hospital treatment, and readmission rates are lower; (c) total time in institutions is a great deal less, both because of the absence of the initial admission and because time in the hospital upon readmission, if it occurs, is briefer; (d) cost of home treatment is estimated to be less than cost of hospital treatment. The following limitations and questions remain, however: (a) for at least a segment of the population treated, the readmission problem remains a significant factor, particularly over time; (b) level of adjustment for a number of patients appears to remain fairly low; (c) the above studies are limited to those patients with families and utilized some kind of family intervention approach. Hence the question remains open of whether or not - and how - patients without a family living situation would be treated in the community.

STUDIES UTILIZING THE COMMUNITY FOR TREATMENT

OF THE SEVERELY DISTURBED THROUGH "TRAINING IN LIVING"

The above data on limited or no hospitalization is encouraging in that such treatment approaches appear to be as effective as, and often more effective than, longer term in-hospital treatment, and has also been found to cost less. Yet it is obvious that for some of the population - those who continue to show high readmission rates - merely eliminating the negative effects of institutions, and/or aiding the individual or family in resolving immediate crises, is not enough. Something else is needed. It is hypothe- sized by the current writers that for this population, the "some- thing else" is training in community living. Indeed, others have also pointed out that a large percentage of the mental population display an "inadequacy syndrome" and a deficit in basic living skills (e.g., Cumming, 1963; Glasscote et al., 1971; Huessy, 1969; Margolin, 1968); furthermore, it has been both observed (e.g., Glasscote, et al., 1971) and empirically documented (Mendel and Rapport, 1969; Paul, 1969) that many patients become and remain hospitalized more as a result of their inadequate social and voca- tional capabilities than because of illness itself. The high re- admission rate of numerous patients may be explained by the fact that this "inadequacy syndrome" is rarely sufficiently treated. As Cumming, (1963) states, "...the patient with an inadequately organized ego recovers from his acute disorganized state no more able to deal with the requirements of a normal environment than he was before his acute illness." Thus it appears that a treatment effort focused on increasing socialization and strengthening ego functioning necessary for daily living is an appropriate direction to follow in attempting both to keep patients out of institutions and to insure achievement of a maximal quality of life in the community.

While the notion and implementation of a treatment philosophy based on education and socialization is far from new (see for example, an excellent historical review by Rausch and Rausch, 1968), what is becoming most apparent recently is the fact that the hospi- tal is particularly unsuited to provide this "training in living" function. Empirical evidence has already been cited which demon- strates the failure of in-hospital programs focusing on the teach- ing of coping skills to have relevance for future community adjust- ment. A series of articles has recently attempted to explain this result by pointing out specific institutional forces that make it difficult, if not impossible, to simulate the "real world" within a hospital setting (see, for instance, Mendel, 1968; Rausch and Rausch, 1968). Therefore, there appears to be a current turning away from the hospital in the direction of the community itself as the most appropriate site in which training in living can effec- tively take place. Day hospitals, halfway houses, and psychosocial

rehabilitation programs are all part of this movement, and results
of these efforts will be reviewed briefly below. More in depth
attention will then be paid to two programs (those of Fairweather
and Marx, Test and Stein) that have carried this trend to a more
extreme degree.

Day Hospital Treatment

Literature reviews of the day hospital movement (e.g.,
Glasscote et al., 1969) revealed that many day centers have a
rehabilitation emphasis, that they are frequently situated apart
from major institutional structures, and that by definition, they
allow the patient to be in his "natural" living setting a good part
of the waking hours. Day centers have been used both as transitional aides to the community and as an alternative to 24 hour care.
Although descriptive discussions regarding day hospital treatment
are enthusiastic, controlled studies comparing the effectiveness
of day vs. inpatient treatment are scarce. In one such study, however, Herz et al., 1971 reported that: (a) time to discharge was
significantly less for patients randomly assigned to a day vs. in-
hospital treatment approach; (b) day patients had a lower readmission rate than inpatients; and (c) that day hospital patients scored
lower on several measures of symptomatology. Along with such favorable results, however, discussions of day hospital treatment point
to several limitations: (a) studies performed thus far have excluded
treatment of a large segment of the hospital population in day
centers, usually because a number of patients are regarded as "too
severely disturbed" to remain out of the hospital for part of the
day or to commute to and from the day center (e.g., Astrachan, et
al., 1970; Glasscote, et al., 1969; Herz, et al., 1971); (b) readmission rates following day hospital treatment remain substantial,
perhaps largely due to an extremely high drop-out rate that occurs
in this kind of treatment (Glasscote et al., 1969).

Halfway Houses

Halfway houses are another treatment modality for the severely
disturbed utilizing a major resocialization emphasis. Such facilities have most often served as transitional living situations
teaching "training in living" for patients going from hospital to
community. The concept of a "halfway-in house" whereby this facility is used as an alternative to institutional care, however, has
not only been suggested (Silverstein, 1968) but occasionally implemented (Glasscote et al., 1971).

Controlled research on Halfway House programs is almost entirely lacking (see Rog and Rausch, 1975), but descriptive reports
(e.g., Landy and Greenblatt, 1965; Rausch and Rausch, 1968) have

much to say in favor of these facilities. A major problem, however, is again a high hospital readmission rate, in part based on the fact that many patients display severe symptomatology when pushed to "move on" to a more independent life after halfway house living. Several investigators have set up "satellite housing programs" (semi-sheltered, terminal living situations) to handle this problem (e.g., Huessy, 1969; Richmond, 1970).

Community Psychosocial Rehabilitation Centers

Recently a number of "psychosocial rehabilitation centers" have been developed in the community in response to concern about the quality of total life and the prevention of rehospitalization of the ever increasing number of marginally adjusted individuals now being discharged from public mental institutions (see Glasscote et al., 1971). Such facilities emphasize living, social and/or vocational adjustment. These centers serve primarily as referral agencies for patients recently discharged from hospitals, and the treatment model is an extremely educational one. Specifically, there is a de-emphasis on symptomatology while attempts are made to work with the healthy portions of the ego. "Thus, a concern is to teach the clients in a variety of ways, such things as how to groom themselves appropriately, how to ride on buses, how to get to events on time, how to shop for food, how to plan and cook a meal, how to behave in a work setting" (Glasscote et al., 1971, p.18). Such facilities are often centralized in one location, thus requiring patients to come there, though various aspects of the program may be quite decentralized.

Research evaluations of these psychosocial rehabilitation centers have been few. Outcome reported, however, appears extremely encouraging for those patients who attend, with hospital readmission rates dropping markedly even for individuals revealing severe inadequacy syndromes (e.g., Beard et al., 1963). A major limitation of these facilities, however, is an extremely high "no show" and "drop out" rate. The proportion of patients referred to such centers who fail to keep even their first appointment is reported to range from 35% to 40%, while those who drop out of the program unilaterally (i.e., before staff agrees they have reached maximum benefit) make up another major segment of the total population referred.

Community Treatment of the Chronic Patient

Limitations of the preceding work suggests that treatment in the community would be most effective if it took place exactly where the patient would ultimately be living (hence, no generalization of learning would be needed, and "drop out" would be more difficult), and that it would be a major part of the treatment program rather than an optional adjunct. Fairweather et al. (1969) and Marx, Test and Stein (1973) have made the most noteworthy attempts in this direction prior to the research presented in the current volume.

The purpose of the Fairweather et al. (1969) study was to compare the effectiveness of a new post hospital community program (a semi-sheltered work-living group) with traditional community programs available. The population for this study were patients who had participated in an intensive in-hospital program (see Fairweather, 1964) and had reached a point where discharge plans were being formulated. The population consisted only of individuals who volunteered to participate in the innovative "lodge" program. Matched pairs of these individuals were placed in the E (lodge) or C (traditional aftercare) group, and shortly thereafter the E group was moved out of the hospital into a group living situation (the "lodge") where a janitorial service was organized. The lodge program, over the course of the project, moved from a stage of high staff supervision and consultation to near autonomy. The C patients, meanwhile, participated in traditional community mental health aftercare programs. Subjects were added to both groups over a three year period, and outcome measures were taken on every patient at six month intervals after entrance into the program.

Results of the Fairweather study indicated that: (a) for every follow-up period, the number of days an ex-patient remained in the community was significantly greater for E than C patients; (b) full time employment was significantly greater for the E than C patients, although employment status of E patients who moved away from the lodge was no better than that of the C group patients; (c) there were few differences between E and C group on other adjustment variables, such as satisfaction with community living, association with friends, verbal communication, symptomatic behavior, drinking behavior, activity level, social responsibilities, or leisure activity; (d) cost of the lodge program during times of maximum staff supervision was about 1/2 as expensive as the state hospital program, and much less during the period when the patient group was fairly autonomous. In summary of these results, Fairweather et al., conclude that the major effect of the lodge situation was to support the Ss stay and productivity in the community, without grossly effecting their individual psychosocial adjustment.

Rather than using community treatment as an aftercare procedure, Marx, Test and Stein (1973) decided to explore its effectiveness as a major treatment modality for patients not yet ready to leave the hospital. Patients who had been in a state hospital from three to 18 months during their current admission and who were given a prognosis by present ward staff of "not currently capable of sustained community living" were randomly assigned to the experimental or one of two control groups. Control patients either remained on their referring wards (Other Unit Controls) or were moved to the Research Unit (Research Unit Controls) where they received progressive in-hospital treatment for five more months, after which they were discharged. Experimental patients were moved to the research ward for a very short period (maximum of eight days.) during which baseline measures were taken. After that they were moved into the community, regardless of symptomatology, and located in a variety of independent living situations. Treatment consisted of staff going out to the community to provide patients with intensive support and the in vivo teaching of coping skills. Staff spent much time "by patients' sides" day and evening helping them learn activities of daily living, employment, and leisure time skills in patients' own homes and neighborhoods. This treatment lasted for five months, after which the experimental patients were linked with existing community aftercare services and followed by research evaluation staff for two years.

Results of the Marx et al. study spoke extremely favorably toward the community treatment approach. Evaluations, performed by an independent research team, revealed that it was feasible to treat this unselected and highly symptomatic group of patients virtually entirely in the community. During the five month treatment period, only one of the 21 experimental patients required hospitalization, and that was only for a day. Furthermore, following treatment these patients had attained significantly more autonomous living and employment situations than controls. Like other studies (e.g., Davis et al., 1974) with a post-treatment follow-up period, the differences between experimental and control groups disappeared over time. During the period in which treatment was in effect, however, the Marx et al. study results pointed to a promising new alternative to institutional treatment.

SUMMARY

The following points have been made clear in the literature review:

1.   Long-term hospitalization has a debilitating effect on many patients, resulting in chronic institutionalization for some.

2.   Attempts to make in-hospital treatment effective have resulted in improved "within hospital" adjustment, but have failed with many patients to make an impact on future community tenure and adjustment.

3.   Efforts to move away from the hsopital and toward the community in the treatment of the severely disturbed appear

advantageous relative to in-hospital treatment, but many of the approaches noted above have serious limitations:

      a.   Shortening hospital stay appears to hold merits over long-term treatment, but has failed to resolve the readmission problem and thus has resulted in the "revolving door syndrome" for a number of patients.

      b.   No hospitalization experiments have demonstrated that severely ill patients can be maintained in the community, but the studies cited here have involved only patients living with families. Additionally, even with this population, readmission rates over time remain substantial, and quality of life while out of the hospital is questionable.

      c.   Programs with a rehabilitation or "training in living" focus reveal encouraging directions for solving the problem of not only discharging but maintaining the previous "treatment failures" in the community. Most attempts in this direction also have limitations, however:

      (1) Often they are not implemeted until severe chronicity has already developed, thus necessitating limited treatment goals such as the placing of patients in semi-sheltered settings;

      (2) Many programs thus far have used only selected patients (e.g., volunteers or those who are relatively unsymptomatic), thus leaving open the question of whether or not more seriously symptomatic individuals can be treated in the community;

      (3) Programs treating patients in the community have experienced extremely high "drop-out" rates. Thus, even if the treatment is effective, it does not reach a significant segment of the population for whom it is intended.

Recently there have been innovative attempts to solve some of the above-mentioned problems. These programs include the use of a community-based team (Stein and Test), a residential treatment center (Mosher and Menn), "enablers" to help patients live in apartment settings (Weinman and Kleiner), and "crisis homes" (Polack). They were all well researced and descriptions of the programs and their evaluations appear as chapters in the next section of this volume.

REFERENCES

Anthony, W.A., Buell, G.J., Sharratt, S., & Althoff, M.E., Efficacy
    of psychiatric rehabilitation. Psych. Bull., 1972, 78, 447-456.

Astrachan, B.M., Flynn, H.R., Geller, J.D., & Harvey, H.M. Systems
    approach to day hopitalization. Arch. Gen. Psychiat., 1970, 22,
    550-559.

Barton, R. Institutional neurosis. Bristol: John Wright and Sons,
    Ltd., 1966.

Beard, J.H., Pitt, R.B., Fisher, S.H., & Goertzel, V. Evaluating
    the effectiveness of a psychiatric rehabilitation program. Amer.
    J. Orthopsychiatry, 33, 701, 1962.

Caffey, E.M., Jones, R.D., Diamond, L.S., Burton, E., & Bowen, W.T.
    Brief hospital treatment of schizophrenia--Early results of a
    multiple hospital study. Hosp. & Com. Psychiat., Sept., 1968,
    282-287.

Cumming, J. Inadequacy syndrome. Psychiat. Quart., 1963, 37,
    723-733.

Davis, A.E., Dinitz, S., Pasamanick, B. Schizophrenics in the new
    custodial community. Ohio: Ohio State University Press, 1974.

Fairweather, G.W., (Ed.) Social psychology in treating mental ill-
    ness. New York: Wiley & Sons, Inc., 1964.

Fairweather, G.W., Sanders, D.H., Maynard, H., & Cressler, D.L.
    Community life for the mentally ill. Chicago: Aldine Publishing
    Co., 1969.

Glasscote, R.M., Cumming, E., Rutman, I.P., Sussex, J.N., &
    Glassman, S.M. Rehabilitating the mentally ill in the community.
    Washington, D.C.: Joint Info. Serv. of APA and Nat'l Assoc. for
    Mental Health, 1971.

Glasscote, R.M., Kraft, A.M., Glassman, S.M., & Jepson, W.W. Partial
    hospitalization for the mentally ill. Washington, D.C.: Joint
    Info. Serv. of APA and Nat'l Assoc. for Mental Health, 1969.

Glick, I.D., Hargreaves, W.A., Drues, J., & Schourstack, J.A.
    Short versus long hospitalization: A prospective controlled study.
    IV. One-year follow-up results for schizophrenic patients.
    American Journal of Psychiatry, 1976a, 133, 509-514.

Glick, I.D., Hargreaves, W.A., Drues, J., & Schourstack, J.A. Short versus long hospitalization: A prospective controlled study. V. One-year follow-up results for non-schizophrenic patients. American Journal of Psychiatry, 1976b, 133, 515-517.

Goffman, E. Asylums. Garden City, N.Y.: Doubleday and Co., Inc., 1961.

Grad, J., & Lubach, J.E., An intensive treatment program for psychiatric inpatients: A description and evaluation. J. Health and Soc. Behav., 1969, 10, 225-236.

Greenblatt, M., Moore, R.F., Albert, R.S., & Solomon, M.H. The prevention of hospitalization. New York: Grune and Stratton, 1963.

Gruenberg, E. The social breakdown syndrome--some origins. Amer. J. Psychiat., 1967, 123, 1481-1489.

Hansell, N., & Benson, M.L. Interrupting long-term patienthood: A cohort study. Arch. Gen. Psychiat., 1971, 24, 238-243.

Herz, M.I., Endicott, J., Spitzer, R.L., & Mesnikoff, A. Day versus inpatient hospitalization--a controlled study. Amer. J. Psychiat., 1971, 127, 1371-1382.

Herz, M.I., et al. Brief hospitalization: A two-year follow-up. American Journal of Psychiatry, 1977, 134, 502-507.

Honigfeld, G., & Gillis, R. The role of institutionalization in the natural history of schizophrenia. Dis. Nerv. System., 1967, 28, 660-663.

Huessy, H.R. Beyond the halfway house. Int. J. Soc. Psychiat., 1969, 15, 235-239.

Kanno, C.K., & Glasscote, R.M. Fifteen indices: An aid in reviewing state and local mental health and hospital programs. Washington, D.C.: Joint Info. Serv. of the APA and the Nat'l Assoc. of Mental Health, 1966.

Landy, D., & Greenblatt, M. Halfway house. Washington, D.C.: U.S. Department of Health, Education, and Welfare, 1965.

Langsley, D.G., Flomenhaft, K., and Machotka, P. Followup evaluation of family crisis therapy. Amer. J. Orthopsychiat., 1969, 39, 753-759.

Langsley, D.G., & Kaplan, D.M. The treatment of families in crisis. New York: Grune and Stratton, 1968.

Langsley, D.G., Machotka, P., & Flomenhaft, K. Avoiding mental
  hospital admission: A follow-up study. Amer. J. Psychiat.,
  1971, 127, 1391-1394.

Linn, L.S. State hospital environment and rates of patient discharge. Arch. Gen. Psychiat., 1970, 23, 346-351.

Ludwig, A.M., & Farrelly, F. The code of chronicity. Arch. Gen.
  Psychiat., 1966, 15, 562-563.

Ludwig, A.M., & Farrelly, F. The weapons of insanity. Amer. J.
  Psychother., 1967, 21, 737-749.

Margolin, R. The concept of mental illness: A new look at some
  old assumptions. Comm. Ment. Health J., 1968, 4, 417-424.

Marx, A.J., Test, M.A., Stein, L.I. Extro-hospital management of
  severe mental illness. Arch. Gen. Psychiatry, 29, 505-511, 1973.

Mechanic, D. Therapeutic intervention: Issues in the care of the
  mentally ill. Amer. J. Orthopsychiat., 1967, 37, 4.

Mechanic, D. Mental health and social issues. Prentice-Hall, Inc.,
  1969, 108-109.

Mendel, W.M. Effect of length of hospitalization on rate and
  quality of remission from acute psychotic episodes. J. Nerv.
  Ment. Dis., 1966, 143, 226-233.

Mendel, W.M. On the abolition of the psychiatric hospital.
  Psychology Newsletter, 1968, 2.

Mendel, W.M., & Rapport, S. Determinants of the decision for psychiatric hospitalization. Arch. Gen. Psychiat., 1969, 20
  321-328.

Newton, J.R., & Stein, L.I. Implosive therapy, duration of hospitalization and degree of coordination of aftercare services with
  alcoholics. Accepted for publication as a chapter in a book on
  proceedings of the First Annual Alcoholism Conference, Washington,
  D.C., June, 1971.

Pasamanick, B., Scarpitt, F., & Dinitz, S. Schizophrenics in the
  community: An experimental study in the prevention of hospitalization. New York: Appleton, Century, Crofts, 1967.

Paul, G.L. Chronic mental patient: Current status--future directions. Psychol. Bull., 1969, 71, 81-94.

Phillips, L. Case history data and prognosis in schizophrenia.
  J. Nerv. Ment. Dis., 1953, 117, 515-525.

Polak, P., & Jones, M. The psychiatric non-hospital: A model for
  change. Comm. Psychiat., in press.

Rausch, H.L., & Rausch, C.L. The halfway house movement: A search
  for sanity. New York: Appleton, Century, Crofts, 1968.

Rhine, M.W., & Mayerson, P. Crisis hospitalization within a psychiatric emergency service. Amer. J. Psychiat., 1971, 127, 1386-1391.

Richmond, C. Expanding the concepts of the halfway house: A satellite housing program. Int. J. Soc. Psych., 1970, 16, 96-102.

Rittenhouse, J.D. Without hospitalization: An experimental study
  of psychiatric care in the home, in press, 1970.

Rog, D.J., & Rausch, H.L. The psychiatric halfway house: How is
  it measuring up? Community Mental Health Journal, 1975, 11,
  155-162.

Rosenburg, M. Society and adolescent self-image, 1965.

Sanders, R., Smith, R.S., & Weinman, B.S. Chronic psychoses and
  recovery. San Francisco: Jossey-Bass, Inc., 1967.

Satir, V. Conjoint family therapy. Palo Alto, Calif.: Science
  and Behavior Books, Inc., 1967.

Schizophrenia Bulletin, At issue: The psychosocial treatment of
  schizophrenia. 1970, 3, 4-5.

Silverstein, M. Psychiatric aftercare. Philadelphia: University
  of Pennsylvania Press, 1968.

Spitzer, R.L., Endicott, J., Fleiss, J.L., & Cohen, J. The psychiatric status schedule. Arch. Gen. Psychiat., 1970, 23, 41-55.

Stein, L.I., & Newton, J.R. Patterns of agency use by male alco-
  holic persons. Paper in preparation.

Towbin, A.P. Self-care unit: Some lessons in institutional power.
  J. Conslt. and Clin. Psychol., 1969, 33, 561-570.

Webb, E.J., Campbell, D.T., Schwartz, R.D., & Sechrest, L. Unobtru-
  sive measures: Non-reactive research in the social sciences.
  Chicago: Rand McNally, 1966.

Weisman, G., Feirstein, A., & Thomas, C.   Three day hospitalization-
   A model for intensive intervention.   Arch. Gen. Psychiat., 1969,
   21, 620-629.

Wing, J.K.   Institutionalism in mental hospitals.   Brit. J. Soc.
   Clin. Psychol., 1962, 1, 38-51.

Wing, J.K., & Brown, G.W.   Social treatment of chronic schizophrenic:
   A comparative survey of three mental hospitals.   J. Ment. Sci.,
   1961, 107, 847-861.

COMMUNITY-BASED TREATMENT AND THE CONSTITUTION:

THE PRINCIPLE OF THE LEAST RESTRICTIVE ALTERNATIVE [1]

David L. Chambers

University of Michigan Law School

Ann Arbor, Michigan

In June 1975, the Supreme Court of the United States decided
a mental-health case. What was newsworthy about the Court's action
was only in part the particular rule of the law the Justices
announced. More newsworthy was the fact that the Court decided
the case at all. For the case, O'Connor v. Donaldson (1975) was
the first major mental-health case not involving criminal behavior
that the Supreme Court had ever decided on the merits. After
forty years of extending broader and broader protections to adults
facing incarceration for crimes and a decade of extending similar
protections to juveniles facing institutionalization for juvenile
offenses, the Court finally began to peer inside the mental hospital.

Why it had taken so long for mental-health issues to reach
the Court is perhaps of little interest to anyone other than lawyers. What is of interest today is what this decision and many
others that have been recently issued by lower federal and state
courts portend for persons involved in the field of mental health
-- either as recipients or providers of mental health services.
Of especial interest is the significance of these decisions for
persons interested in the relationship of inpatient hospitalization
to treatment in other settings.

The range of mental-health issues that are beginning to come
before courts is as diverse as the range of persons who become involved as recipients of mental-health care. Many of these issues
should be of concern to persons involved in developing alternatives
to hospitalization, though some do not on their surface appear to
be relevant to community-based care. Let me give a couple of
examples of issues that arise in the context of inpatient hospitalization but that have important indirect implications for other

23

alternatives will probably find itself without sufficient resources
to insure that an adequate search occurs. Even in Michigan, with
broad new legislation requiring the use of alternatives, no new
funds were made available for professionals to explore for alternatives for individuals. Nor, to be sure, did any great infusion
of new funds occur for community-care programs. A recent District
of Columbia decision used a local statute to compel the creation
of new community-based programs, but it is uncertain how far
Congress, the District's "legislature", will fulfill the Court's
order through necessary appropriations (Dixon v. Weinberger, 1975).

The Constitutional Arguments for the Requiring

Searches for Alternatives to Commitment

If applicable statutes will not bear a reading that alternatives may or must be used or if courts refuse to read the statutes
broadly, the United States and State Constitutions may provide the
necessary force. On dozens of occasions, the United States Supreme
Court and state supreme courts have compelled state governments to
achieve clearly legitimate goals by methods of regulation less
constrictive of some important constitutionally protected interest
than the methods being used. The decision in Shelton v. Tucker
(1960) contains the most frequently quoted recent statement of the
principle. There the Court declared that in judging governmental
actions "even though the governmental purpose be legitimate and
substantial, that purpose cannot be pursued by means that broadly
stifle personal liberties when the end can be more narrowly
achieved." Though not yet explicitly held applicable by the
Supreme Court to the mentally ill, such precedents have obvious
relevance to issues concerning alternatives to mental hospital
treatment.

Two decisions of the United States Supreme Court offer illus-
trations. In 1951, the Supreme Court struck down a ban placed by
the city of Madison, Wisconsin, on the sale of milk processed
more than twenty-five miles from the city (Dean Milk Co. v. City
of Madison, 1951). The court invalidated the ordinance because it
found that a less drastic method of inspection could fully serve
the city's legitimate interest in protecting its citizens from
spoiled or adulterated milk without entirely prohibiting the sale
of non-local milk. In another case, decided in 1972, the Court
examined a Tennessee statute requiring that newcomers reside in the
state for ninety days before becoming eligible to vote (Dunn v.
Blumstein, 1972). Tennessee sought to justify the statute in part
on the ground that it served to prevent fraud by persons who had
not truly made the decision to become residents of Tennessee.
Preventing fraud was a legitimate goal, but the 90-day residency
requirement could not stand when there was an alternative (checking

drivers' licenses and car registrations) that did not deny constitutionally protected rights to bona fide new residents.

The reasoning of these cases has obvious application to civil
commitment of persons considered mentally ill: Courts should not
permit involuntary commitment if care at home or at a community
group home or outpatient care through a mental health clinic can
offer whatever protection or treatment is needed.

The application is obvious, but attorneys must leap one hurdle
before they can be confident that courts will require courts and
agencies to apply the principle of the least restrictive alternative to state action affecting mentally ill citizens. The obstacle
is that the Supreme Court and other courts do not apply the principle to all forms of regulations. Courts insist upon the use of
less restrictive alternatives as a matter of constitutional right
only when the method of regulation used by the state affects
interests that are considered especially sensitive under the
Constitution, such as free speech, or are directed at groups
against whom discrimination is regarded with especial suspicion by
the court, such as Black Americans or aliens.

For example, the Supreme Court upheld a state regulation requiring sprinkler systems in apartment buildings without inquiring
whether an alternative form of protection to tenants less financially onerous for the landlord was available (Queenside Hill
Realty Co. v. Saxl, 1946). It has even upheld restrictive welfare
legislation that discriminates against larger families without
examining claims that narrower legislation not working such hard-
ships would serve the state's interests (Dandridge v. Williams,
1970). The Madison, Wisconsin, milk ordinance imposed a burden
on interstate commerce, an activity expressly mentioned in the
Constitution. Tennessee's voting residency requirement affected
two rights afforded special protection under the Constitution:
voting in political elections and travel among the states. On
the other hand, the law requiring fire sprinklers and those providing a lesser portion of needs to larger families on welfare
than smaller families were immune from constitutionally compelled
inquiry into alternatives because they affected no constitutionally
sensitive group or interest. Despite the fact that those laws
were of critical importance to certain individuals' livelihood and
sustenance, they were found to have no special place in the
Constitution.

Thus, the first task for lawyers or others seeking to persuade
courts to find a constitutional obligation to use or explore alternatives to the hospitalization of mentally ill persons is to
develop arguments that the regulations affect a constitutionally
preferred interest or constitutionally protected group--or, at a
minimum, that there is something especially worrisome about

compulsive hospitalization. Some commentators have argued that all regulation of the mentally ill as a class should be subjected to skeptical examination by courts (Burt, 1976). Like regulations based on race or national origin (both highly disfavored by the courts), regulations of persons labelled as "mentally ill", involve punishing people for conditions beyond their control and stigmatizing them in ways that ought if at all possible be avoided. To date, however, it is, I believe, sufficient to say that no court so far as I know has been willing to go anywhere near this far.

If the courts did begin to treat as suspect regulation of the mentally ill as a separate class, all special regulation adversely affecting the mentally ill would presumably be subject to examination for less restrictive alternatives. If, as is far more likely, the courts refuse to recognize mental illness as a suspect classification, arguments that courts should compel inquiries into alternatives (or order the creation of alternatives) must focus on special constitutional protections for particular forms of conduct.

Civil commitment of the mentally ill intrudes on their constitutionally protected rights of travel and free association (Chambers, 1972). The right to travel protects the freedom of individuals to journey where they want when they want to, except when government has compelling reasons to curtail it. The right of association protects both people's freedom to participate in group political activity and their right to more mundane associations with companions of their choice. Both rights have been accorded protection by the Court over a substantial range of important cases. Moreover, some Supreme Court decisions indicate a special sensitivity to regulations permitting incarceration, without reference to other specific freedoms that incarceration inhibits (Chambers, 1972). Reflecting this concern, three recent federal court decisions have held that prior to involuntary hospitalization of the mentally ill, the Constitution requires a demonstration that there are no suitable less restrictive alternatives (Covington v. Harris, 1969, see ref.). In addition, the order entered by the trial court in Wyatt v. Stickney bars commitment of a mentally handicapped person to an institution "unless a prior determination shall have been made that residence in that institution is the least restrictive habilitation setting feasible for that person" (Wyatt v. Stickney, 1974).

The Supreme Court's decision in 1975 in O'Connor v. Donaldson has also important, if oblique, application here. The case involved a man who had been hospitalized for fifteen years in Florida, even though acknowledged by all to be harmless to himself or others. The Court held that states violate the Constitution when they confine a nondangerous person without at least providing treatment.

It left open the possibilities that it would later hold that states cannot involuntarily confine a nondangerous person at all and or, conversely, that states must provide treatment even to ill persons considered dangerous. Indeed, Donaldson is perhaps most significant for all the possibilities it left open. To this reader, the Court was making a small initial foray into a new territory, letting lower courts know that it was troubled by what it had learned about hospitals, and inviting the organic development of a body of remedial law. In the course of its discussion, the Court did in fact drop a hint that it was ready to adopt the principle of the least restrictive alternative in mental health cases. In discussing the commitment of nondangerous persons such as the plaintiff in the case before it, the court said:

> "While the State may arguably confine a person to save him
> from harm, incarceration is rarely if ever a necessary con-
> dition for raising the living standards of those capable
> of surviving safely in freedom, on their own or with the
> help of family or friends. See Shelton v. Tucker, 364 U.S.
> 479, 488-490, 81 S.Ct. 247, 252-253, 5 L.Ed. 2d 231."

The Court's citation to the Shelton case is significant, for Shelton is a first amendment case that is the most commonly cited explicit statement of a constitutionally required obligation to use lesser alternatives when important liberties are at stake.

THE SEVERAL APPLICATIONS OF THE PRINCIPLE TO MENTAL HEALTH

Whenever it is properly applied, the principle of the least restrictive alternative requires first an articulation by the affected court or agency of the interests the state seeks to serve through the law (or regulation) at issue, for it is only through identifying the state interests that the court can determine what alternative methods may be substituted. In the process of articulating interests courts are forced (if they act properly) to identify and reject impermissible interests that may have been the basis of the law. Thus, for mentally ill citizens, alternatives to commitment should be assessed in terms of whether they provide needed protection or habilitation, not in terms of their effectiveness in serving the improper function (as the Supreme Court has made clear in O'Connor v. Donaldson) of simply screening from sight those who make others in society feel uncomfortable. In defending its ban on milk processed at a distance from the city, Madison, Wisconsin, was similarly precluded from relying on its constitutionally improper interest of protecting its local milk producers from outside competition.

Once interests are identified, the principle can secure valid forms of relief. The most narrow but perhaps most significant relief is in the context of methods of regulation requiring case-by-case determination of a mentally ill person's appropriateness for inpatient hospitalization. In such cases, the principle calls at a minimum for an individualized inquiry into the current availability of less restrictive alternatives that would serve the state's interests.

The principle (coupled with well-developed notions of due process of law) (Goldberg v. Kelly, 1970) also can properly be used to insure that the search for less restrictive alternatives occurs before and not after the more restrictive placement occurs. A second extension of the principle would be to require case-by-case determinations where none are currently required. For example, the principle could be used to require individualized inquiries into and use of alternatives under statutes imposing absolute bans on marriage for institutionalized mentally ill persons. Similarly, the principle can easily be used to compel individualized periodic re-examination of placements or restrictions to determine their continued necessity (Covington v. Harris, 1969).

Yet bolder uses of the principle lie in waiting. The principle may be a useful tool to lawyers in securing the removal of legal barriers to the use of currently available alternatives. For example, if a public or private agency is repeatedly blocked by zoning regulations from placing a group home for mentally ill persons in a residential area (Chandler & Ross, 1976), attorneys can argue that the state may not continue to confine mentally ill persons in institutions and retain their zoning regulations when group homes would adequately serve the needs of the institutionalized individuals. In such a case a court striking down a zoning regulation would have to find either that the purposes underlying the zoning regulation would not be adversely served by permitting placement of the home or that (and here is an extension of the principle) the value of permitting the less restrictive home justifies some intrusion in the state's interests in permitting restrictive zoning.

Striking out even further, the principle may be used to compel the creation of new alternative programs or facilities (such as group homes in the community) even when no agency as yet stands ready to erect them. Many Supreme Court decisions have compelled states to choose between foregoing regulation of certain conduct altogether (such as the regulation of nonlocal milk) or adopting a new method of regulation not currently in existence (Shelton v. Tucker, 1960 and Dean Milk Co. v. City of Madison, 1951). Courts might similarly hold that states need not create systems of involuntary (or fictionally voluntary) commitment of mentally ill persons, but if they do they must create a full range of less

confining residential settings so that no one is confined in a
setting more restrictive of his freedom than necessary (Chambers,
1972). In a recent decision, a federal district court in Texas
has explicitly drawn upon the principle in ordering the state of
Texas to create new community-based alternative facilities for
juvenile delinquents, rather than continuing to rely heavily on
incarcerative institutions (Morales v. Turman, 1974; Dixon v.
Weinberger, 1975).

The right to treatment or habilitation, developed in the
celebrated case of Wyatt v. Stickney (e.g., Wyatt v. Stickney,
1972), has in this context essentially the same potential for
encouraging the creation of new programs. Under either rubric,
courts have to assay the costs that government must pay as the
price for continuing to incarcerate many mentally ill citizens.
In determining the forms of treatment to be required, courts will
find that experts disagree on the precise components of an adequate
system of residential alternatives for mentally ill individuals.
Courts may be even more puzzled by state claims that they cannot
afford to create the alternatives but cannot humanely give up the
institutions altogether. This seems in part to be Alabama's
claimed dilemma in Wyatt argued through the veil (as seductive as
Salome's) of the inappropriateness of judicial intrusion into this
essentially legislative domain. But the judiciary has a duty to
protect individual liberty, even if a consequence of that duty is
to compel a redirection of funds away from programs not involving
such constriction on individual liberty.

THREE OBSTACLES FOR LAWYERS AND
MENTAL HEALTH PROFESSIONALS

Three obstacles to successful application of the principle
merit special discussion. The first--state claims that placement
in the restrictive setting under attack is "voluntary"--may lead
courts to hold that the principle does not apply at all. The second
obstacle--claims by the state that the placement or regulation is
the only one adequately serving the state's goal of maximum protection for the mentally ill person--may lead courts to apply the
principle and still routinely permit the use of the most restrictive
placement. The third--the inadequacy of current systems for exploring alternatives in individual cases--may not deter courts from
holding that the principle applies, but may render useless any
favorable holding that they do reach.

The Somewhat Red Herring of Voluntariness

For persons who are admitted as "voluntary" or "nonprotesting" residents at institutions, courts may reject arguments that states must explore existing alternatives to residential care. The courts might reason that the obligation to exercise alternatives that maximize freedom applies only when the government is seeking by force to take the freedom away. As to many forms of separate treatment for the mentally handicapped today, states are likely to claim that participation is voluntary or that those held are free to leave at any time (N.Y. Assn. of Retarded Children v. Rockefeller, 1973).

One attack on claims that programs are voluntary is that they really are not--at least not in the peculiar sense that lawyers use the term "voluntary." As used by lawyers a "voluntary" decision in order to be considered "voluntary" must not have been without a gun at the temple. Moreover, it must also have been made without a threat of some drastic governmentally-threatened consequences or under misapprehensions about the consequences that will occur (Rogers v. Richmond, 1961). A mentally ill person's "voluntary" admission to a hospital is often made under a barely veiled threat that he will be judicially committed if he does not volunteer. Even without threats, a "voluntary" admission might appropriately be considered involuntary if not made with full disclosure about conditions in the institution, available alternatives, and the reduced likelihood of the person's reintegration into the outside world. (Here, as you can see, the gathering and dissemination of information about alternatives can be seen as part of the state's duties in insuring informed choice. The state has no general duty to insure that all choices people make are informed. Before courts will upset a choice as "involuntary" it must generally first decide that the choice involves the waiver of a constitutional right. The argument, somewhat strained, would essentially be that people have a constitutional right to be free of unnecessary government-ally-provided institutionalization.)

Finally, a parent's "voluntary" decision to commit a mentally ill child should almost never be considered voluntary as to the child, for the interests of parent and child (especially when the parents are considering expelling him from their home) may greatly conflict (J. L. v. Parham, 1976). The consequence of refusing to recognize the parents' choice as voluntary would be that courts or agencies would make an independent inquiry into alternatives. The parents' own attitude about placing their child would, of course, be one important factor in judging the adequacy of a home-based alternative program.

The State's Goal of Protecting the Mentally
Handicapped Person

Courts can be expected to require the use of less restrictive alternatives only when they serve the state's legitimate goals at least as well as (or, at the most, not much less satisfactorily than) the more restrictive program the state is seeking to impose on the mentally ill person.

One goal of many governmental restrictions of the mentally ill person is to protect him from his own inadequacies. The most restrictive form of regulation--for example, commitment to a distant institution--will nearly always maximize that protection at least for the short run. Judges are often concerned solely or primarily with assuring such protections and are understandably reluctant to bear the risk that their failure to have ordered the most restrictive alternative will later lead to some calamity for which the judge will feel blameworthy (or be blamed). Judges may thus honestly apply the principle and still reject the mentally ill person's plea for greater freedom.

Attorneys and mental health professionals must be well armed to respond to this protective instinct. They must try to show that protection is not the only goal of the legislation in issue and point to other goals, if they exist, such as treatment or maximizing the capacity for independent living. Even accepting the primacy of a goal of protection, they should try to show that many mentally ill persons need far less protection than is commonly believed and that a high degree of protective segregation for the present may largely undermine the long-term capacity of the mentally ill person to look out for himself in the future. Attorneys and others should in short be sympathetic to the judge's concerns but show him that a greater degree of freedom may best serve the judge's own goals. Less, as Mies van der Rohe told us, is often more.

Systems To Ensure That Alternatives Are Explored

The most likely use of the principle for the mentally handicapped citizen will lie in compelling reliance on existing less restrictive alternatives. Champions of community care need to devote special emphasis to assuring that explorations for alternatives actually occur, even after appellate courts decree that such explorations are mandatory. In 1966, the United States Court of Appeals for the District of Columbia Circuit ordered that alternatives to hospitalization for the mentally ill be explored in all cases and used where appropriate (Lake v. Cameron, 1967). The government, according to the court, bore the burden of performing

the search. In the vast bulk of commitment proceedings since
conducted in the District, however, little or no exploration of
alternatives has occurred because, at least until recently, there
was no one to perform the search--attorneys were ignorant of the
alternatives and too overworked to explore them, the committing
authority and the reviewing court had no staff to perform explorations, and the mentally ill person was often unaware of what was
available.

Much the same story is being retold in Michigan today: broad
new legislation called for a search for alternatives in all cases.
In Detroit in the first years under the new act, the judges simply
ignored the new provisions because no staff existed to perform a
search.

The same problem is likely to arise in other jurisdictions
that recognize an obligation to search for alternatives. Thus,
a bare holding, without more, that alternatives to any compulsory
procedure must be explored on a case-by-case basis is by itself
of small value--and attorneys who secure them will have advanced
their client's cause very little. The best cure will come through
legislation or from aggressive mental health professionals. New
Mexico has, for example, recently amended its mental health code
to require an examination for alternatives through community mental
health centers in advance of commitment (New Mexico Statutes).
Formal links between courts and community mental health centers
can occur without mandatory legislation. In Battle Creek, Michigan,
the court routinely refers all cases on its own motion to the local
clinic for screening.

The task of searching for alternatives might also be entrusted
to court personnel, not now existing anywhere so far as I know,
but comparable in function to probation officers now generally
hired by adult criminal and urban juvenile courts to advise them
on community placement. The analogy is more compelling than may
instantly appear. Such "probation" personnel may not merely help
locate community alternatives but may also play a role in monitoring the individual's progress. They may also infuse the judges
with enthusiasm for developing new community programs. Alterna-
tively, information about alternatives might be generated through
a separate staff of lay or professional advocates, perhaps attached
to an agency providing legal representation. Some legal service
agencies for the mentally ill have been highly pleased with the
results. Examples include, the public defender agency in the
District of Columbia, the Mental Health Information Service in New
York's First Judicial Department (Manhattan and the Bronx), and
Cleveland's Legal Aid Society.

Finally, the state may prefer to rely on an investigation of
alternatives conducted by staff of the hospital or institution in

which the individual has been placed. Such searches may or may
not prove adequate depending on the degree of the staff's acceptance
of the principle, but the danger does exist that the staff will
have an unconscious need to affirm the decency of the institution
by recommending placements there. Such institutions may also
attract as employees those with the greatest confidence in inpatient treatment.

Whatever the system created, the important point is this:
any court that accepts the principle of the least restrictive
alternative must also concern itself with the structure for vinci-
cating the principle. Attorneys filing class suits or appealing
individual cases and mental health professionals cooperating with
them need to address explicitly not merely the abstract constitutional principle but its implemental as well.

Mental health professionals bear a heavy burden of responsibility to insure searches for alternatives occur. In many parts
of the country, judges will have been long accustomed to relying
on hospitalization as the preferred mode of care. They cannot be
expected to educate themselves about the new era of alternatives
to mental hospital treatment. Attorneys, however well informed,
will often appear to judges to be starry-eyed idealists spouting
high-sounding moral nursery rhymes. Mental health professionals
need to get to know judges, gently educate them, cajole them into
cooperative projects. Take a judge to lunch.

A WARNING ABOUT THE LIMITATIONS OF THE PRINCIPLE
AND THE LIMITATIONS OF ATTORNEYS

The principle of the least restrictive alternative cannot
ensure by itself that government will respond wisely to the needs
of the mentally disabled. The principles cannot alone, even if
broadly accepted by courts, compel the creation of exactly the
right mix of affirmative programs and broad freedoms for mentally
handicapped persons. Those who seek community programming walk a
wobbly tightrope. They do not seek the elimination of special
programs. Far from it. They often want elaborate but subtle programs to help the mentally ill person learn to survive in the
community without crippling anxiety and without interfering unduly
with the peacefulness of other persons' lives.

The natural vector of the principle of the least restrictive
alternative lies in the dismantling of restrictions. To the
extent that it is a useful tool in arguing for the creation of
new community-based programs or more flexible regulation, its
utility is premised on the continued existence of more restrictive
programs. If acceptance of notions of community treatment leads

states to close the most confining and "abnormal" of its institutions there will be fewer and fewer more restrictive alternatives
to serve as the magnetic point for requiring the use or creation
of the next least restrictive. If a state abandoned all special
residential programs for the mentally ill, the principle would
offer no aid in compelling the creation of new ones, even desirable ones in the community. I do not intend to suggest that we
retain heavy reliance on involuntary hospitalization so that the
principle can flourish. Rather, I want to point out that the
principle is not itself an affirmative right that can compel
special programs, if the state decided to do nothing. Today,
while many restrictions remain, the principle, if accepted, can
do much. But, even today, attorneys seeking special programs
should couple the principle with statutory and constitutional
arguments that are less intrinsically negative in their tone.

A broader warning is in order. A heavy responsibility falls
upon the lawyer seeking alternatives for mentally ill, or other
segregated groups. Class actions that fail may appear to vindicate
current practices and impede efforts for change for the lawyer's
own clients and thousands of others across the country. Class
actions that succeed may produce hastily devised alternative placements or the release of institutional residents with nothing to
support them in the community. When lawyers seek to persuade
courts to do what legislatures ought to have done, they bear a
weighty burden to do what legislatures ought to do before they act
--that is, to avoid being propelled alone by high sounding slogans
like the principle of the least restrictive alternative or even
by their anger at the vile conditions at an institution. Rather,
they must first become well informed about the problem they seek
to cure. In this context, lawyers need to inform themselves about
the varying capacities and needs of retarded and mentally ill
citizens and the range and effectiveness of alternatives to whatever confining institution, program or regulation they seek to
dismantle. They need to visit the institutions and special programs for mentally handicapped persons and sit down and get to
know some of their children.

When attorneys induce a court to order a lesser alternative
that is far less wise than another, they are responsible for
helping plant dead or dying trees. If attorneys act to force
states to give up confining institutions because of the prohibitive
cost of developing alternatives, we run the risk that for many
persons, the grass will not prove greener on the other side of the
fence. In some ways, attorneys involved in test case work are
uniquely situated to act irresponsibly--having no accountability
to an electorate, no responsibility to bear the brunt of a judicial
opinion as their own, and often no real client other than their own
moral convictions. The attorneys who have been involved in the

major cases for mentally ill persons to date have generally, but not always, borne well the burden of becoming informed, keeping informed, and acting with caution. As suits proliferate, attorneys must strive to meet the same high standards. I hope that other mental health professionals will work with us to meet these goals.

Footnote

1. The author has written at greater length on the subject of this piece in an article entitled Alternatives to Civil Commitment of the Mentally Ill: Practical Guides and Constitutional Imperatives, 70 Mich. L. Rev. 1107 (1972), and in chapters of books issued by the President's Committee on Mental Retardation entitled The Mentally Retarded Citizen and the Law (M. Kindred et al, eds. 1976) and the Practicing Law Institute, Legal Rights of the Mentally Handicapped (Volume II, Ennis et al, eds., 1973). Parts of the chapter here are borrowed directly from these earlier works. For aid in checking my assertions here, I am grateful to Arthur M. Luby, a student at the University of Michigan Law School.

REFERENCES

Burt. Beyond the right to habilitation. In Kindred (ed.), The mentally retarded citizen and the law, 418-36, 1976.

Cal. Welfare and Institutions Code, sec. 5358 (Derring's Supp. 1977); Illinois Ann. Stat., ch. 91 1/2, sec. 9-6 (Smith-Hurd Supp. 1977); Ohio Revised Code Ann., sec. 5122.15 (C) (Page's Code Supp. 1976).

Chambers. Alternatives to civil commitment of the mentally ill: practical guides and constitutional imperatives, 1107, 1155-68 (1972).

Chambers. Alternatives to civil commitment of the mentally ill: practical guides and constitutional imperatives, 1180-1200 (1972).

Chandler and Ross. Zoning restrictions and the right to live in the community. In Kindred (ed.), The mentally retarded citizen and the law, 305-43 (1976).

Covington v. Harris, 419 F.2d 617 (D.C. Cir. 1969); Lessard v. Schmidt, 349 F. Supp. 1078 (E.D. Wis. 1972), vacated for entry of definitive decree, 414 U.S. 473 (1974) (holding the trial court's order to be insufficiently specific and detailed under the Federal Rules of Civil Procedure), clarified, 379 F. Supp.

1376 (E.D. Wis. 1974), vacated on procedural grounds, 95 S. Ct. 1943 (1975); Dixon v. Attorney General, 325 F. Supp. 966 (M.D. Pa. 1971).

Covington v. Harris, 419 F.2d 617 (D.C. Cir. 1969) (a case dealing with the degree of confinement within a hospital after the initial hospitalization had occurred long before).

Dandridge v. Williams, 397 U.S. 471, 484, 486 (1970).

Dean Milk Co. v. City of Madison, 340 U.S. 349 (1951).

Dixon v. Weinberger, 405 F. Supp. 974 (1975).

Dunn v. Blumstein, 405 U.S. 330 (1972).

Goldberg v. Kelly, 397 U.S. 254 (1970).

J.L. v. Parham, 412 F. Supp. 112 (1976).

Lake v. Cameron, 364 F.2d 657 (D.D.C. 1967).

Lessard v. Schmidt, 349 F. Supp. 1078 (E.D. Wis. 1972), vacated for entry of definitive decree, 414 U.S. 473 (1974), clarified, 379 F. Supp. 1376 (E.D. Wis. 1974), vacated on procedural grounds, 95 S. Ct. 1943 (1975).

Michigan Statutes Annotated, sec. 14.800 (469) (1976)

Morales v. Turman, 383 F. Supp. 53, 121-26 (E.D. Tex. 1974). See also Dixon v. Weinberger, 405 F. Supp. 974 (1975) (based on a District of Columbia statute).

New Mexico Statutes Annotated, sec. 34-2-5E.

New York Assn. of Retarded Children v. Rockefeller, 357 F. Supp. 752 (E.D.N.Y. 1973).

O'Connor v. Donaldson, 422 U.S. 563 (1975).

Queenside Hill Realty Co. v. Saxl, 328 U.S. 80 (1946).

Rogers v. Richmond, 368 U.S. 534 (1961).

Shelton v. Tucker, 364 U.S. 479, 488 (1960)

Shelton v. Tucker, 364 U.S. 479 (1960); Dean Milk Co. v. City of Madison, 340 U.S. 349 (1951).

Wyatt v. Stickney, 344 F. Supp. 387, 344 F. Supp. 373 (M.D. Ala. 1972), 344 F. Supp. 1341, 325 F. Supp. 781 (M.D. Ala. 1971), aff'd. sub nom. Wyatt v. Aderholt, 503 F. 2d 1305 (5th Cir. 1974).

Wyatt v. Stickney, 344 F. Supp. 387, 396 (M.D. Ala. 1972), aff'd sub nom. Wyatt v. Aderholt, 503 F.2d 1305 (5th Cir. 1974).

Part II

CONTROLLED EXPERIMENTS OF ALTERNATIVES TO MENTAL HOSPITAL TREATMENT PROGRAMS

AN ALTERNATIVE TO MENTAL HOSPITAL TREATMENT

Leonard I. Stein* and Mary Ann Test**

*University of Wisconsin, Madison, Wisconsin

**Mendota Mental Health Institute, Madison, Wisconsin

Two recent papers, Becker and Schulberg (1976) and Bachrach (1976), have comprehensively reviewed the historical antecedents and the current debate concerning deinstitutionalization. Their conclusions are not surprising. They both agree that limiting hospital treatment is a rational goal, but reaching that goal is markedly hampered by the woeful inadequacy of our present system of community care for the chronically disabled psychiatric patient.

Testimony supporting their conclusions are replete in the literature and can be summarized as follows. Limiting hospitalization is based on several factors. First and foremost inpatient treatment has an insignificant effect on post-hospital adjustment (Fairweather, 1964; Sanders, Smith & Weinman, 1967; Caffey et al, 1968; Paul, 1969, Anthony et al, 1972; Glick et al, 1976). One of the few controlled studies with a contrary finding was that by Glick (1976) which was lethally confounded by differences in degree of post-hospital treatment in the two groups studied. Furthermore, the debilitating effects of institutional treatment (Paul, 1969; Goffman, 1961; Barton, 1966; Gruenberg, 1967; Ludwig and Farrelly, 1966; Honigfeld and Gillis, 1967), and the fact that the more often a patient has been in the hospital, the more likely he is to return (Rosenblatt and Mayers, 1974), are well documented negative consequences of hospitalization. In addition, continued use of the hospital relieves the pressure from community agencies to develop programs for this population. On the other hand, the recommendation of Becker and Schulberg and Bachrach to limit hospital treatment in favor of community treatment is based on well-accepted principles in mental health and supported by the fact that controlled studies of alternatives to hospital treatment consistently find that mode

of treatment superior to hospitalization (Rittenhouse, 1970;
Weinman et al, 1970; Langsley et al, 1971; Marx et al, 1973).

In spite of the research noted above, community treatment for
this population remains inadequate. One can speculate about the
factors which have inhibited the development of adequate care for
the chronically disabled psychiatric patient. In addition to insufficient funds some of the more frequently mentioned factors are:
treatment goals based on "cure" rather than stabilization, the
patients are unattractive to work with and thus do not meet the
needs of the providers (Allen, 1976), inadequate training of mental
health professionals in working with this population, poor modeling
by the faculty in our training institutions, insufficient attention
to continuity of care, insufficient attention to the psychosocial
needs of patients, and inappropriate use of treatment models designed for healthier outpatients. All of the above, of course,
interact with one another and help explain the lack of adequate
community treatment. In addition, they point to the absence of a
conceptual framework upon which to base treatment models for this
population of patient.

This paper is divided into two sections. The first section
describes a conceptual model, based on patients' needs, for developing community based treatment programs for the chronically disabled
psychiatric patient. The second section describes a treatment program entitled Training in Community Living (TCL) which was based on
the conceptual model and developed as an alternative to mental
hospital treatment. The next chapter reports the first year's
results of a controlled experiment which compared TCL with our
present system of treatment, namely, short-term hospitalization
plus aftercare.

CONCEPTUAL MODEL

It is our contention that the inadequacies of current models
of community treatment are caused by the fact that they do not
effectively address certain factors required by patients to achieve
a satisfactory life in the community. Absence of one or more of
these factors lead to a tenuous community adjustment keeping
patients on the brink of rehospitalization. These requirements
were derived from our clinical experience and similar ones are also
clearly delineated in Professor Mechanic's chapter - Alternatives
to Mental Hospital Treatment: A Sociological Perspective. The
requirements are as follows:

    1. Material resources - food, shelter, clothing, medical care,
        recreation, etc.

Although the hospital may try to make arrangements for these resources to be available, the hospital can contribute little to help the patient with these requirements after discharge. Community treatment programs must assume responsibility for helping the patient acquire these resources.

2. Coping skills to meet the demands of community life.

These are the kinds of skills we all take for granted, such as using public transportation, preparing simple but nutritious meals, budgeting money, etc. Hospitals have attempted to teach these skills through simulating a community in the hospital. However, the evidence is clear - that approach is ineffective (Fairweather, 1964). We are convinced that the learning of these skills must take place _in vivo_ where the patient will be needing and using them.

3. Motivation to persevere and remain involved with life.

Our patients experience a good deal of stress and their motivation to remain in the community becomes easily eroded. A ready available system of support to encourage the patient, to help him solve real life problems and to help him feel he is not alone and that others are concerned about his welfare is crucial in keeping his motivation intact.

4. Freedom from pathological dependent relationships.

We define a pathological dependent relationship as one which inhibits personal growth, re-enforces maladaptive behaviors, and generates feelings of panic in its members when its loss is threatened. Many of our patients have been pathologically dependent on families or institutions all their lives. Unfortunately, hospitalization deepens pathological dependency and upon discharge the patient is usually returned to a highly conflictual family situation where the ingredients for another crisis and hospitalization are omnipresent. This cycling has been termed the revolving door syndrome. In order to break that cycle, community programs must help the patient become free of pathological dependent relationships, and in so doing must provide sufficient support to keep the patient involved in community life and encourage growth toward greater autonomy.

5. A supportive system which _assertively_ helps the patient with the above four requirements.

Chronically disabled patients are frequently passive,
interpersonally anxious, and prone to develop severe
psychiatric symptomatology. Such characteristics often
lead these patients to fail to keep appointments and to
"drop out" of treatment, particularly when they are becoming more symptomatic. Hence, a program designed for
their care must be assertive in involving patients in
their treatment program and be prepared to "go to" the
patient to prevent drop out. Additionally, it must
actively insure continuity of care among treatment
agencies rather than assume that a patient will successfully negotiate the often difficult pathways from one
agency to another on his own.

TREATMENT PROGRAM

TCL is a clinical research program that radically departs from
the present system of short-term hospitalization plus aftercare.
It is unique among "alternative to the hospital" programs in that,
unlike the others which accepted only patients whose families were
willing to take them back home (Rittenhouse, 1970; Langsley et al,
1971), TCL accepts an unselected sample of adult mentally ill
patients coming to the state hospital for admission. As will be
described in more detail in the next chapter, the patients are
people who by and large have a long history of poor community
adjustment with multiple admissions to the hospital.

The treatment program was designed to attend to the very requirements discussed in the last section. Its base of operation is
the community and its goal is to help patients develop and maintain
a satisfactory community adjustment. Use of the hospital is
virtually eliminated. The program will be described in terms of
work with patients, work with families, work with the community
and a description of the staff and how it functions. Finally a
case study is presented to illustrate the operation of the program.

Work With Patients

Patients coming to the hospital for admission are immediately
interviewed by a member of the community staff, and are then taken
from the admission office to the community to begin their treatment
program. Every effort is made to avoid hospitalization, with use
of hospital reserved for patients who are imminently suicidal or
homicidal or who require such high doses of medication necessi-
tating the hospital's structured environment. In the rare instances when hsopitalization is used, it is of short duration so
that "community treatment" can begin with minimal delay.

The community treatment approach focuses directly on an in vivo teaching of coping skills as well as treating the acute problem that precipitated the patient coming to the hospital. The patient's "treatment" consists of participation in a full schedule of daily living activities in the community with pharmacotherapy utilized where appropriate. The therapeutic input from staff consists of motivating, supporting, and often being "by patients' sides" day and evening. More specifically, staff members "on-the-spot" in patients' homes and neighborhoods, teach and assist them in daily living activities such as laundry upkeep, shopping, cooking, restaurant utilization, grooming, budgeting, and use of transportation. Additionally, patients are given sustained and intensive assistance in finding a job or sheltered workshop placement, and staff then continue daily contact with patients and their supervisors or employers to help with on-the-job problem solving. Furthermore, patients are aided in the constructive use of leisure time and the development of effective social skills by staff "prodding" and supporting their involvement in relevant community recreation and social activities. This frequently includes staff members accompanying patients to such functions until the patient is comfortable enough to attend by himself. In all these activities, a "can do" philosophy is transmitted from staff to patient, with the assets of patients stressed and symptomatology downplayed. Daily, even hourly, contact of staff with patients is emphasized initially and is gradually diminished according to each patient's progress in the treatment program. Even after there is relatively little staff contact, staff remain aware of the patient's functioning and are assertive in intervening early at the first sign of regression. Thus the treatment model is efficient. The patient gets specifically what he needs, when he needs it and it is provided to him at the site of where it will do the most good.

We believe that an important therapeutic effect of the program is the tremendous amount of support patients experience through their day to day contacts with staff during the activities mentioned above. Over time patients learn that the staff members indeed care about them and are concerned with them as individuals.

Work With Families

Work with families is primarily directed towards breaking pathological dependency ties. With married patients structured meetings with patient and spouse are held to facilitate increased symmetry in the relationship. Most of the patients, however, are unmarried. In these cases families (parents, parent surrogates, siblings) are evaluated to determine whether the patients' problems are significantly contributed to by a pathological family relationship. When this is found to be the case a highly specialized treatment approach termed "constructive separation" is utilized

(Marx et al, 1973). Operationally it consists of meeting with
family and identified patient, describing the community treatment
program to family members and then explaining to them in a firm,
though supportive manner that the patient's living with or receiving any support whatsoever from his relatives would be anti-
thetical to the program's goals. Specific guidelines are set up
to regulate interactions such as visits, phone contact, and letter
writing. Frequently complete curtailment of these activities for
an indefinite period of time is requested. Both parents and
patient are given enormous support in maintaining the "separation",
with staff being constantly available to families to provide guidance and reassurance. Finally, structured visits between patient
and family are initiated when the patient has gained sufficient
independence to relate to his family in a more adult to adult
fashion.

Work With Community

     A program of this nature could not survive without the
community being carefully prepared for its implementation. Prior
to beginning clinical work with patients, conferences were held
with every relevant community agency to establish the closest of
working relationships. We described our program in detail and
helped them understand what we wanted to achieve. We clearly outlined the role we expected them to play which, briefly stated,
encompassed the following:

    I.   We did not expect them to be mental health workers.

    2.   We did expect them to operate solely in their own area
          of expertise, i.e., we wanted police to do police work,
          landlords to be landlords, etc.

    3.   We advised them to expect from our patients and to
          respond to them as they would to any other citizen.

    4.   Finally we gave them our phone number and encouraged
          them to call us at any time, 24 hours per day, if they
          felt they needed our help. We assured them we would be
          constantly available.

     Our major effort was to influence them to respond to patients
in a manner that would promote responsible behavior rather than
reinforce maladaptive modes of coping with stress. For example,
if a patient's behavior was disruptive to other tenants in his
apartment building, we would encourage the landlord to talk to the
patient directly about his behavior and tell him he would be evicted
if it continued. This is in contrast to the community's usual
response, which is to see to it that the patient's disruptive

behavior leads to rehospitalization. That action implicitly gives
the patient the message that he is not responsible for his behavior,
teaches the patient a maladaptive mode of coping with stress and
leads to a hardening of the chronic patient role.

We received excellent cooperation from the community. We
believe the most important factors positively influencing community
cooperation were living up to our commitment by responding promptly
whenever called and not asking community members to change their
social and professional roles.

The Staff

To carry out the program, we retrained a typical mental
hospital ward staff, i.e., psychiatrist, psychologist, social
worker, occupational therapist, nurses and aides. As outlined
above, this staff spend their time dispersed throughout the community working with patients in their homes, places of work, super-
markets, recreational facilities, etc., helping them learn the
requisite skills necessary to sustain a satisfactory community
adjustment. The staff gather twice a day at the community headquarters, a rented house in downtown Madison, to share information,
revise treatment programs as necessary, and plan the next shift's
work schedule. There are two shifts so that the program is well
staffed from 7:00 a.m. until 11:00 p.m., seven days a week. A
member of the professional staff remains on call at night to give
24 hour per day coverage for patients as well as community agencies.

Utilization of mental hospital personnel in this kind of extro-
hospital program has advantages as well as disadvantages (Stein
and Test, 1976). The advantages include experience in, and commitment to, working with severely ill patients and an orientation
towards working with patient behaviors as well as feelings and
cognitions. Additionally, they have experience in a team approach
and have a willingness to rotate shifts so that the program can
be operational at all times. The major disadvantage lies in making
the transition from working in a highly structured hospital setting
where there is relatively little in the way of individual decision
making to working in the inevitably unstructured setting of the
community where a great deal of initiative and willingness to make
decisions on the spot becomes vital. Fortunately, with training
and support this transition could be made and staff have increasingly welcomed the taking on of increased responsibility. Moreover, working in a program where the fruits of their labors are
demonstrable has proven most gratifying to them.

Case Example

The following case illustrates how the program was operation-
alized:

John, a 30-year-old, single male, is brought to the hospital
by his parents for voluntary admission. They bring with them
admission papers signed by a physician, stating the patient is in
need of hospital treatment. This hospitalization would have
represented the sixth hospital admission for John with an accumulation of 11 prior months in a psychiatric hospital. John had
been living at home and had been unemployed for the past year.
Prior to that he had a poor work history, having had many jobs,
none lasting over six months. Although he had lived away from home
several times for very brief periods, he virtually lived as a
"child" in his parental home, contributing nothing financially to
the support of the family. Since his last discharge, the patient
had been maintained on phenothiazine medication and was seen at a
mental health clinic as an outpatient for periodic medication
checks. Over the past two months he had become increasingly
irritable, irrational, and precipitated frequent arguments with
his parents. During this time he began missing mental health
center appointments and it was questionable whether he was taking
his medication faithfully. This whole pattern was one that the
family had become very familiar with and invariably in the past
had led to the patient being hospitalized.

When John came to the admission office, the hospital registrar
picked up an envelope which randomly assigned the patient to either
the extrohospital, "Training in Community Living" program, or to
the acute treatment ward in the hospital. In this case, the
envelope indicated "Training in Community Living" and the registrar
called our community-based program headquarters to inform us that
our patient was in the admission office.

Almost immediately a psychiatrist and nurse came out to meet
John and the family. It was soon evident that John was in the
midst of a schizophrenic episode, but was not imminently suicidal,
homicidal, or required such high dosages of phenothiazines as to
necessitate the structure and nursing care of the hospital. Therefore, hospitalization was ruled out. Our program was then described
to John and his family, they agreed to accept a non-hospitalization
treatment approach, and they were taken down to the community headquarters where plans were initiated for John's treatment program.

The immediate plan included increasing John's medication,
arranging for him to stay at the YMCA at night until a more permanent community living arrangement could be worked out, and giving
the family instructions that we would essentially "take over" with
John, and requesting of them, at least for the time being, to

curtail all contact with him in order to prevent the continuation of the pathological relationship between John and his family. For support, the family was encouraged to get in touch with us whenever they wished and were given a 24 hour per day contact phone number. The rest of the afternoon and evening John spent time with the staff, going to supper with a staff member, going to the YMCA to rent his room, and going to an evening activity with another staff member, as well as receiving a thorough physical examination.

The next morning he was picked up by a staff member and taken to breakfast at a nearby coffee shop. Later that morning he met with the vocational rehabilitation counselor, who felt John could benefit from a workshop experience. That afternoon he was taken over to one of the community's sheltered workshops and allowed to look the place over; plans were then made with him to start work the next day.

Within a week John was clinically much improved and he indicated he wanted to move into a rooming house where he could have kitchen privileges. Staff spent time with him, looking through the classified ads and visiting prospective housing sites. After choosing a place to live, staff time was allocated to help John learn how to keep his place livable, to plan simple menus, shop for food, and budget his money.

Staff time was also allocated to help John discover leisure time activities and to make use of those in which he manifested an interest. At the onset staff frequently accompanied him to these social-recreational activities.

During his first month in the treatment program John's performance in the sheltered workshop continued to improve and he was becoming more autonomous in his living situation. His family did require repeated reassurance that John was able to manage without continuous supervision and they were strongly supported for not seeing John and reinforcing his dependency in other ways.

However, not unexpectedly, difficulties arose. The day after John received a very positive evaluation at the workshop indicating he was close to being ready for competitive employment, he got into an argument with the floor supervisor at the workshop and walked off the line. Since he was on a contingency program where he got paid only if he worked, he did not get that day's pay. John then stormed into the program's headquarters and demanded money for supper. A staff member spent the next hour with John going over the events at work, attempting to delineate resolvable problem areas, but emphasizing to him that he would not receive money he did not earn. The next morning he did not show up at the sheltered workshop. A staff member immediately went to his place

of living and urged John to get out of bed and to get back to work.
While he complied at that time, within the next two weeks several
more disruptive episodes occurred - one at work, the other at the
rooming house, eventuating in his eviction. Finally, John appeared
at his parents home asking to move back in with them. All these
episodes were handled firmly and consistently. He again was held
to the contingency program at work, he learned most directly that
certain behaviors would lead to eviction from his residence, his
family was given extra support to help them resist John's becoming
dependent on them again, and most importantly, John found that this
gamut of disruptive behaviors would not get him back into the
hospital! Our consistent message to him was that while we were
always available to help him learn to adapt to the community, we
could not be coerced into treating him as an "irresponsible child."

       At this time our work with John continues. He is now in a
competitive job, but still requires some support from us, implemented by our getting together with him several times a week to
talk about how things are going at work. He also still needs some
help learning to budget his money better. Overall, John is managing his autonomous living arrangement quite well and does his own
shopping and meal preparation. At this point in time, we spend
approximately two hours per week with him. He is no longer
struggling against us and his family has come to see him as a
person with more potential than they believed possible. They
appear to experience satisfaction in having played their part in
letting John "grow up", and relieved not to have him as a continuous burden. John now has ties with several community agencies.
His medication is being given via depot injection by the Visiting
Nurse Service. He takes part in an aftercare program sponsored by
the Mental Health Center and utilizes the City's Community Center
for recreational activities. As each day of independent community
living passes, even during the inevitable "ups and downs" he under-
goes, John's ties to the "sick role" lessen.

                              COMMENT

       The lack of an effective model to treat the chronically dis-
abled psychiatric patient is one of our nation's major health care
problems. The results reported in the next chapter suggest that
there is considerable hope for a solution to this problem when
community programming is based on the concepts of assertively
helping patients to: (1) acquire material resources, (2) learn
necessary coping skills in vivo, (3) gain sufficient support to
stay motivated and involved with treatment and (4) help free themselves from pathological dependent relationships; the TCL program
is an example of such an effort.

Although the TCL program was designed as an alternative to hospitalization and every effort was made to minimize its use, the hospital was used, albeit for very brief periods, for some of the patients. Thus it is clear that the hospital does have a role to play in the treatment of the chronically disabled psychiatric patient. We believe our study is useful in helping define what the hospital's role can optimally be. First and foremost it must be understood that the role of the hospital, for any community, must be seen in the context of what kinds of programming are available in the community for the chronically disabled psychiatric patient. Although hospitalization has undesirable effects on patients, there may be greater patient harm and certainly greater burden to the community if use of the hospital is denied on "principle" without providing adequate community programming in its place. The more comprehensive the community program the less the need to use the hospital. With a program such as TCL available, we believe the hospital need be used only for the following cases:

1. For protection of the individual or others when patients are imminently suicidal or homicidal. Care must be taken not to hospitalize patients who utilize self-destructive behavior as a means of getting help. This presents a very burdensome clinical judgment, but one that can be learned and made if the clinician is willing to do so. In our experience, if the patient is provided with the support he needs, the danger is minimal.

2. For patients whose psychosis is so severe that they require the structure and good nursing care only a hospital can provide. The goal here is to medicate the patient and interrupt the psychotic process as quickly as possible. We have used the hospital for this purpose with patients in the midst of a very manic episode or highly disruptive schizophrenic episode where we were unable to insure that the patient was being adequately medicated. Length of hospitalization in these cases was rarely over two weeks and often a matter of days.

Importantly we found that psychosis per se was not necessarily an indication to hospitalize. We were able to successfully treat many patients presenting as acutely psychotic without use of the hospital. In short, given adequate community programming, we recommend use of psychiatric hospitalization only in the specific instances described above.

Although we have come to respect the severity of our patient's disabilities, we continue, in most cases, to set expectations for improved functioning and provide sufficient support to help the patient move toward greater autonomy. Most of our patients will

require some help from us for the rest of their lives and some
will need an increasing amount of help as time passes. We have
learned that "cure" is not a useful concept in thinking about
most of our patients and that growth, stability and adequate
quality of life, or even prevention of deterioration, are worth-
while goals in the treatment of such individuals.

REFERENCES

Allen, P. Response: A consumer perspective. Proceedings of the
    conference "Community Living Arrangements for the Mentally Ill
    and Disabled: Issues and Options for Public Policy." NIMH,
    1976.

Anthony W.A., et al. Efficacy of psychiatric rehabilitation.
    Psychol. Bull. 78, 447-456, 1972.

Bachrach, L. L. National Institute of Mental Health Deinstitution-
    alization: An analytical review and sociological perspective.
    DHEW Publication No. (ADM) 76-351. Superintendent of Documents,
    U. S. Government Printing Office, Washington, D.C. 20402, 1976.

Barton, R. Institutional neurosis. Bristol, England: John Wright
    and Sons Ltd., 1966.

Becker, A., Schulberg, H.C. Phasing out state hospitals - a
    psychiatric dilemma. N. Eng. J. Med. 294, 255-261, 1976.

Caffey, E.M., Jones, R.D., Diamond, L.S., Burton, E., Bowen, W.T.
    Brief hospital treatment of schizophrenia--Early results of a
    multiple hospital study. Hosp. Community Psychiatry, 282-287,
    Sept. 1968.

Fairweather, G.H. (ed). Social psychology in treating mental
    illness. New York: Wiley & Sons, Inc., 1964.

Glick, I.D., Hargreaves, W.A., Drues, J., Schourstack, J.A.
    Short versus long hospitalization: A prospective controlled
    study. V. One year follow-up results for nonschizophrenic
    patients. Am. J. Psychiatry, 133, 515-517, 1976.

Glick, I.D., Hargreaves, W.A., Drues, J., Schourstack, J.A.
    Short versus long hospitalization: A prospective controlled
    study. IV. One year follow-up results for schizophrenic
    patients. Am. J. Psychiatry, 133, 509-514, 1976.

Goffman, E. Asylums. Garden City, N.Y.: Doubleday & Co. Inc.,
    1961.

Gruenberg, E.   The social breakdown syndrome: Some origins.
    Am. J. Psychiatry, 123, 1481-1489, 1967.

Honigfeld, G., Gillis, R.   The role of institutionalization in the
    natural history of schizophrenia.   Dis. Nerv. Syst. 28, 660-663,
    1967.

Langsley, D.G., Machotka, P., Flomenhaft, K.   Avoiding mental
    hospital admission: A follow-up study.   Am. J. Psychiatry, 127,
    1391-1394, 1971.

Ludwig, A.M., Farrelly, F.   The code of chronicity.   Arch. Gen.
    Psychiatry, 15, 562-568, 1966.

Marx, et al.   Extrohospital management of severe mental illness.
    Arch. Gen. Psychiatry, 29, 505-511, 1973.

Paul, G.L.   Chronic mental patient: Current status - future
    directions.   Psychol. Bull., 71, 81-94, 1969.

Rittenhouse, J.D.   Endurance of effect: Family unit treatment
    compared to identified patient treatment, in the Proceedings of
    the Annual Convention of American Psychological Association.
    Washington, D.C.: American Psychological Association, 2,
    535-536, 1970.

Rosenblatt, A., Mayers, J.E.   The recidivism of mental patients:
    A review of past studies.   Amer. J. Orthopsychiat., 44,
    697-706, 1974.

Sanders, R., Smith, R.S., Weinman, B.S.   Chronic psychoses and
    recovery.   San Francisco: Jossey-Bass, Inc., 1967.

Stein, L.E., Test, M.A.   Retraining a hospital staff for work in
    a community program in Wisconsin.   Hosp. Community Psychiatry,
    27, 266-268, 1976.

Weinman, B., Sanders, R., Kleiner, R., Wilson, S.   Community based
    treatment of the chronic psychotic.   Community Mental Health J.,
    6, 13-21, 1970.

Experimental Design

Subjects meeting the above criteria were randomly assigned to either the experimental ("community treatment") or control group by the admissions office staff. Control Ss were treated in the hospital for as long as deemed necessary and then linked with appropriate community agencies. Experimental Ss did not enter the hospital (except in the cases mentioned in the clinical description), but instead received the "Training in Community Living" approach for 14 months, after which they received no further input from the experimental unit staff. Assessment data on all patients were gathered at baseline (i.e., time of admission) and every four months for a span of 28 months through "face-to-face" interviews by a research staff which operated totally independently of both clinical teams. In cases where experimental Ss were hospitalized, these data are included in the results reported. Thus no patients were excluded from the study on the basis of severity of symptomatology or for any reason other than failure to meet the three admission criteria specified above.

Description of the Control Treatment

Patients assigned to the control group were immediately screened by a member of the hospital's acute treatment unit serving Dane County. The patients were usually (though not necessarily) admitted to the hospital where they received progressive treatment aimed at preparation for return to the community. The Dane County Unit served as a stringent control for the experimental program as it had a high staff to patient ratio and offered a wide variety of services: in-patient, partial hospitalization, and out-patient follow-up. It was by no means a custodial unit as its median length of stay was only 17 days. In addition, the unit made liberal use of aftercare services available in Madison for their discharged patients.

Assessment Instruments

The effects of the two treatment models were assessed on a variety of "hard" and "soft" patient outcome measures, with our own strongest interest being in the area of autonomous behavioral functioning. Those instruments utilized are summarized in Table 1.

Measures given at baseline were the following: 1) Demographic Data Form--to collect standard demographic data on life situation and economic variables; 2) Community Adjustment Form--our major assessment instrument, with scales tapping behavioral functioning in the areas of living situation, time in institutions, employment, leisure time activities, and social relationships, as well as

TABLE 1

Major Instruments and Their Measurement Times

Baseline	One Month	Subsequent Four-Month Periods
Demographic Form		Community Adjustment Form
Community Adjustment Form		- Living situation
- Living situation		- Time in institutions
- Time in institutions		- Employment
- Employment		- Leisure time activities
		- Social relationships
		- Quality of environment
		- Subjective satisfaction with life
Self-Esteem Scale		Self-Esteem Scale
Symptomatology Rating		Symptomatology Rating
	Family Burden Form	Family Burden Form (given the first four-month period only)

scales measuring quality of environment and subjective satisfaction with life (not all scales were given at baseline); 3) Rosenburg Self-Esteem Scale (Rosenburg, 1965)--a self-report measure of self-esteem; 4) Short Clinical Rating Scale (French & Heninger, 1970)-- a measure of symptomatology. Measures taken at the subsequent four-month intervals were the Self-Esteem Scale, the Short Clinical Rating Form, and the Community Adjustment Form.

In addition to the instruments which were administered to patients, a "Family Burden Scale" was administered to the most "significant other" in the family if such a person lived within Dane County. This measure was given to the family one month and four months after treatment of the patient began. The purpose of this scale was to assess whether or not the experimental approach of treating the patients in the community placed more of a burden, emotional and economic, on family members than did the control approach of treating patients in the hospital and then linking them with aftercare services.

Finally, a detailed cost benefit analysis of the two models is being carried out in collaboration with an economist in order to assess the short range and long range costs and benefits of the new versus the traditional treatment model.

RESULTS

The results reported here represent those on 65 experimental (E) and 65 control (C) subjects through their first year in the study. In tables and discussion below n's of less than 65 are the result of missing data in cases in which it was impossible to obtain the scheduled follow-up interview for reasons of patient nonavail-ability or lack of cooperation. Through assertive data collection, however, 89% of all possible interviews were completed.

Characteristics of the Sample

Characteristics of the sample at the time of entry into the study appear in Table 2. This table indicates that the E and C groups were quite similar on basic demographic factors. About 73% of the patients in both groups were either single, separated, or divorced; the mean age was fairly young (approximately 31), and patients had accumulated substantial prior time in psychiatric institutions before presenting for the current admission. Addi-tionally, data not described in Table 2 indicated that the E and C groups did not differ significantly on any of the major measuring instruments given at the time of admission with the exception of Self-Esteem, which will be discussed later.

TABLE 2

Characteristics of the Two Treatment Groups at
Time of Entry Into the Study

Characteristic		E Group (N = 65)	C Group (N = 65)	Significance
Sex				
Male		36	36	n.s.*
Female		29	29	
Marital Status				
Single		30	30	
Divorced or Separated		17	18	n.s.*
Married		18	17	
Age (years)	X̄	31.46	30.77	n.s.**
	SD	10.49	11.29	
Prior time in Psychiatric Institutions				
(months)	X̄	16.65	12.52	n.s.**
	SD	30.99	28.91	

* Tested at .05 significance level (chi-square)
** Tested at .05 significance level (t-test)

Decision to Hospitalize

Among the most significant feasibility data are the matters
of how many patients in each group were hospitalized at Mendota
during the first year in the study and how much time was spent
there. Data on the number of subjects hospitalized appear in
Table 3. In the E group only 12 of 65 patients were hospitalized
at Mendota at any time during their first year in the study,
whereas in the C group, 58 of 65 were hospitalized in Mendota.
The mean number of days spent in Mendota by the Ss in each group
also are shown in Table 3. Not indicated in the table is the
additional fact that 21 of the 58 C patients hospitalized were

TABLE 3

Number of S's Hospitalized at Mendota During the First
Year Post Entry Into the Study

		E Group (N = 65)	C Group (N = 65)	Significance
Not Hospitalized		53	7	p.<.001*
Hospitalized		12	58	
Mean number of days for those hospitalized	X̄	11.17	36.60	p.<.001**
	S̄D	18.12	41.75	
Mean number of days for entire group	X̄	2.06	29.35	p.<.001**
	SD	8.69	33.09	

 * Chi-square
** t-test

readmitted at least once, for a readmission rate of 37.5% in the
first year. Thus, many of the patients treated in the traditional
manner were becoming involved in the familiar "revolving door syndrome."

Living Situation

Table 4 summarizes the amount of time that subjects in the two
groups spent at various kinds of living situations during each of
the first three four-month long data collection periods. The data
in Table 4 indicate that throughout the first year E subjects spent
very little time in psychiatric institutions as compared to controls.
This avoidance of use of the mental hospital for the E patients did
not lead to a greater utilization of medical or penal institutions,
nor of supervised living situations in the community. In fact, the
E group spent significantly more time than the C group in independent living situations in the community.

A closer look at the E data regarding time in psychiatric
institutions in Table 4 indicates an increase in the 12 month period
as compared to the four and eight month periods. Additional data
indicate that 97% of the psychiatric institutional time at 12 months

TABLE 4

Mean Percentage of the First Three Data Collection Periods
Spent in the Various Living Situations[+]

		4 months		8 months		12 months	
		E (n = 62)	C (n = 60)	E (n = 62)	C (n = 60)	E (n = 58)	C (n = 59)
INSTITUTIONS							
Psychiatric	X̄	1.59 ***	21.20	1.38 ***	11.63	4.71 *	13.13
	SD	5.35	20.62	3.99	22.88	16.61	26.56
Medical	X̄	.97	1.12	.11	.53	.77	.81
	SD	4.89	3.19	.44	1.85	3.83	2.17
Penal	X̄	4.42	3.53	5.14	5.27	3.47	6.06
	SD	15.39	10.65	19.96	15.45	14.37	21.24
TOTAL	X̄	7.06 ***	25.85	6.64 *	17.44	8.96 *	20.00
	SD	17.47	21.31	20.99	28.14	23.39	31.74
NON-INSTITUTIONAL							
Supervised	X̄	7.83	10.73	6.37	12.02	8.95	12.27
	SD	20.49	21.58	22.39	24.69	26.38	26.90

Table 4 (continued)

		4 months		8 months		12 months	
		$\underline{E}$ (n = 62)	$\underline{C}$ (n = 60)	$\underline{E}$ (n = 62)	$\underline{C}$ (n = 60)	$\underline{E}$ (n = 58)	$\underline{C}$ (n = 59)
Independent	$\overline{X}$	85.20	63.41	86.99 **	70.54	82.09 *	67.73
	SD	26.06	31.02	34.22	37.02	32.50	38.49
TOTAL	$\overline{X}$	93.02 ***	74.15	93.36 *	82.56	91.04 *	80.00
	SD	17.50	21.31	20.99	28.14	23.39	31.74

[+]Differences between $\underline{E}$ and $\underline{C}$ groups within each of the data collection periods that are significantly different are indicated by an asterisk(s) between the two means:

* $p < .05$
** $p < .01$
*** $p < .001$

was due to six patients who left the program against our advice and then gained admission to institutions other than Mendota. Since at the time they left the program none of these patients were psychotic or in acute difficulty, it is our judgment that had they continued in the program, hospitalization would have been avoided.

Employment Status

Data concerning time spent in various employment categories by Ss in both groups are displayed in Table 5. It can be seen that E subjects spent significantly less time unemployed and significantly more time in sheltered employment than did C patients. There was no significant difference between groups in percentage of time spent in competitive employment situations. Additional data, however, indicate that the E approach indeed did have a favorable effect on competitive employment. Table 6 demonstrates that during two of the three data collection periods, E subjects earned significantly more income through competitive employment than did C subjects. Other data indicate this was probably the result of the fact that E subjects spent significantly more time in full time competitive employment situations than did C subjects, who spent more time in part time competitive employment.

Leisure Time Activities, Social Relationships,
and Quality of Environment

Leisure time activities and social relationships were not measured across the entire four-month long data collection periods. but instead were assessed by asking Ss at the 4, 8, and 12 month follow-up interviews a series of objective questions about specific activities they had engaged in during a designated interval of time preceding the interview (e.g., past three days, last week, last month). The two scales developed from these items to measure Leisure Time Activities revealed no significant differences between the E and C groups at any of the three data collection points. Likewise, several of the scales derived to measure Social Relationships revealed no significant differences. One scale measuring "Contact With Trusted Friends", however, revealed that E subjects had significantly more contact ($p < .05$) than did C subjects at the 12-month period. Additionally, Table 7 reveals that the mean score for E subjects on a scale measuring "Social Groups Belonged to and Attended in the Last Month" is significantly greater than the mean C group score at all three of the data collection points.

"Quality of Environment" was measured by asking Ss about the number of meals they regularly ate, the quality of their living situations, and whether or not they had a number of common

TABLE 5

Mean Percentage of the First Three Data Collection Periods Spent in the Various Employment Situations[+]

		4 months		8 months		12 months	
		E (n = 61)	C (n = 60)	E (n = 61)	C (n = 60)	E (n = 57)	C (n = 59)
Unemployed	X̄	33.76 ***	61.74	22.97 ***	53.97	30.31	56.76
	SD	36.48	37.04	36.23	42.93	41.34	43.31
Sheltered Employment	X̄	26.68 ***	5.06	22.50 ***	2.00	22.39 ***	1.10
	SD	38.33	13.53	37.69	9.79	38.64	8.24
Competitive Employment	X̄	39.63	33.20	54.52	44.03	47.30	42.14
	SD	42.29	36.03	46.27	43.07	45.86	42.69

+ Difference between E and C groups within each of the data collection periods that are significantly different are indicated by an asterisk(s) between the two means:

*** $p < .001$

TABLE 6

Mean Amount of Competitive Income (Dollars) Earned by $\underline{S}s$

in Both Groups During the First Three Data Collection Periods +

	4 months		8 months		12 months	
	$\underline{E}$ (n = 61)	$\underline{C}$ (n = 59)	$\underline{E}$ (n = 61)	$\underline{C}$ (n = 59)	$\underline{E}$ (n = 57)	$\underline{C}$ (n = 59)
$\overline{X}$	610.00	308.80	872.30 *	436.00	759.80 *	418.90
SD	1053.40	622.80	1260.00	834.00	1063.50	711.60

+ Differences between $\underline{E}$ and $\underline{C}$ groups within each of the data collection periods
   that are significantly different are indicated by an asterick between the two
   means:

* p<.05

TABLE 7

Mean Scores on a Scale Measuring

"Social Groups Belonged To and Attended in the Last Month"

	4 months		8 months		12 months	
	$\overline{E}$ (n = 41)	$\overline{C}$ (n = 48)	$\overline{E}$ (n = 47)	$\overline{C}$ (n = 48)	$\overline{E}$ (n = 51)	$\overline{C}$ (n = 47)
$\overline{X}$	2.05 **	.67	1.66 *	.79	1.88 **	.55
SD	2.30	1.81	2.30	1.83	2.45	1.49

+ Differences between $\underline{E}$ and $\underline{C}$ groups within each of the data collection periods that are significantly different are indicated by an asterick(s) between the two means:

* p<.05
** p<.01

"creature comforts" (e.g., private bath, radio, TV, easy chair).
There was no significant difference between groups on these
measures.

The above cited results on leisure time activities, social
relationships, and quality of environment are important since they
indicate that even though E patients were spending a significantly
greater percentage of their time in the community, there was no
reduction in their quality of life relative to controls. On some
measures, in fact, their social adjustment was enhanced.

Satisfaction With Life and Self-Esteem

The patient's subjective satisfaction with various aspects of
his or her current life situation (e.g., living situation, friends,
food, work, etc.) was tapped through use of an 8-item self-report
scale adapted from work by Fairweather et al (1969). Scores on the
items were summed to produce a Total Satisfaction score, and the
means of the E and C groups on the score revealed E subjects to be
significantly more satisfied with their present life situations
than C subjects at the 12-month data collection point (p<.05).

Self-esteem was measured by a 10-item scale and a single total
score was derived as described by Rosenburg (1965). On this measure
the E group revealed significantly higher self-esteem than C subjects at baseline (p<.05). While the two groups may have actually
represented different populations on this variable, this would seem
unlikely in view of the fact that E and C groups differed significantly on no other variable baseline. An alternative explanation
is that, since this measure was taken a few days after the patient's
admission to the study, a lower self-esteem in the C group may be
related to the fact that almost all C patients were initially
hospitalized while almost all E patients were kept in the community.
Subsequently, meanwhile, both t-tests and analyses of covariance
of self-esteem scores at the 4, 8, and 12-month data collection
periods revealed no significant differences between E and C groups.

Symptomatology

Symptomatology was measured through the Short Clinical Rating
Scale (French & Heninger, 1970), a 13-item scale filled out by the
program evaluator after performing a mental status examination of
the patient. The severity of twelve different symptoms were
assessed (on a nine point scale) along with a final item assessing
"Global Illness." Scores on the individual items were analyzed
separately since there was no rationale for either totalling or
weighing the separate items to form a single score. Means of the
E and C groups on each of the 13 items were compared at the 4, 8,

TABLE 8

Significant Differences Between E and C Group Means On
Items of the Short Clinical Rating Scale [+]

Items	4 months	8 months	12 months
Depressed Mood	--	--	.01
Suicidal Trends	--	--	.001
Anxiety or Fear	.001	.01	.01
Expression of Anger	--	--	--
Social Withdrawal	--	--	--
Motor Agitation	.05	.01	--
Motor Retardation	--	--	--
Paranoid Behavior	--	--	.001
Hallucinations	--	--	--
Thought Disorder	--	.01	.001
Hyperactivity- Elation	.05	--	.01
Physical Complaints	--	--	--
Global Illness	.05	.001	.01

+ Items on which the means of E and C groups differed significantly
   are indicated by the above figures which represent the level (p)
   of statistical significance. In all cases of significant differences, C subjects were more symptomatic than E subjects.

and 12-month periods, using analysis of covariance with the baseline score serving as the covariant. Results of these analyses
appear in Table 8. It can be seen from the table that at each of
the three data collection points E subjects revealed less symptomatology than C subjects, indeed revealing better functioning on
seven of the 13 scales by the 12-month period. Additional data
are being analyzed to shed light on the reasons for this favorable
outcome.

Suicide and Other Dangerous Acts

It is a common concern that severely disturbed individuals
being treated virtually totally in the community may either kill
themselves or harm others to a greater extent than their

hospitalized counterparts, who often have been "locked up" for their own protection or the protection of others. There is no evidence to substantiate this concern from our study. During the first year of the program, one of the 65 E patients committed suicide as did one of the 65 C patients. Meanwhile, there were no homicides in either group and few felonies, and, as already indicated, there was no difference between groups in time spent in penal institutions. Precise data on all law-breaking behaviors in both groups have been collected and are currently being analyzed.

Family Burden

The Family Burden Scale tapped behavioral measures of burden (e.g., time missed from work; disruption to social life, etc.) as well as economic and subjective experience of burden by families of patients. Thus far only a global rating of burden has been analyzed. Results of this measure appear in Table 9. The relatively small numbers of 18 and 16 for E and C groups respectively reflects the fact that a high percentage of patients who seek admission to public mental hospitals do not have a family living near them. The results show that at four months there was a significant drop in the burden on families of E subjects; however, there was no such decrease in the burden of C families. These preliminary results indicate that our community approach did not shift burden from the hospital to the family, but in fact reduced family burden relative to the traditional approach.

Cost-Benefit Analysis

A detailed cost-benefit analysis of the project is being carried out by Professor Burton Weisbrod of the Department of Economics at the University of Wisconsin. The study deals not only with the totals of costs and benefits of E and C treatment approaches, but also with the distribution of these costs and benefits among governmental levels, community groups, and private individuals. Results of the cost-benefit analysis will be published at a later date.

DISCUSSION

The above results clearly indicate that the "Training in Community Living" model is an effective alternative to mental hospital treatment. Specifically, virtually without use of the hospital it was possible to treat in the community an unselected group of patients presenting for admission to a public mental hospital. This was accomplished without shifting the burden to the family. While most of the control Ss were admitted to the

TABLE 9

A Measure of Family Burden* at One Month and Four Months

Post Entry Into the Study

		E Group (N = 18)		C Group (N = 16)		
		One Month	Four Months	One Month	Four Months	Differential Change**
Family Burden Rating	$\overline{X}$	1.89	1.44	1.81	1.81	p <.05
	SD	.76	.70	.75	.75	
Within-group *** Change		p <.01		n.s.		

* Family burden based on a 3 point scale (1 - no burden to 3 - severe burden)

** t-test on change scores

*** Correlated t-test

hospital and many subsequently readmitted, almost all E patients experienced a sustained community tenure without suffering the disruption to life and reinforcement of the patient role frequently incurred through hospitalization. Additionally, and most important, the data indicate that their sustained community living was not gained at the expense of their quality of life, level of adjustment, self-esteem, or personal satisfaction with life. Instead, relative to C patients the E patients showed enhanced functioning in several significant areas and manifest less subjective distress and greater satisfaction with their lives.

Two methodological issues bear brief mentioning. First, it is obvious that the "Training in Community Living" approach differed from the traditional approach in a number of significant ways. Therefore, much hard work remains in sorting out which of the factors carry the greater part of the variance in accounting for the favorable results. What seems already apparent, however, is the importance of the site of treatment--the "sane" community-- since some rather high powered attempts at "training in community living" inside of an institution have failed remarkably.

A second issue requiring mention is the apparent tautological nature of some of the results--that is, that they may be highly dependent on our treatment input and may have little "carry-over" value. Our post-treatment follow-up data will provide objective evidence regarding this matter. Early observations indeed indicate, however, that without ongoing services, a number of patients will return to the chronic patient role--e.g., evidence a pattern of frequent hospitalizations and a poor community adjustment between admissions. Meanwhile, additional economic data show that it re-quires very little input to prevent patients from experiencing the above regression. These factors lead to the conclusion that the "Training in Community Living" approach may need to exist as an ongoing treatment modality that remains available to clients over an indefinite period of time. If society opts for such a model of treating "the insane" in "sane places", however, our data provide clear hope that the next generation of chronic patients can be prevented.

Footnotes

1. This study was supported in part by Grant 05-R 000009 from the National Institute of Mental Health. The authors wish to acknowledge the major contributions of their skillful research staff: Rick Bowman, Carl Schwanz, Suzanne Senn, and Gene Jackson.

REFERENCES

Fairweather, G. W., Sanders, D. H., Maynard, H., and Cressler, D. L.
    Community life for the mentally ill. Chicago: Aldine Publishing
    Company, 1969.

French, M. H., and Heninger, G. R. A short clinical rating scale
    for use by nursing personnel. I. Development and design.
    Archives of General Psychiatry, 1970, 23, 233-240.

Rosenburg, M. Society and the adolescent self-image. Princeton,
    N.Y.: Princeton University Press, 1965.

LOWERED BARRIERS IN THE COMMUNITY: THE SOTERIA MODEL[1,2]

Loren R. Mosher* and Alma Z. Menn**

Center for Studies of Schizophrenia, Rockville, Maryland*

Mental Research Institute, Palo Alto, California**

BACKGROUND

Serious students of the mental hospital scene in the United States frequently remark on the isolation and quasi-penal appearance of many state hospitals. Most of these institutions were built in the second half of the 19th century, an era when tuberculosis was a scourge and social Darwinism was a fairly widely held philosophy in the West. As is usual in the development of new institutions, the mental hospital movement was highly influenced by the cultural context of its era. It is not surprising then that these new "hospitals" often looked like a cross between sanatorium and prison. In this regard, the United States was different than older European civilizations whose insane and criminal members had been incarcerated together; until the 1800's, there had been no such precedent in the relatively young American nation. The penal aspects of the mental hospitals built between 1850 and 1900 would seem to reflect the culture's ambivalence about mental illness: Was it a medical disease like tuberculosis and therefore to be treated in a hospital? Or, on the other hand, was it a reflection of basic unfitness (the perspective of social Darwinism), whose demise should be ensured by keeping its victims safely locked up to prevent reproduction with more "fit" members of society? Although overstated and oversimplified, this view reflects some of the functions society ascribed, as least implicitly, to these institutions.

If the mental hospital was created to shield society from mad-persons, the century-old barriers have now been eroded by changes in the cultural context since World War II. The new context is reflected in changing public attitudes, legal activity on behalf of the mentally

75

ill, the development of psychiatric wards in general hospitals, and
the appearance of community mental health centers--to name but a
few examples.

This meeting, focused on alternatives to mental hospitals, is
a logical outgrowth of the new context. Unfortunately for those of
us who have spent time working in and around today's mental hospitals,
the barriers within the hospital--between patients and staff--seem
more resistant to change and have not kept pace with developments
outside. The project I will describe, Soteria (the word for deliv-
erance in Greek), is our response to the relatively unchanged inter-
nal barrier structure of most psychiatric hospitals. For us, hospi-
tals--even well staffed, "progressive" ones--usually have institutional characteristics that create barriers to establishing the
types of relationships we believe to be critical for the facilitation of the process of recovery from psychosis.

Thus, Soteria House was established to provide a home-like
alternative for schizophrenics who would otherwise have been hospitalized, a place where they are allowed to experience their psychosis
at their own pace in the context of warm, protective, supportive
and, we hope, facilitating relationships with a specially selected
and trained nonprofessional staff. Of course, because it is an
open institution located very much in the community, it is likely
that Soteria will, over time, contribute to the further closing of
the distance between society and its madpersons.

In this report we address four aspects of inpatient settings
(present to varying degrees in different settings) that create in-
ternal barriers to which Soteria is a response: theoretical model,
size, social structure and neuroleptic medications.

Theoretical Model

Although a variety of other models may be mixed in, or explicitly avowed, most psychiatric wards function primarily with a medical model: Doctors have final authority and decision-making powers;
medications are accorded primary therapeutic value and used extensively; the person is seen as having a disease, with attendant disability and dysfunction that are to be "treated" and "cured"; and
labeling and its interpersonal consequences, objectification and
stigmatization, are almost inevitable. Although we have no quarrel
with the demonstrated heuristic value of the medical model, we do
believe its application to the treatment of psychiatric disorders
can have long-lasting unfortunate (although unintended) consequences
for individual patients. In our view, the most deleterious consequences stem from the fact that the medical model, with its primary
emphasis on sickness rather than health, almost inevitably fosters
the "mental patient" identity. The development of this identity can

be traced--with oversimplified strokes--as follows: The disorganized
person arrives at his first intake point with a poorly formed notion
of "what's wrong." He and his family have come (or been brought) to
the hospital to obtain the answer to the "problem" from the powerful,
high status doctor. The answer will vary depending on the doctor's
own personal background and training. But the model answer--often
not openly communicated--will be that the person hospitalized and
diagnosed "schizophrenic" (a notoriously unreliable term) is the
victim of an inherited disease (i.e., he and his family are not
responsible for the affliction and therefore can do little about it);
the disease is believed to have a predictable, deteriorating course
(in practice, excellent recovery tends to call the diagnosis into
question); it does, however, respond to medication (nonsomatic forms
of treatment are considered interesting but of peripheral value),
which only the doctor can prescribe. The patient is admitted to a
ward where his sometimes troubling or troublesome behavior is often
related to and explained by his diagnostic pigeonhole. Because he
is often seen as manifesting a disease (i.e., an endogenously driven
process) the effects of interactional and contextual factors in
determining his behavior are usually given little credence. As a
consequence, the patient may begin to call into question his own
experience of himself as other wiser and more powerful people do--
i.e., as a powerless victim of a disease process over which he has
little control and no responsibility. This is obviously also a
view that is easy for his family to accept--especially since it is
proffered to them at a time of crisis when they are assailed by
guilt over the admission of their offspring. Thus, the medically
based treatment system leads to a cycle of spiraling negative expectations that may induct the patient into a career as a mental
patient or schizophrenic. His identity, never very secure, has been
redefined and will be reinforced as long as he remains within the
system--an excellent example of mutual dependence! Although his
relationships may have been altered by his experience of madness,
the treatment tends to leave him feeling less able to understand,
cope with or modify these relationships than before. His new mental
patient identity and its attendant erosion of self-confidence and
self-esteem certainly do not prepare him to confront the competitive
work world of this society. However compassionately motivated, his
family's view of him as "sick", "dependent", and nonresponsible will
only hinder any attempts he may make at assuming a mature adult
status--usually through work.

In planning the Soteria project, we identified as a major goal
the comparison and evaluation of one setting (Soteria) in which the
input of the medical system was minimized with one (CMHC) in which
it was more important and pervasive. Our hypothesis was that
Soteria's nonmedical orientation would mitigate the effects of labeling and stigmatization. Soteria-treated patients, we predicted,
would show less tendency to assume a mental patient identity and

their psychosocial competence would be enhanced as compared with patients treated in the more medically oriented control facility.

Although we believe application of the medical model to the treatment of schizophrenia may be premature or incorrect--given the present state of our knowledge--we are not proposing an alternative theoretical model. We know of none that can organize, encompass, integrate and make comprehensible the diversity, uncertainty and ambiguity of knowledge about psychiatry's most persistent conundrum --schizophrenia. We do, however, propose an alternative attitude or stance; basically, we advocate a phenomenologic approach to schizophrenia, an attempt to understand and share the psychotic person's experience without judging, labeling or derogating it. Although we purposely eschew theories, as they make it more diffi- cult to assume a phenomenologic stance, we do have a loose, rela- tively nonspecific "developmental crisis" framework within which we find it easier to work (Mosher, Menn, & Goveia, 1972).

Put most simply, we view psychosis as a crisis in the course of an individual's development, which in our specially selected sample usually first occurs in late adolescence or early adulthood. As with nonpsychotic crises (from which most crisis theory has evolved), we view the psychotic crisis state as especially suscep- tible to change; properly dealt with, this change can be growth en- hancing, leaving the individual with a greater sense of integrity, identity, and "togetherness" and, as a result, more psychosocially competent than he had been before his psychosis.

Size

Most psychiatric hospital wards have at least 20 patients. Thus, the staff/patient group is apt to be 40-60. For us, this is too large and complex a social group for severely disorganized per- sons to cope with. A social reference group of no more than 10-12 persons seems more natural, less complex, and of a size to which we are all accustomed. A group of this size, when combined with a home- like atmosphere, would seem to maximize the possibility of the dis- organized person's getting to know and trust a new environment and to find a surrogate family in it; at the same time, because it is generally consonant with the individual's previous life, small group size might contribute importantly to minimizing the labeling, stig- matization and mental patient identity process described above. Interestingly, 10-12 is about the maximum number of persons in one extended family household, or in a single commune, and is also the upper limit for group therapy and experimental psychology's small task group membership. Thus, rather than a 20-bed ward, Soteria is a home that sleeps 8-10 comfortably, with six beds occupied by resi- dents (our term for patients) and two by staff. We also hypothesized

that the setting's intimacy would be particularly well suited to
developing the sense of trust and willingness to explore the inner
self, without fear of punishment, that seems so important if recovery
from psychosis is to result in enhanced competence. Again, we believe this freedom to explore will lead to better outcome among
Soteria-treated patients as compared with our CMHC-treated controls.

Social Structure

This aspect interacts closely with size. To function effectively every organization, large or small, needs structure; generally
speaking, the larger the organization, the greater the structure.
Unfortunately, more elaborate structures have consequences that im-
pinge negatively on persons undergoing psychotic disorganization:
Inflexibility, reliance on authority, institutionalization of roles,
and decision-making power residing in the hierarchy outside patients'
purview. As a result, those at the bottom of the hierarchy feel
relatively powerless, irresponsible and dependent. To obviate this
problem at Soteria, we are attempting to be as unstructured as is
commensurate with adequate function. Structure which develops to
meet functional needs is dissolved if the need is not a continuing
one. There is no institutionalized method of dealing with a particular type of occurrence. We hypothesize that this relative lack of
structure will lead to more highly individualized programs in which
the resident/patient feels involved, responsible and independent--
which will, in turn, lead to enhanced psychosocial competence among
Soteria-treated, as compared with CMHC-treated patients.

Medication

We live in an overmedicated, too frequently drug-dependent
culture despite Calvinist-based ambivalence about these "crutches."
Our ambivalence is resolved by creating two categories of drugs--
good ones (e.g., alcohol) and bad ones (e.g., L.S.D.). In action,
our society is basically pro-drug. Psychiatry's attitude is no
different from that of the wider social context; it seeks the magical
answer from a pill. The antipsychotic drugs have provided psychiatry with real substance for their magical cure fantasy with regard
to schizophrenia. As is the case with most such exaggerated expectations, the fantasy is better than the reality. After two decades,
it is now clear that the phenothiazines do not cure schizophrenia.
It is also clear that they have serious, sometimes irreversible
toxicities (Crane, 1973), that recovery may be impaired (i.e., unnecessary disability produced) by them in at least some schizophrenics (Goldstein, 1970; Rappaport et al, 1974) and that they have
little effect on long-term psychosocial adjustment (Niskanen & Achte,
1972). For us, the main damaging effect of drugs is their introduction of a barrier within the person which prevents his experiencing

himself, especially the disavowed aspects of himself that come to the fore in psychosis. This is not to deny the extraordinary helpfulness of drugs in reducing and controlling symptoms, shortening hospital stays and revitalizing the interest of psychiatrists in schizophrenia as a potentially treatable problem. They also have two less often noted effects--both of which serve to reinforce the medical model. First, as only a doctor can prescribe neuroleptics, they serve to maintain his power and control of the treatment system. Second, as pills are given to individuals, they maintain medicine's traditional focus on a person as "sick." This prevents the doctor and the system over which he presides from looking at family and wider social contextual factors that might have exerted important influences on the development of psychosis--and might also therefore be amenable to intervention. Thus, medications tend to narrow conceptual sights and may actually deprive the system of important treatment possibilities. An aim of the Soteria project is to seek a viable informed alternative to the overuse of, and excessive reliance on, these drugs. We use neuroleptics infrequently and, when prescribed, they are kept primarily under the individual resident's (patient's) control. That is, he is asked to monitor his responses to the drug very carefully, to give us feedback so we can adjust dosage, and after a trial period of two weeks he is given a major role in determining whether he will continue on them.

In each of the four areas mentioned above, Soteria is a reaction to criticisms of existing facilities. Much of what is involved in the program is, however, based on the positive contributions of a variety of other researchers, clinicians and theorists. In fact, we have come to recognize that no individual element of the Soteria program is new; it is their combination in one setting we believe to be unique. Some of Soteria's roots may be traced to the era of moral treatment in American psychiatry (Bockover, 1963); the tradition of intensive interpersonal intervention in schizophrenia (Sullivan, 1962; Fromm-Reichman, 1948); therapists who have described growth from psychosis (Menninger, 1959; Perry, 1962); and the current group of psychiatric heretics (Laing, 1967; Szasz, 1961).

Table 1 summarizes, in somewhat exaggerated and oversimplified terms for purposes of explication and contrast, the characteristics of Soteria and those of more usual inpatient facilities like our control ward.

Table 1

Differences Between the Two Treatment Models

Soteria   Community Mental Health Ward

Institutional Variables

Soteria	Community Mental Health Ward
Non-medical	Medical
Non-hospital	Hospital
Open	Closed (or restrictive)
Varied work schedules	8 hour staff shifts
Minimal use of medication	Medication--"usual" treatment
Labeling, stigmatization minimized	Labeling, stigmatization inevitable
Behavior of residents and staff open to scrutiny and discussion	Staff behavior usually reviewed in closed sessions

Social Structure

Soteria	Community Mental Health Ward
Non-authoritarian	Authoritarian
Non-hierarchical	Hierarchical
Peer/fraternal relations	Parent/child relationships
Program flexibility	Inflexibility
Role differentiation minimized	Institutionalized role definitions (e.g., nurse, social worker)
Resident	Patient
Equality	Patient submissive to authority
Dyadic, triadic units emphasized	Group emphasized
Individuals usually responsible for and in control of their lives	Hospital/doctor/ward assumes responsibility and control

Table 1--Continued

Soteria	Community Mental Health Ward
Power resides equally in each resident and staff member	Power resides in hierarchy; head nurse/doctor/hospital administration
Minimal structured activities	Emphasis on structured activities
Continuity of relationship after discharge	Outside hospital contact discouraged
Family-like atmosphere	Hotel/boarding house atmosphere

Staff Attitudes

Psychosis a valid experience	Psychosis an illness, therefore not an intimate part of person
"Being with" the individual	Maintain objectivity and distance
Important event, should be taken seriously	Getting over it most important
Understanding the experience important	Putting the experience behind important
Allow individual to experience his psychosis	Shore up defenses to suppress, repress, and abort psychosis
Regression allowed	Regression prevented or interrupted when possible
Containing, holding environment	"Moving on" environment
Growth and learning from psychosis valued	Getting over psychosis quickly valued
Minimal pressure to "get going"	Length of stay seen as critical

Family

Vacation from psychotic offspring	Continued involvement necessary

Table 1--Continued

Soteria	Community Mental Health Ward
Aftercare decided upon by individual; therefore perhaps not involving family	Aftercare determined by M.D.-- usually family (if available)
Degree of involvement determined by family	Involvement dictated by institutional policy

RESEARCH DESIGN

Sample Selection

All subjects are obtained from a large screening facility that is part of the CMHC complex containing our control wards. Approximately 600 new patients are seen there per month, of whom about 200 are hospitalized. Anyone meeting the following basic criteria is a potential study candidate:

(1) Clearly schizophrenic [3]

(2) Deemed in need of hospitalization

(3) No more than one previous hospitalization for two weeks or less with a diagnosis of schizophrenia

(4) Age 16-30 (either sex)

(5) Unmarried, separated, widowed or divorced

About 5-8 subjects per month meet these criteria.

The selection criteria are designed to provide us with a relatively homogenous sample of individuals diagnosed schizophrenic, but a group "at risk" for prolonged hospitalization and/or chronic disability (early onset and being unmarried both predispose to chronic care) (Rosen et al, 1971). In addition to its value in homogenizing our sample, our elimination of individuals with extensive previous hospitalization reflects our wish not to deal with the learned patient role before actually involving the person as himself in the Soteria program. We recognize that these criteria limit our study's generalizability, but we feel that the advantages of relative homogeneity outweigh the disadvantage of more limited generalizability when it is possible to study only a relatively small number of subjects.

Independent Research Assessment

All patients referred to the study are screened by a research
psychologist to be sure they meet admission criteria. If they do,
he then completes a pretreatment packet consisting of:

(1) Independent diagnosis (DSM II)

(2) Diagnostic Symptoms: At least four of the following
     symptoms must be present for acceptance into the study
     (Cole, Klerman, & Goldberg, 1964); thought disorder,
     catatonic motor behavior, paranoid ideation, hallucin-
     ations, delusions (other than systematized paranoid),
     blunted or inappropriate emotion, disturbance of social
     behavior and interpersonal relations.

(3) Diagnostic certainty (Mosher, Pollin & Stabenau, 1971):
     A 1 to 7 rating of the assessor's certainty the patient
     is schizophrenic (1 = definitely not, 7 - definite).

(4) Mode of Onset (Mosher, 1972; Vaillant, 1964): Four
     elements make up this scale; time (more or less than
     6 months), confusion (present or absent), precipitants
     (yes or no), and schizoid adjustment (yes or no). This
     scale allows us to dichotomize patients into acute or
     insidious onset types as the scales measuring process/
     reactive or good/poor premorbid adjustment are not
     applicable to this special sample.

(5) Paranoid/Non-Paranoid Status (Venables & O'Connor, 1959):
     This 10-item measure contains five items (each having a
     5-point range) for rating paranoia: delusions of external
     control, ideas of reference, feelings of persecution,
     grandiosity and overtly expressed hostility.

(6) Inpatient Multidimensional Scale for Rating Psychotic
     Patients (Lorr & McNair, 1963) (IMPS). An 88 item
     interview-based symptom rating instrument yielding 10
     symptom variables (e.g., excitement, hostility).

Milieu Assessment

The most frequently used research instrument in the field of
milieu assessment has come from Moos and Houts (1968) who developed
a Ward Atmosphere Scale (WAS) and a reworded version of it, the
Community Oriented Program Evaluation Scale (COPES) (Moss & Otto,
1972; Moos, 1973), to be used in non-hospital based programs. It
contains ten subscales subsumed under three more inclusive classes:

I.   "Relationship" Dimensions:

    A.   Ward Involvement - Social involvement of patient in day-to-day social functioning of the ward including pride in the ward, enthusiasm and group spirit.

    B.   Support - Extent to which patients provide support to other patients on the ward as well as degree to which staff supports and encourages patients.

    C.   Spontaneity - Extent to which environment encourages patients to act openly and express their feelings toward other patients and staff.

II.   "Treatment Program" Dimensions:

    A.   Autonomy - Patients' self-sufficiency and independence in personal affairs and relationships with staff.

    B.   Practical Orientation - Extent to which patients are practically prepared for release from the hospital (e.g., job training).

    C.   Personal Problem Orientation - Extent to which patients are encouraged to examine their problems and openly deal with them with other patients and staff members.

    D.   Anger and Aggression - Extent to which patients are allowed and encouraged to argue openly with other patients and staff.

III. "The Administrative Structure" Dimensions:

    A.   Order and Organization - Importance of order on the ward in terms of patients' scheduling (e.g., do they follow a regular routine?), staff activity (e.g., do they keep appointments?) and physical appearance of the ward.

    B.   Program Clarity - Patients' awareness of ward rules and procedures.

    C.   Staff Control - Extent to which staff uses measures (rules, schedules) to control patient behavior.

Staff and patients in both settings are assessed at 6-month intervals on the WAS (Community Mental Health Center) and COPES (Soteria). This instrument is particularly useful in this study as it allows us to assess systematically, and to some extent independently, the characteristics of the two programs and compare them to those hypothesized to exist in the settings.

Treatment Assignment

The study requirements are explained, and informed consent is obtained from the patient and his family or significant other, if available. Group assignment is on a consecutively admitted, space available basis. As only six residents can be accommodated in the experimental setting, intake is limited by bed availability. Therefore, after a subject is admitted to the experimental program the next one who fulfills all study requirements becomes a control.

Subsequent Independent Assessments

The admission assessment battery (see above) is repeated at 3 days, 6 weeks, 6, 12, 18 and 24 months post-admission. In addition, a composite measure of community adjustment (Soskis, 1970) is obtained at discharge and at the above intervals. Data on work, social life, school, rehospitalization and other aspects of community adjustment are included in our Patient Progress Report.

Other Data

Although this report focuses primarily on independently derived research assessments and milieu data, family, staff and therapeutic process data are also obtained in the study. Some have already been reported (Mosher et al, 1973; Wilson, 1974). We have also compared and contrasted the characteristics of the two programs in greater detail previously (Wendt et al, 1974; Mosher et al, 1975; Mosher, 1974) or as ways of dealing with day-to-day problems as seen from a sociologic perspective (Wilson, 1974), the two programs are different enough to reassure us we are, in fact, comparing two very different programs.

PROGRAM DESCRIPTIONS

Experimental

Soteria is a 1915-vintage, 12-room house located on a busy
street in a "transitional" neighborhood of a San Francisco Bay
Area city. Bordering Soteria on one side is a nursing home and,
on the other, a two-family home. The neighborhood has a mixture
of small businesses, medical facilities (a general hospital is one
block away), single family homes and small apartments (usually
homes that have been remodeled for this purpose). It is a designated poverty area inhabited by a mixture of college students,
lower class families and ex-state hospital patients. Some 15-20
percent of residents in the area are Mexican-American, and there
is a sprinkling of blacks.

Due primarily to licensing laws, the house can accommodate
only six residents at one time, although as many as 10 persons can
sleep there comfortably. There are six paid nonprofessional staff
plus the project director and a 1/4 time project psychiatrist. One
or two new residents are admitted each month. In general, two of
our specially trained nonprofessional regular staff, a man and a
woman, are on duty at any one time. In addition, there are usually
one or more volunteers present, especially in the evening. Most
staff work 36- to 48-hour shifts to provide themselves the opportunity to relate to "spaced-out" (their term) residents continuously over a relatively long period of time. Staff and residents
share responsibility for household maintenance, meal preparation
and cleanup. Persons who are not "together" are not expected to
do an equal share of the work. Over the long term, staff do more
than their share and will step in to assume responsibility if a
resident cannot do a task to which he has agreed. The project
director acts as friend, counselor, supervisor, and object for dis-
placed angry feelings by staff, whereas our part-time project
psychiatrist supervises the staff and is seen as a stable, reassuring presence (in addition to his formal medico-legal responsibilities).

Although staff vary somewhat in how they see their roles, they
generally view what psychiatry labels a "schizophrenic reaction"
as an altered state of consciousness in an individual who is experiencing a crisis in living. Simply put, the altered state involves
personality fragmentation, with the loss of a sense of self.

Few clinicians would disagree with a description of the evolu-
tion of psychosis as a process of fragmentation and disintegration.
But, at Soteria House, the disruptive psychotic experience is also
believed to have unique potential for reintegration and reconstitu-
tion if it is not prematurely aborted or forced into some

psychologically strait-jacketing compromise. Such a view of
schizophrenia implies a number of therapeutic attitudes. All facets
of the psychotic experience are taken by Soteria House staff members
as "real." They view the experiential and behavioral attitudes
associated with the psychosis--the clinical symptoms, including
irrationality, terror, and mystical experiences--as extremes of
basic human qualities. Because "irrational" behavior and mystical
beliefs are regarded as valid and as capable of being understood,
Soteria staff try to provide an atmosphere that will facilitate
integration of the psychosis into the continuity of the individual's
life. Thus, psychotic persons are not to be considered nonhuman;
nor are they to be related to in a depersonalized way, for to do
so would invalidate the experience. When the fragmentation process
is seen as valid and as having potential for psychological growth,
the individual experiencing the schizophrenic reaction can be
tolerated, lived with, related to, and validated, but not "treated"
or used to fulfill staff needs. Limits are set if the person is
clearly a danger to himself, others, or the program as a whole--
not merely because others are unable to tolerate his madness.
Phenothiazines are ordinarily not used for six weeks. If the
resident shows no change at that time and is either paranoid or
has an insidious onset, Thorazine (300 mg/day or more) is given.

One final word about the background for our use of specially
trained nonprofessionals as primary staff in the house might be
valuable. We believe that **relatively untrained**, psychologically
unsophisticated persons can assume a phenomenological stance vis-
a-vis psychosis more easily than highly trained persons (e.g.,
M.D.'s or Ph.D.'s) because they have learned no theory of schizophrenia, whether psychodynamic, organic, or a combination of both.
Because they lack the preconceived ideas of professionals, our nonprofessional staff members have the freedom to be themselves, to
follow their visceral responses, and to be a "person" with the
psychotic individual. Highly trained mental health professionals
tend to lose this freedom in favor of a more cognitive, theory-
based, learned response that may invalidate a patient's experience
of himself if the professional's theory-based behavior is not
congruent with the patient's felt needs. Professionals may also
use their theoretical knowledge defensively when confronted, in
an unstructured setting, with anxiety-provoking behaviors of
psychotic persons. This pattern of response is not so readily
available to our unsophisticated nonprofessional therapists; nor
is it reinforced by a professional degree with its accompanying
status and power.

Control

The Community Mental Health Center's inpatient service consists of two locked wards of 30 beds each. About 250 patients are admitted (including readmissions) per month. It is a well-staffed (1.5/1 staff/patient ratio), active treatment facility oriented toward crisis intervention, which employs high doses of phenothiazines, rapid evaluation and placement in other parts of the County's treatment network as its immediate goal. All of the 27 control patients reported here received therapeutic courses of phenothiazines during their inpatient stays. Only one was discharged off drugs.

When possible, the service refers patients to one of the four open, private inpatient facilities in the County. The staff is generally well trained, experienced, and enthusiastic; they see themselves as doing a good job. Patients are assigned to one of five treatment teams on each ward which meet daily to decide treatment plans. The upstairs ward is directed toward slightly longer term care, and usually receives transfers from the downstairs admitting ward. Patients are assigned a therapist who provides 1/2 hour of psychotherapy daily and takes a major role in treatment planning. The therapist may be a technician, community worker, or any of the other treatment specialists. There are 1-1/2 hours/day of occupational therapy and a daily community meeting led by any member of the treatment team. A crisis group meets for 1-1/2 hours five times per week (all patients); a couples group, two hours per week (married patients and spouses); a psychodrama group, two hours per week (all patients who are able); a women's group, two hours per week; and a survival group 1-1/2 hours (for readmitted patients) three times each week.

Because the Center inpatient service takes patients from all over the County (it is the only facility with a 24-hour-a-day psychiatric emergency service and locked wards), most patients are referred back to one of four regional centers nearest their homes for outpatient care. This care may include partial hospitalization (day or night care), individual, family or group therapy, and medication follow-up. The county also has an extensive board and care system and eight halfway houses for adolescents and adults. A sub-acute facility (30 beds) and various locked (so-called "L") facilities intended to shorten hospital stay are also being utilized. As is the case with many programs these days, this one is frequently in flux--usually because of changing economic circumstances.

The above description does not convey very well actual day-to-day life on this ward. To fill out the picture we asked Holly Wilson, Ph.D., a sociologist who had studied Soteria previously (Wendt, Mosher, Matthews, & Menn, 1974), to describe the setting

from the point of view of a participant observer. As a former
nurse, she is uniquely well qualified to describe hospital ward
processes. Her report is based on 120 hours of participant
observation on the ward, which included time spent on all shifts,
attendance at all meetings, review of all the ward's written
documents (e.g., guidelines for medical coverage, nursing notes)
and informal interviews with all types of staff. She describes
the ward's primary overall functioning as a "dispatching process"
with a variety of subprocesses as follows (Wilson, 1975):

1.   Patching. Staff's initial contact with patients often
revolves around the imposition of a variety of behavioral
controls such as use of seclusion rooms, mechanical restraints,
verbal instructions, and particularly heavy doses of psycho-
tropic medications such as Haldol, Prolixin, or Thorazine.
In essence, violent, out of control or inappropriately bizarre
patients are patched together by subduing their socially un-
acceptable symptoms as quickly as possible.

2.   Medical Screening. Because the psychiatric dispatching
process (a term used to encompass the multiple, complex
operations employed for "processing patients through" a clear-
ing house model of care) takes place in a "medical" setting
under the direction of physicians for the most part, a
standardized routine of physical testing and diagnostic procedures is immediately initiated for all new admissions.
These procedures include a physical exam, blood work, urin-
alysis, E.E.G., and a selected variety of others. Such
screening also serves as an information-gathering strategy in
that on occasion, a patient's psychiatric problem is discovered to be a consequence of a medical or physiological
disorder. Properties of this process of screening are that
it is extremely time-consuming for staff, that it requires
accurate and proper completion of a multitude of requisitions
and forms, and that it is rigidly imposed even though a patient
who is readmitted may have undergone the same screening process within the same week.

3.   Piecing together a story. Proportionately speaking, the
most staff time and energy is devoted to this dimension of
the dispatching process. In order to make subsequent decisions about distributing a patient to the appropriate aftercare placement as well as the more immediate decision of which
course of medications to begin, a diagnosis must be made.
Thus, information gathering and intelligence operations con-
sume staff's focus during the first 72 hours of a patient's
confinement. The interaction of staff attempting to sleuth
out and uncover information about a patient in order to engage
in fate-making decisions, with patients who are attempting to

cover up what they believe is damaging data about themselves,
constitutes another key focus for staff/patient contact. The
major modalities for this contact are the "Group Intake
Interview" wherein a newly admitted patient is confronted by
a group of staff in an interview room and questioned, and
the "Second-hand Report" where bits and pieces of data are
passed along from shift to shift verbally and on the patient's
chart and then used to make generalizations about the patient.
Properties of this process are its preconceived tendency, a
reliance on speculations which easily become "truth", and
the trickery involved in "finding things out."

4.   Labeling and Sorting. Once there is sufficient data to
justify some decisions, patients are stamped with a psychiatric
label. For the most part, patients in the study setting fell
into the following diagnostic categories: schizophrenic,
manic-depressive, alcohol or drug abuse, or violent character
disorder of some type. Labeling acts as a key in deciding
which medications to order and which aftercare placements to
begin exploring. It also provides staff with an additional
source of control in their dealings with patients, for with
diagnoses comes an increased sense of being able to predict
patient behavior and the ability to deal with patient communications and behaviors as typifications--"That's her
hysterical personality coming out; Those are just delusions,
etc."

5.   Distributing. The official goal of Community Mental
Health legislation in California also includes a goal of
moving mentally ill persons back into "the community" as
rapidly as possible. Yet, psychiatric professionals in the
study setting are constantly balancing this mandate against
their perceived mandate to act as protectors of society and
their patients. Consequently, staff act as fate-makers by
distributing their "charges" to one of a variety of placement
options for follow-up and aftercare. A property of the distributing stage of dispatching is its revolving door nature.
Many of the setting's patients are "old familiars" who period-
ically rotate through the study setting and back out again.
A number of patients are tracked by community liaison workers
which contributes additional data taken into account when
distributing decisions are made. Reports include that one
aftercare facility or another "won't take her back again" so
the options become limited by virtue of exhausting some of
them over time.

The above conceptualization of "usual psychiatric care" in the
study setting conveys, I hope, the complex nature of the
psychiatric decision-making and deposition process that goes
on. Consequences of these operations include: (1) A very

hectic and busy pace of work for staff while the hours "drift
by" for patients; (2) A low accessibility of staff for
patients--sitting and talking with patients has very low
priority in view of all the tasks that must be accomplished;
(3) A substitution of technology for potential face-to-face
contacts (e.g., there's a mechanical cigarette lighter on the
wall to discourage patients from bothering busy staff for
lights, medications are announced over a loud speaker instead
of passed out by a nurse who seeks out patients around the
ward, etc.); (4) Staff spend the majority of their time in
interaction with other staff--in report, team meetings, intake
interviews, and other meetings. (This observation differed
on the two wards with more staff/patient contact on Ward 1,
in ritualized formats such as "anger group, feelings group,
etc.", but these contacts were low on spontaneity, low on
openness, and high on superficiality and control). (5) Staff
are the constants on the units with patients only passing
through--thus, a lot of energy is devoted to intra-staff
conflict, problems, and the distribution of labor; (6) Most
staff have a lot of integrity about their work--their value
systems are relatively congruent with conventional psychiatric
and medical model explanations of madness.

RESULTS

Reliabilities

Interrater reliabilities are high, whether calculated as
intraclass correlations or percent agreements (if the scale contains too few points for intraclass computations). The reliabilities are conveyed in Table 2.

Pretreatment Characteristics

Demographic Data. There are no significant differences between the experimental and control groups (see Table 3).

Independent Research Assessments. All subjects received a
diagnosis of schizophrenia from three independent raters. There
are no significant group differences in number of diagnostic
symptoms, certainty of diagnosis, mode of onset, paranoid/non-
paranoid status, or global psychopathology (see Table 4). Table 5
separates the groups according to mode of onset-paranoid-non-
paranoid status. Also, the IMPS profile reveals no intergroup
differences at baseline assessment.

Table 2

Interrater Reliabilities

MEASURES	RELIABILITY	INTRACLASS	RANGE
	N*		
IMPS (10 subscales)	9	.98	.95-1.00
Paranoia	5	.63	0-1.00
Global Psychopathology	6	1.00	-----
BFUR	5	1.00	-----
		% AGREEMENT	
Diagnostic Symptoms	5	.86	
Onset	4	.81	
Certainty	4	.75	

*N = number of subjects simultaneously rated by 2 or more raters.

The striking overall similarity of the groups is especially important in view of the lack of random assignment to treatment.

Milieu Characteristics

Analyses of the Soteria staff and patient data as well as the CMHC patient data involve in each case, small Ns. However, at Soteria the total staff/patient group is only 10-12. Therefore, the limited number of subjects included at each testing is, in fact, representative of the total number of persons involved in the Soteria Program at any given time. The control patients included in each testing are representative proportionally to the total number of patients who meet our research criteria at the Center.

Standard scores based on the WAS normative reference group of 160 wards were derived for the Soteria and the CMHC-ward staff and residents/patients and are depicted in Figures 1 and 2. The WAS rather than COPES norms were used for the comparison because Soteria residents were all deemed in need of hospitalization and came into the program in lieu of admission to Center inpatient wards.

Table 3

DEMOGRAPHIC DATA

	Experimental (N-30)	Control (N-27)*
AGE **		
Mean	20.73 ± 3.1	22.37 ± 4.4
Range	15-27	16-31
SEX		
Male	16 (53%)	17 (63%)
Female	14 (47%)	10 (37%)
SOCIAL CLASS ***		
Mean	3.07 ± 1.1	2.83 ± 1.1
Range	1-5	1-5
EDUCATION		
College Degree	2 (7%)	2 (7%)
Some College	15 (50%)	12 (44%)
High School Diploma	3 (10%)	4 (15%)
Some High School	10 (33%)	4 (15%)

* Data not available on 5 control subjects for social class and education.

** Upon admission to project.

***Hollingshead-Redlich for father

Figure 1 shows the two environments as perceived by the residents/patients. Soteria is two or more standard deviations higher than the CMHC on Involvement, Support, Spontaneity and Personal Problem Orientation. It is more than two standard deviations lower on Practical Orientation. Although the differences are somewhat less striking than those noted above, the programs are at least one standard deviation different on four of the five

Table 4

ADMISSION PSYCHIATRIC ASSESSMENTS

DIAGNOSTIC SYMPTOMS (Max = 7)	Experimental (N=30)	Control (N=27)
Mean	4.8 ± 1.4	5.1 ± .9
Thought Disorder	93%	96%
Hallucinations	70%	67%
Delusions	60%	81%
All Three	43%	56%
DIAGNOSIS		
Day 1 & 3	All Schizophrenic	All Schizophrenic
CERTAINTY (Max = 7)		
Mean	6.1 ± .8	6.2 ± .7
Range	5-7	5-7
ONSET		
Mean	2.4 ± .9	2.7 ± .7
Acute (3 or 4)	50%	59%
Insidious (1 or 2)	50%	41%
PARANOID/NON-PARANOID (Max = 25)		
Mean	11.1 ± 4.8	12.4 ± 4.7
Paranoid	40%	41%
Non-Paranoid	60%	59%
GLOBAL PSYCHOPATHOLOGY (Max = 7)		
Mean	4.8 ± 1.2	5.4 ± .8

Table 5

MODE OF ONSET/PARANOID - NONPARANOID STATUS

	Experimental		Control	
	Paranoid *	Nonparanoid	Paranoid	Nonparanoid
Insidious	5	10	3	8
Acute **	7	8	8	8

*   Score = 13 on Venables & O'Connor (1959) Short Scale for
Rating Paranoid Schizophrenia.

**   Score = 3 on Mosher Onset Scale (from Vaillant, 1964).

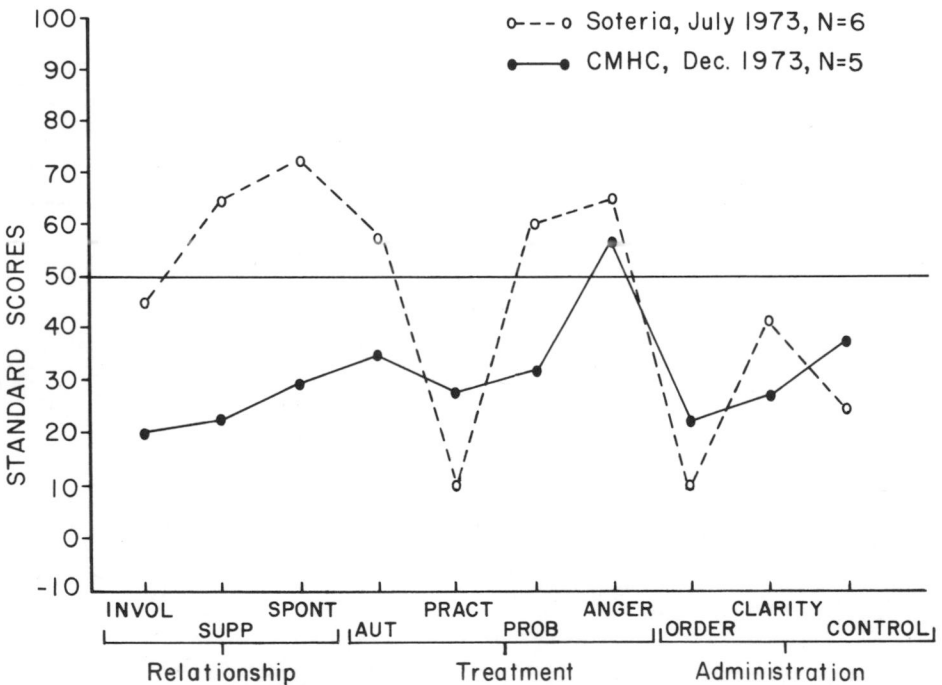

Figure 1. Comparison of Soteria resident COPES and CMHC patient
WAS real testing based on patient norms for 160 wards.

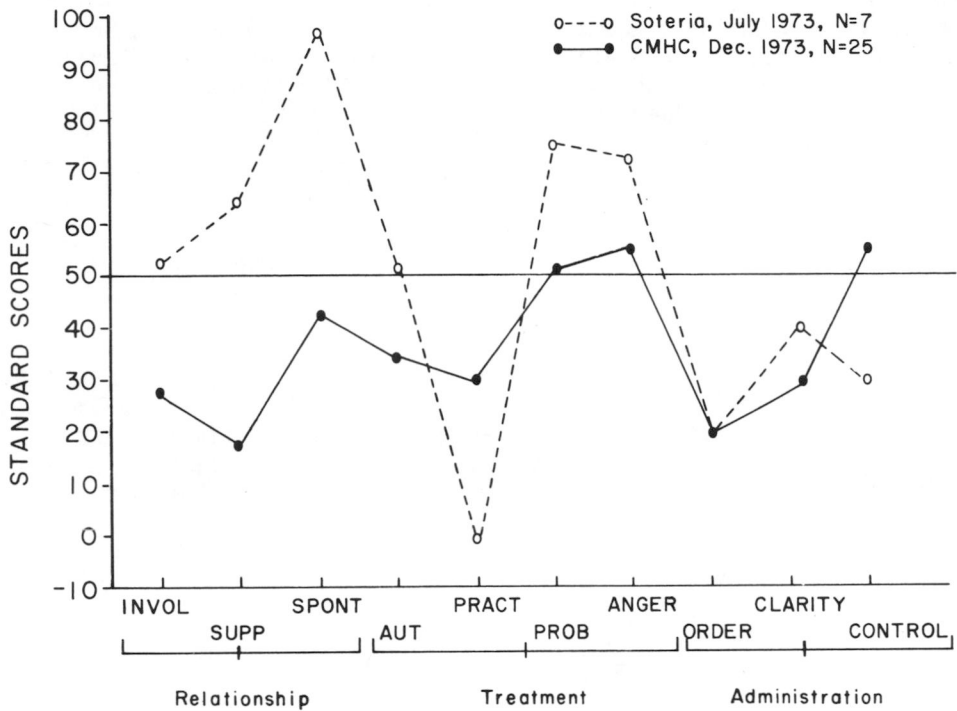

Figure 2. Comparison of Soteria staff and CMHC staff WAS real testing based on staff norms for 160 wards.

remaining variables as well (Soteria higher on Autonomy and Program Clarity, lower on Order & Organization and Staff Control). Both environments are perceived by residents/patients as encouraging about the same amount (slightly more for Soteria) of angry and aggressive behavior. Overall, the two programs are very different, with Soteria conforming well to our theoretical expectations. The Center program's scores, which yield a flatter pattern, are diffi-cult to compare with expectations because of the lack of clearly defined theoretical predictions.

In general, as Figure 2 illustrates, the overall patterns of the two settings as perceived by the staff coincide closely with the perceptions of the patient/residents (Figure 1). When the staff and residents/patients' standard scores are based on the same reference group (e.g., WAS staff norms for 160 programs), compari-son shows that staff members in both settings perceive equal or greater emphasis on nine of 10 subscales than do their respective

residents/patients. The Soteria staff score Staff Control lower
than do the residents and the Valley staff score Order and Organization lower than do the patients. The magnitude of the differences
between the two staff groups on Support (4 standard deviations),
Spontaneity (5 standard deviations), and Practical Orientation (3
standard deviations) is remarkable.

Treatment Experience

Experimental subjects stay significantly longer on their
initial episode of care (167 days vs. 21 days). Significantly fewer
receive courses of antipsychotic medications (17% vs. 100%) or are
maintained on them as outpatients. (A course of antipsychotic medications is defined for purposes here as two weeks or more of antipsychotic medication at a level equal to or greater than 300 mg/day
of Thorazine.) Fewer experimental subjects are readmitted during
the first six months post discharge (29% vs. 42%); during the second
six months there are no differences in readmissions (11% vs. 14%).

Table 6

GLOBAL PSYCHOPATHOLOGY*

	Experimental	Control
Admission	4.8 + 1.2 (N=29)	5.4 + .8 (N=17)
Six Weeks Post-Admission	4.0 + 1.5 (N=28)	4.0 + 1.6 (N=14)
One Year Post-Admission	2.6 + 1.4 (N=13)	3.1 + .7 (N=13)

*Maximum score = 7.

Outcome

Sample sizes reported vary because of three factors: (1) Subjects are acquired slowly so that the number reaching follow-up
points decreases progressively. (2) Some assessments were missed
(e.g., six months) although the subject was later found (e.g., for
the one year data point). (3) We recently pegged all data gathering to admission; thus, post-discharge data on recent subjects are
no longer gathered.

Scores on Global Psychopathology appear in Table 6. At six
weeks and one year post-admission there are no significant differences, although at one year there is a trend favoring the experimental group on this measure. Both groups changed significantly
at each point in time as compared with pretreatment levels.

As was previously mentioned, there were no intergroup differences at the baseline assessment on the IMPS profile (see Figure 3). At six weeks and one year <u>from admission</u> (Figures 4 and 5) there are no significant intergroup differences in any of the 10 IMPS subscales.

When we look at the IMPS data in terms of change over time within each treatment group (paired t-tests of matched subjects at admission vs. six weeks and one year), control patients show significant change on four IMPS variables (EXC, PAR, PCP, CNP) at six weeks (n=16), whereas experimental subjects show significant change on one variable (RTD). At one year (N=13), control patients show significant change on six variables (HOS, PAR, GRN, PCP, INP, CNP), whereas experimental subjects also show change on six variables (PAR, GRN, PCP, INP, RTD, CNP) (see Figure 6). No experimental subject included in this analysis received therapeutic courses (as previously defined) of antipsychotic drugs between admission and six weeks, whereas all control subjects included received them while inpatients and 64% of controls were maintained on them continuously for the first year (Table 7).

Table 7

Phenothiazine Treatment

	EXPERIMENTAL		CONTROL	
SIX Months Post-Discharge:				
Continuous	3/16*	(19%)	14/20*	(70%)
Intermittent	1/16	(6%)	3/20	(15%)
None	12/16**	(75%)	3/20**	(15%)
TWELVE Months Post-Discharge:				
Continuous	3/13***	(23%)	9/14***	(64%)
Intermittent	----	-----	2/14	(14%)
None	10/13*	(77%)	3/14*	(21%)

*Significant intergroup difference, p <.01, two-tailed chi square test.

**Significant intergroup difference, p <.001, two-tailed chi square test.

***Significant intergroup difference, p <.05, two-tailed chi square test.

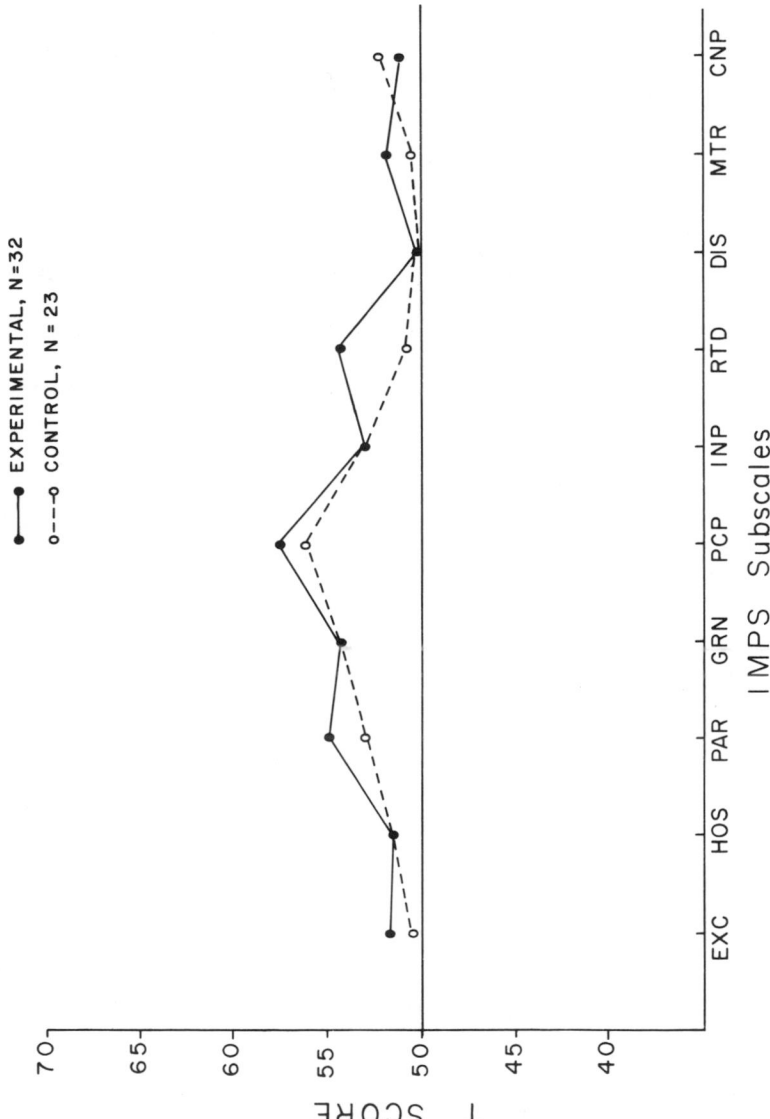

Figure 3. Admission analysis of IMPS profile sheet for combined raters, male and female acute patients.

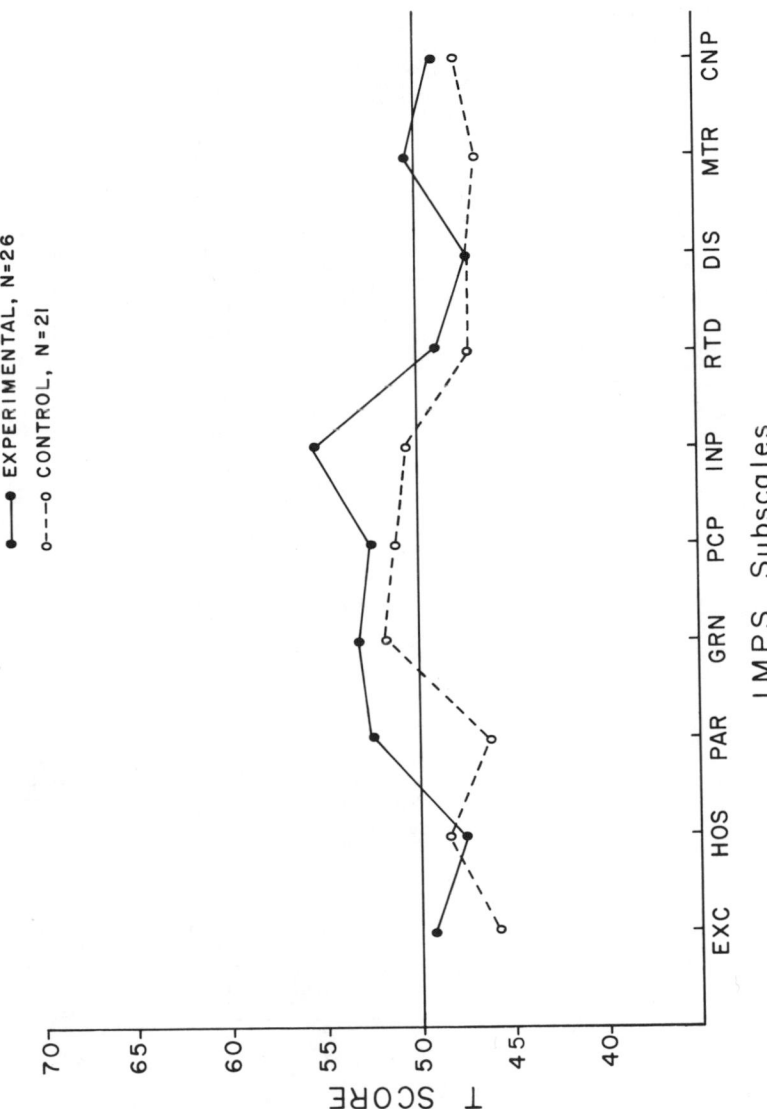

Figure 4. Six week (Day 45) analysis of IMPS profile sheet for combined raters, male and female acute patients.

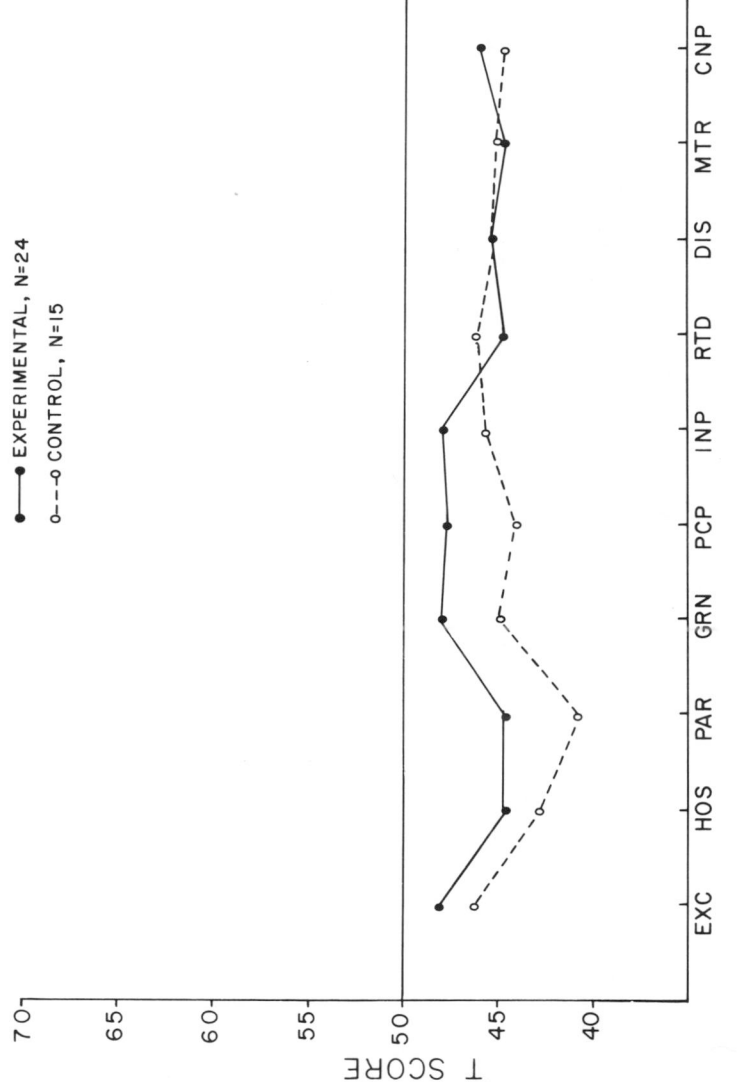

Figure 5. One year post-admission analysis of IMPS Profile
sheet for combined raters.

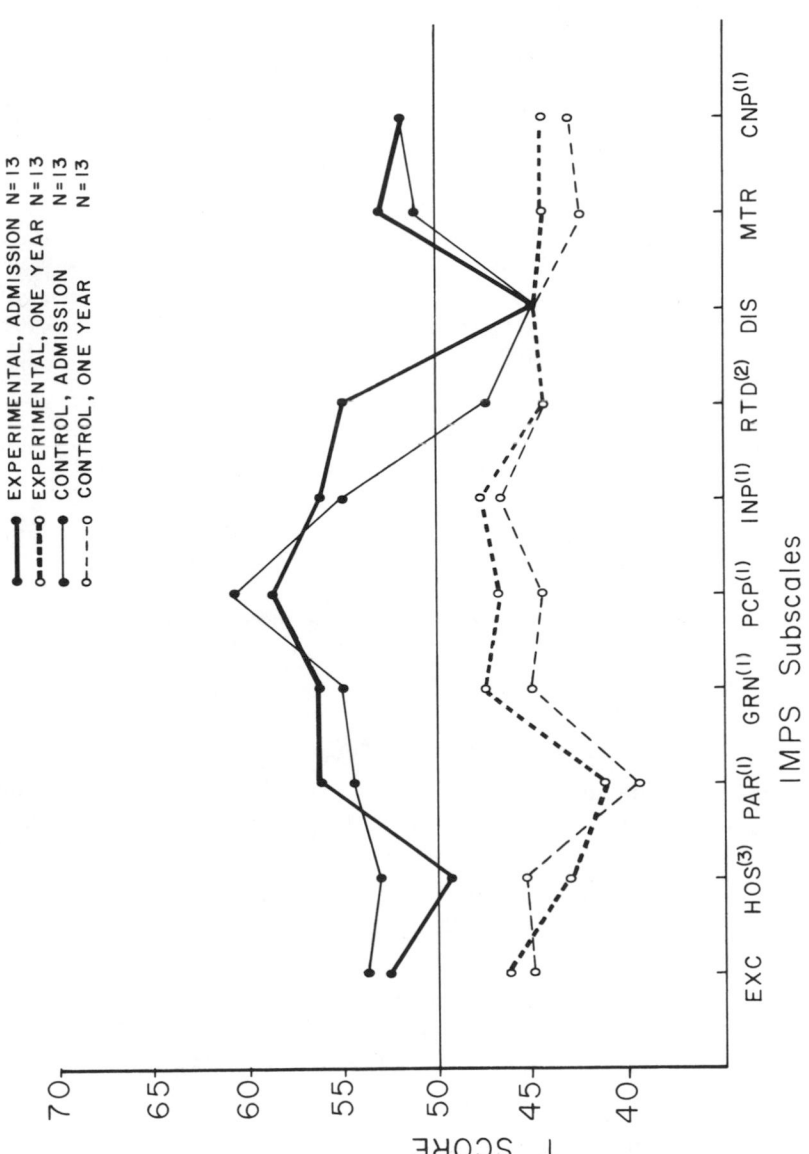

Figure 6. Analysis of change over time (Admission vs. One Year Since Admission) of IMPS profile sheet for combined raters. Subscales labelled (1) = significant change over time, P<.05, both E and C groups; (2) = significant change over time, P<.05, E group only; (3) = significant change over time, p<.05, C group only.

Community Psychosocial Adjustment

Although arguable, we have until recently collected these
data pegged to discharge since, by definition, a patient who is
in the hospital (or Soteria) is not in the community. Thus, in
contrast to the psychopathology measures reported above, these
will be reported in terms of time since initial discharge.

Results of the Brief Follow-up Rating appear in Table 8. This
composite measure of community adjustment covers rehospitalization,
work, and interpersonal relationships, and is first obtained at
discharge. Therefore, in terms of community psychosocial adjustment, discharge scores (maximum possible = 44) represent baseline
values. As may be seen in Table 8, experimental patients are
significantly healthier at discharge; but at six months and one year
post-discharge there are no significant group differences. Between
discharge and one year both groups improve further.

Results related to work appear in Table 9. In the first year
post-discharge there are no significant differences between the
groups in amount of time spent working. However, there is a

Table 8

Psychosocial Adjustment: Brief Follow-Up Rating

OVERALL BFUR (Max. = 44)	Experimental	Control
Discharge	16.2 ± 11.1* (N=17)	7.1 ± 5.3* (N=10)
Six Months Post-Discharge	18.6 ± 12.5 (N=10)	12.4 ± 10.2 (N=14)
One Year Post-Discharge	20.3 ± 12.5 (N=15)	15.1 ± 11.4 (N=18)

*Significant intergroup difference, $p < .05$, two-tailed t-test.

a nonsignificant trend for the percentage of controls who are working at one year to decrease as compared to their prehospitalization
work records. This decrease is not found among experimental subjects.

Data on living arrangements appear in Table 10. At six months
post-discharge, significantly more experimental subjects are living
alone or with peers (60% vs. 4%). This trend is maintained at one
year but does not reach significance due to the small numbers of
subjects.

Table 9

Psychosocial Adjustment: Work

		EXPERIMENTAL		CONTROL	
		N	%	N	%
I.	Prior to Admission:				
	Full time	12/29	41%	15/24	62%
	Part tune	12/29	41%	5/24	21%
	Not working	5/29	17%	4/24	17%
II.	Six Months Post-Discharge:				
	Full time	6/20	30%	4/23	17%
	Part time	4/20	20%	6/23	26%
	Not working	10/20	50%	13/23	57%
III.	Twelve Months Post-Discharge:				
	Full time	7/17	41%	6/19	32%
	Part time	4/17	24%	7/19	36%
	Not working	6/17	35%	6/19	32%

Cost

The average cost of the initial six months of treatment per patient for the control group is $4,450; for Soteria residents, $4,400 (excluding research costs).

DISCUSSION

This presentation has been long and, in many respects, overly detailed. The data speak for themselves. As of this moment, we view them as interesting but too preliminary (e.g., N's are small, follow-up short) to warrant firm conclusions. Therefore, in presenting our current thinking about the practical implications of the Soteria model for lowering barriers within residential treatment facilities, we must stress that our views should be regarded as tentative. Each area of Soteria's departure from current "usual" practice will be addressed in turn.

Table 10

PSYCHOSOCIAL ADJUSTMENT: LIVING ARRANGEMENTS

		EXPERIMENTAL		CONTROL	
		N	%	N	%
I.	PRIOR TO ADMISSION:				
	With Parents/relatives	21/29	72%	17/24	71%
	Alone/peers	7/29	24%	4/24	17%
	Spouse/children	----	--	2/24	8%
	Board-and-care, etc.	1/29	3%	1/24	4%
II.	SIX MONTHS POST-DISCHARGE				
	With Parents/relatives	6/20*	30%	16/24*	67%
	Alone/peers	12/20**	60%	1/24**	4%
	Spouse/children	-----	--	1/24	4%
	Board-and-care, etc.	2/20	10%	6/24	25%
III.	TWELVE MONTHS POST-DISCHARGE				
	With Parents/relatives	8/17	47%	9/18	50%
	Alone/peers	8/17	47%	4/18	22%
	Spouse/children	1/17	6%	1/18	6%
	Board-and-care, etc.	----	--	4/18	22%

*   Significant intergroup difference, p <.05, two-tailed x^2.

**   Significant intergroup difference, p <.001, two-tailed x^2.

Theoretical Model

After four years experience, we believe we have demonstrated that the medical model and the hospital trappings attendant upon it are not necessary for the treatment of newly admitted schizo- phrenic persons. Although we have a 1/4 time psychiatrist on the project, we are convinced that we would be able to operate with only occasional psychiatric consultations now that Soteria is firmly established. Ideally, these consultations would be focused on the proper psychopharmacologic treatment of Soteria residents who require (as per our protocol) neuroleptics. Current medico- legal, insurance and social welfare system requirements, however, make it mandatory for us to continue to use the same amount of professional time. These requirements seem to increase unneces- sarily the cost of a basically low cost care facility.

Most ex-Soteria residents give little evidence of the mental patient identity and only one (who refused to return to Soteria and then had extensive hospitalization) seems to have embarked on a career as a chronic mental patient. The model ex-Soteria resident is living with peers, leading a life much in keeping with the life style of his age group in that particular cultural context. Al- though we would ideally like to see more subjects working regularly, we do not make much of this in a country with an 8.4% unemployment rate--and one probably more than double that in our lower social class, 21 year group. More importantly, ex-Soteria residents are not interacting with their environment in a way that makes them look like backward patients who happen to live at home or in board and care. They are actively engaged in living--they have not had their passion suppressed or taken away.

Let us stress again; the fact that the medical model and context are not currently necessary for the treatment of schizo- phrenia says nothing about the etiology of this disorder. The schizococcus may yet be isolated.

Size

Here we have only inferential data to support our view that a total social group of 10-14 is better for psychotic persons than one of 30-40. As reflected in our Moos data, however, the two sizes are associated with strikingly different milieu character- istics. At a minimum, we can say that outcomes are no worse in patients treated in a small setting and that the residents them- selves view their experience at Soteria as generally positive-- whereas control patients tend to regard their inpatient experience as neutral at best and, more often, negative. In addition, we be- lieve the combination of small size, longer stays and like-aged

nonprofessional staff is what makes it possible for Soteria-
treated residents not to return home on leaving. If one believes
(as we do) Brown et al's data (Brown, G., Birley, J., and Wing, J.,
1972) on differential outcome among schizophrenics who go home
versus those who do not, it may mean that this aspect of Soteria's
impact on the person will be crucial over the long term.

Social Structure

Soteria's being so seemingly unstructured raises questions
for many people who have worked in the mental health field. A
question we hear frequently is, how do you keep things under control (usually referring to sex and aggression) when there are so
few rules and there is so little program structure? While it is
not always easy or pleasant to be at Soteria, there have been
relatively few untoward incidents in or just outside the house.
No one has been seriously hurt; there has been no sexual exploitation; and no one has killed himself while in residence there (we
have had two serious attempts).

How do we account for our ability to manage without extensive
rules, regulations, well-organized program, authoritarian imposition of control and a vertical hierarchy? Simply put, we believe
that our emphasis on close interpersonal contact, within which
one person doesn't feel exploited by the other, both encourages
residents to maintain self-control and allows control, when necessary, to be a part of this relationship. Thus, as with life
everywhere, persons at Soteria are willing to compromise their
own needs if the needs of someone else for whom they care are in
conflict with them. This is not so much "control" as interpersonal
negotiation with constant feedback to allow adjustment to changing
circumstances. Furthermore, Soteria's home-like qualities elicit
guest-like behavior at first, ans ownership-like behavior later,
from the residents. Both of these attitudes tend to normalize
potentially destructive behaviors via self-control.

Medication

The Soteria project has, we believe, established that withholding neuroleptics from newly admitted schizophrenics is, at a
minimum, not harmful in terms of symptom remission and subsequent
psychosocial functioning. Questions have been raised by many as
to whether our practice is ethical. Given that no harm is done by
withholding drugs, we can state with conviction that our procedure
is ethically justified. We cannot yet say whether there is an
advantage to being drug-free, although there are data which suggest
this is the case (Goldstein, M., 1970; Rappaport, M., et al, 1974; &

Schooler, N., et al, 1967). Because we recognize the proven ability
of neuroleptics to reduce symptoms and shorten hospital stays, we
were very surprised at the absence of group differences in symptoms
at six weeks. We initially predicted that, at Soteria, the non-
drug treated patients would have more symptoms than the controls--
all of whom would be receiving "good" pharmacotherapy. We did believe our interpersonal efforts would result in significant symptom
reduction but had thought it would take perhaps six months to be
evident. The rapidity of the response actually noted is probably
due to the relatively acute nature of our sample. However, it
strengthens a cost-effectiveness argument (especially if psychosocial adjustment can be enhanced) (Gunderson, J., and Mosher, L.,
1975) in favor of withholding drugs if a favorable response to
interpersonal efforts can be expected within six weeks rather than
six months. If our psychosocial adjustment trends favoring the
experimental group continue and achieve significance with the accumulation of subjects and the passage of time, then a major re-
evaluation of the use of these chemicals would seem to be in order.
In fact, given their known toxicities and less well-known subjective effects on motivation, motor and sexual performance, and sense
of being in control of oneself, we believe this re-evaluation is
long overdue. The use of medications is clearly a complex matter,
and we do not wish to propose a simple-minded position about them--
i.e., that they are never of value. This is not what we believe.
However, we do believe more effort should be devoted to character-
izing subjects who should or should not receive drugs during residential care or follow-up or both. Presently, there are minimal
data by which inpatients could be assigned to drugs or not. The
only data we know that would allow a prediction to be made for outpatients come from Brown et al (Brown, G., Birley, J., & Wing, J.,
1972) in England; ironically enough, these data reveal it is a
family characteristic (negative overinvolvement) that indicates
drugs should be continued if the discharged person is to live at

home. We would, of course, rather see more non-family living
alternatives become available so that long-term medication could
be avoided. In our more facetious moments, we are moved to inquire;
Why not treat the emotionally overinvolved family members with
neuroleptics? After all, why should the patient be obtruded so he
won't respond to their critical comments? It seems in that situation the psychiatrist is acting as the family's agent for enforcing
social control on one of its members. This is, of course, a model
problem again; that is, doctors have traditionally been trained to
treat only manifest individual patients--not social contexts.

Where have we failed to lower barriers; or, where are the
thorns on the Soteria rose? Our most consistent concern is with
our staff. Paying one person to take care of another--even in the
hands-off, nondoing, being-with, Soteria style--inevitably builds
a barrier. One brief example; recently our staff was feeling over-

burdened (as usual). Upon inquiring as to ways in which this burden could be lightened for them, we soon realized that they had gradually taken charge of meal preparation. This take-charge attitude had implicitly excluded residents. At first, staff felt they were doing their job; residents felt left out and incompetent. In time, though staff began to feel overburdened and residents increasingly demanded to be waited on because the staff was, after all, being paid to do so! This example is not unique; similar barriers are constantly being erected in other spheres. We cannot prevent them, we can only attempt to deal with them as they arise. Our other choice would be not to have a paid staff. Unfortunately, we have found very few individuals willing to give of themselves as is demanded at Soteria for purely altruistic reasons. The practical reality is that even altruistic people like to eat regularly.

Finally, we have an important philosophic thorn. That is, how can we conduct research of a logical positivist vein in a basically existential setting? Note that our research data bear only tangential relationship to several of the barrier issues with which we are concerned. Poor research design? Yes, in part. No adequate methodology to deal with these issues? Yes, in part. Funding agencies' demands for precise quantitative measures? Yes, in part. Underlying all of the partial reasons, however, is the basic contradiction I set out above. Our discussion addresses this issue by adding some of our clinical, qualitative impressions to our quantitative, but rather sterile and lifeless, data. We believe this additional input is vital if Soteria's current and potential contributions are to be adequately represented. As with our other thorns, we have no answer; we can only draw your attention to contradiction by having attempted to present both sides as valid; it is too bad one can be called "research" and the other not.

Taken as a total gestalt we hope the Soteria project will provide a model with which others interested in lowering barriers, both within and outside residential settings, can identify. Perhaps it will, over time, allow us all to interact with disturbed persons as H. S. Sullivan's description of them would have us do-- "More than anything, they are simply human."

Footnotes

1. The opinions expressed in this paper are those of the authors and do not necessarily represent any official position of the National Institute of Mental Health.

2. Research reported here is supported by NIMH Grant #20123.

3.   If the diagnostic assessment at day 3 is other than schizo-
     phrenia, the subject is excluded from the research (but still
     treated). This means that every subject must be diagnosed
     schizophrenic by three different interviewers to be included
     in the study.

REFERENCES

Bockover, J. Moral treatment in American psychiatry. New York:
   Springer Publishing Co., 1963.

Brown, G., Birley, J., and Wing, J. Influence of family life on
   the course of schizophrenic disorders: A replication. British
   Journal of Psychiatry, 1972, 121, 241-258.

Cole, J. Klerman, G., and Goldberg, S. Effectiveness of phenothiazine treatment in acute schizophrenics. Archives of General
   Psychiatry, 1964, 10, 246-261.

Crane, G. Clinical psychopharmacology in its 20th year. Science,
   1973, 181, 124-128.

Fromm-Reichmann, F. Notes on the development of treatment of
   schizophrenia by psychoanalytic psychotherapy. Psychiatry,
   1948, 11, 263-273.

Goldstein, M. Premorbid adjustment, paranoid status, and patterns
   of response to phenothiazine in acute schizophrenia.
   Schizophrenia Bulletin, 1970, 3, 24-37.

Gunderson, J. and Mosher, L. The cost of schizophrenia. American
   Journal of Psychiatry, 1975, 132(9), 901-906.

Laing, R. The politics of experience. New York: Ballantine
   Books, 1967.

Lorr, M., Klett, C., and McNair, D. Syndrome of psychosis.
   New York: MacMillan, 1963.

Menninger, K. Psychiatrist's world: the selected papers of
   Karl Menninger. B. Hall (ed.). New York: Viking Press, 1959.

Moos, R. Community-oriented programs environment scales:
   Technical report. Social Ecology Laboratory, Dept. of
   Psychiatry, Stanford University, 1971.

Moos, R. Community-oriented program environment scale manual.
  Social Ecology Laboratory, Dept. of Psychiatry, Stanford
  University, 1973.

Moos, R. and Hoots, P. Assessment of the social atmospheres of
  psychiatric wards. Journal of Abnormal Psychology, 1968,
  73, 595-604.

Moos, R. and Otto, J. The community-oriented programs environment
  scale: A methodology for the facilitation and evaluation of
  social change. Community Mental Health Journal, 1972, 8, 28-37.

Mosher, L. A research design to evaluate a psychosocial treatment
  of schizophrenia. Hospital and Community Psychiatry, 1972,
  23, 229-234.

Mosher, L. Psychiatric heretics and the extra-medical treatment
  of schizophrenia. In: R. Cancro (ed.), Strategic intervention
  in schizophrenia. New York: Behavioral Publications, 1974.

Mosher, L., Menn, A. and Goveia, L. Schizophrenia and crisis
  theory. Paper presented at the 49th Annual Meeting of the
  American Orthopsychiatric Association, Detroit, Mich., 1972.

Mosher, L., Menn, A. and Matthews, S. Soteria: Evaluation of a
  home-based treatment for schizophrenia. American Journal of
  Orthopsychiatry, 1975, 45, 455-467.

Mosher, L., Pollin, W. and Stabenau, J. Identical twins dis-
  cordant for schizophrenia: neurologic findings. Archives
  of General Psychiatry, 1971, 24, 422-430.

Mosher, L., Reifman, A. and Menn, A. Characteristics of nonprofessionals serving as primary therapists for acute schizophrenics. Hospital and Community Psychiatry, 1973, 24, 391-395.

Niskanen, P. and Achte, K. The course and prognosis of schizophrenic psychoses in Helsinki: A comparative study of first
  admissions in 1950. Monograph No. 2 from the Psychiatric Clinic
  of the Helsinki University Central Hospital, 1972.

Perry, J. Reconstitutive process in the psychopathology of the
  self. Annals of the New York Academy of Sciences, 1962,
  96, 853-876.

Rappaport, M., Hopkins, H., Hall, K., Belleza, T., and Silverman, J.
  Selective drug utilization in the management of psychoses.
  Progress Report, NIMH Grant 16445, 1974.

Rosen, B., Klein, D. and Gittelman-Klein, R. The prediction of
   rehospitalization: the relationship between age of first
   psychiatric treatment contact, marital status, and premorbid
   asocial adjustment. Journal of Nervous and Mental Disease,
   1971, 152, 17-22.

Schooler, N., Goldberg, S., Boothe, H., and Cole, J. One year
   after discharge: Community adjustment of schizophrenic patients.
   American Journal of Psychiatry, 1967, 123, 986-995.

Soskis, D. A brief followup rating. Comprehensive Psychiatry,
   1970, 11, 445-449.

Sullivan, H. Schizophrenia as a human process. New York:
   W. W. Norton and Co., 1962.

Szasz, T. The myth of mental illness: Foundations of a theory
   of personal conduct. New York: Hoeber-Harper, 1961.

Vaillant, G. Prospective prediction of schizophrenic remission.
   Archives of General Psychiatry, 1964, 11, 509-518.

Venables, P. and O'Connor, N. A short scale for rating paranoid
   schizophrenia. Journal of Mental Science, 1959, 105, 815-818.

Wendt, R., Mosher, L., Matthews, S., and Menn, A. A comparison
   of two treatment environments for schizophrenia, 1974, (in
   preparation).

Wilson, H. Infra controlling: the social order of freedom in an
   anti-psychiatric community. Dissertation, University of
   California, Berkeley, CA., 1974.

Wilson, H. Conventional psychiatric treatment: A dispatching
   process. Unpublished draft report, 1975.

A COMPREHENSIVE SYSTEM OF ALTERNATIVES

TO PSYCHIATRIC HOSPITALIZATION

Paul R. Polak

Southwest Denver Community Mental Health Services

Denver, Colorado

INTRODUCTION

The key deficiency, both of psychiatric hospitals and of many existing models for hospital alternatives, is that treatment efforts are focused on the individuals who are admitted as patients, rather than on the social forces that are the primary determinants of admission. Our work in Scotland and the United States indicates that social forces, usually disturbances in small social systems around the patient, are the most frequent primary cause of admission (Polak, 1967; Morrice, 1968). It follows that direct intervention in the social environment of the patient should be the cornerstone of a comprehensive system of alternatives to psychiatric hospitalization. In those instances when separation from the real world setting is needed, the artificial social environments to which clients are admitted should be designed to facilitate changes in the social systems around the client as well as encouraging the client's own growth and learning.

The present paper describes a comprehensive system of community treatment which places primary emphasis on intervening directly in social systems disturbances in the real-life setting of the client. Through routine use of home visits and social systems intervention, and the treatment of individual clients within the real-life setting, the majority of clients who would normally be hospitalized are treated at home. A back-up system of small community-based social settings is used for situations requiring brief or long-term separation from the real-life setting. The total system of community care in southwest Denver has resulted in a use of psychiatric hospital beds of approximately 1/100,000 population. The present paper

115

will describe the southwest Denver model for community care and
present initial research results evaluating the inpatient alternative system.

INTERVENTION IN THE SOCIAL ENVIRONMENT
OF THE CLIENT

A 42-year-old man who had trouble thinking straight was
admitted to a psychiatric hospital in Scotland because he was
hearing voices. When the patient's living situation was investigated by the admission ward nurse, it was found that he had been
hearing voices off and on for more than 10 years, but this didn't
interfere much with his ability to hold a low-key job and get
along well outside the hospital. The real reason he was admitted
was that his brother's wife, who took care of the household where
the patient lived, and managed the tourist guest home where both
the patient and his brother worked, was feeling overwhelmed for a
number of quite understandable reasons. She initiated the steps
involving the family doctor that led to the patient's admission.
It became quickly apparent that working constructively with the
household where the patient lived, and providing specific services
to the living group which included the patient, his brother, and
the brother's wife, would have crucial impact, both on the patient's
symptoms and on the forces which would likely lead to his future
readmission. When we systematically explored the social setting
prior to hospitalization of 100 consecutive admissions, we found
that the picture illustrated by this case was in no way exceptional.
Social forces, especially the patient's living group, were the
main determinant of admission in approximately 60% of the cases.
For this reason, when we designed the comprehensive community
treatment system in southwest Denver, direct intervention in the
social forces leading up to admission became a primary focus of
treatment. The techniques for assessing and intervening in social
systems disturbances were developed at Dingleton Hospital in
Melrose, Scotland, (Polak, 1967) and in the crisis division at
Fort Logan Mental Health Center (Polak, 1971).

In current practice in southwest Denver, initial evaluation
procedures usually take place at home, at work, or in other real-
life settings. While the concept of home-based evaluation and
treatment is attractive (Polak, 1971), actual implementation has
involved substantial problems. Staff members need to learn how to
operate in much less controlled and predictable environments than
in office practice. This often threatens therapist authority,
competency and potency. To facilitate staff learning of home
visiting skills, we pair an experienced staff member as a co-
therapist with a less experienced clinician during home-based
social systems sessions, followed by a staff review of the
process.

Before the actual home evaluation session, there are several phone contacts with key members of the social system to determine who should be involved in the first meeting and where it should take place, and enlist the cooperation of participants in the evaluation session. For individual or social systems crises, we provide evaluation within an hour, 24 hours a day, seven days a week. For non-emergent routine intake, we initiate clinical contact within 24 hours for 80% of the cases.

What is learned by one clinician at the initial assessment of the client and his family at home is difficult to communicate accurately to another staff member. Additional obstacles to treatment can be created when separate staff teams are assigned to different clinical functions such as intake, outpatient, partial care, and 24-hour care. The client must retell his story and re-develop many trust relationships. To avoid these problems and promote continuity of care in the southwest Denver treatment system, the same staff member who does the intake evaluation becomes the primary therapist through virtually all phases of treatment, whether the primary modality of treatment is outpatient care or one of the community homes. Clearly, this emphasis on generalized, rather than specialized, clinical functioning requires that staff be sufficiently experienced and skilled to handle a wide variety of clinical problems.

ON TERRITORIALITY AND THE USE OF OFFICE SPACE

To be effective, the majority of social systems work needs to be carried out in the real-life setting where the problems originated. No single factor influences the level of comfort of staff in doing frequent home visits as much as the location and organization of staff office space.

It is no accident that we use the term "occupied" to describe the space inhabited by humans. Man is a highly territorial animal, and the split rail fence around the boundaries of a property in suburbia carries the same signals as the urine trail of a brown bear that marks the borders of his territory.

Members of the helping professions have a particular affinity to territoriality in the use of space. A welfare worker, whose overt professional objective can be described as altruistic, is much more likely to operate out of an office setting which communicates that she is one up on the client, than a life insurance salesman with more materialistic overt goals. The mecca of

territorial battles for space is the academic department in the
social sciences, whose members have given up both materialistic
careers and decent wages.

A territorial map of space occupied by any organization makes
a shorthand statement of that organization's social structure and
distribution of power. Such territorial maps of a psychiatric
hospital usually display some striking features. Space owned by
staff, such as the nurses' station, is rigidly taboo to patients.
On the other hand, a corner of the dayroom may evolve into
territory owned by patients, and such territory is often governed
by an unwritten agreement that staff will not intrude, even if
they see rule-breaking activity take place.

In community mental health settings, once a staff member is
assigned an office, the majority of his interactions with patients
will take place in that office. Each treatment session is likely to
be preceded by non-verbal signaling reaffirming the dominant position
of the therapist. Patient-staff contact is decreased and stereotyped, and the clinician is highly unlikely to be exposed to the
real-life territorial space of the patient. Our experience at the
Fort Logan Mental Health Center Crisis Division was that although
staff members were strongly committed philosophically to home
visiting, once they were assigned their own offices, the majority
of their treatment sessions took place on their turf. Like the
male stickleback, the courage of the mental health professional
decreases in direct proportion to the distance from the nest.

Our solution to this problem in southwest Denver was quite
simple. We eliminated all staff offices. A small amount of
communal space was available for telephone work, paperwork and
patient interviews, but no clinician was assigned an office.

We first rented an 850 square foot, two-bedroom residence to
house 25 clinicians, 2 secretaries, and a medical records system.
This provided two client interview rooms and a living room for
staff paperwork and communication. Due to the emphasis on home
visits, there were rarely over eight staff in the residence at any
one time, but even this number proved unworkable because of problems
of confidentiality, communication, overcrowding, and frustration.

Although the home visiting rate remained at over 65%, our
initial experience convinced us that we had gone from one extreme
to the other. In analyzing our experience, we concluded that
there are four justifiable functional needs for office space by
mental health staff:

1. Small, private, soundproof space for telephone calls;
2. Similar space for paperwork and writing;
3. Space for clinical interviews where interviews in the
    real-life settings are not indicated;
4. Private storage for papers and other materials.

None of these needs requires specific assignment to an office.
Needs 1 and 2 can be carried out through the provision of private,
soundproof cubicles, which can be used in common, similar to the
teaching cubicles in language labs. Need 4 can be met through
provision of filing cabinet space and mail boxes. Need 3 can be
met through a few communal conference rooms.

The 30 adult psych staff have now moved to 2500 square feet
of office space, which more specifically fits the four needs
described above. A major feature is a large workroom which has
been subdivided into ten small, soundproof compartments, each with
a telephone and a table for paperwork. As before, no clinician has
been assigned his own office. Each clinician does have his own
filing cabinet and cubicle storage space.

SOCIAL ARCHITECTURE

If the immediate social environment is as powerful a predictor
of behavior as the characteristics of the individual (Raush et al.,
1959; Gump et al., 1957), it follows that the field of psychiatry
should pay as much attention to the systematic design of specific
social environments as it does to the development of techniques of
individual psychotherapy. I use the term "social architecture" to
describe the systematic design of social environments. Social
architecture concerns itself with the characteristics of physical
space, and social climate factors such as cohesiveness and expres-
siveness. It incorporates social structural variables such as the
degree of role definition and the optimal size of the social environment to be designed. Finally, social architecture delineates the
characteristics of the individuals who are to be involved in various
facets in the social setting.

The design requirements of optimal physical and social space
for a residential community correctional facility for adults will
differ significantly from those for a private open educational
junior high school setting. The relationship of the facility to
the surrounding physical and social environment, and the design of
space within it need to be integrated with the design of the social
organization and its subunits. In this process, social systems
factors such as desired communication patterns, decision making
processes, flexibility or rigidity of boundaries, the optimal

characteristics of the participants, and cost factors all are
varied systematically to meet the specific objectives of the
social environment to be designed.

The southwest Denver model represents a working application of
the principals of social architecture in the design of a comprehensive system of alternatives to psychiatric hospitals. The design
of such a system is strongly influenced by the assumptions underlying the conceptual framework in which treatment takes place. If
treatment has a primary focus on the problems of the individual
patient, the design of treatment environments begins by delineating
the common patterns of the individual problems to be treated.
Several different social settings can then be designed with each
social environment responsive to a different subgroup of individual
treatment needs.

In the conceptual framework underlying the southwest Denver
model, the problems to be worked on in treatment consist of a combination of problems within small social groups in the real-life
setting, and problems experienced by individuals who are members of
these small social systems. The design of a system of social environments to replace psychiatric hospitals then must incorporate
common patterns of social systems problems, as well as common
patterns of individual problems. A dependent, suicidal housewife
may be part of a marriage that is in a state of chronic semi-
separation with very poor communication between husband and wife,
and a strong, at times domineering husband. Treatment objectives
include the improvement of communication in the marriage, the
facilitation of a decision on whether the couple should separate,
work with the client to facilitate her development of more constructive ways of dealing with dependency, and improvement in the client's
symptoms of depression. To meet these objectives, such a client
might best be admitted into the specific social environment of a
healthy family with high skills in open communication, and which
is currently dealing constructively with the emancipation of two
teenage daughters.

The design of a comprehensive system of community treatment
incorporated the following considerations:

Facilitation of Social Systems Work

The mental health delivery system was structured to facilitate
intervention in the social environment of the client by decentral-
izing office locations, eliminating assignment of staff to offices,
encouraging home visits, and replacing a clinical personnel system
based on degrees with a clinician series based on ability to carry
out specific tasks, with emphatically included social systems skills.

Volunteers with specific skills in resolving social systems crises
were enlisted as co-therapists. The structuring of crisis respon-
siveness 24 hours a day, seven days a week, was an important contributor to effective social systems work.

Size and Location of Hospital Alternative Settings

Because of many observations of the specific disadvantages of
large isolated psychiatric institutions, we felt a hospital alternative setting should be small, with an upper limit of eight to
ten in one setting, and easily accessible to the client's home.

The Message in the Medium of
Hospital Alternative Settings

We feel that the instantaneous strong non-verbal messages
carried to a client on the point of entering the social environment of a treatment setting are important determinants of later
transactions in that setting. Large doors opening onto a vestibule
with a prominent sign saying "SHOES MUST BE WORN" followed by a
long, white corridor with a faint disinfectant smell, make a very
different statement than a small brick house in a residential
neighborhood with flowers and a waterfall in the back and plenty
of unguarded plate glass windows inside. The non-verbal message
in a treatment environment should be designed carefully rather
than be allowed to develop haphazardly.

Generalizability of Learning

The social structure of the hospital alternative setting
should closely enough resemble the real-life setting of the
client and his social system that learning can easily generalize
to the real-life setting and vice versa.

Preexisting Social Structure

To meet the specific needs normally served by an acute admission ward, our experience is (Brook, 1973) that a clearly defined
preexisting social structure with a predetermined role for the
client which supports easy entry and exit is preferable to a more
loosely defined therapeutic culture which is expected to emerge
from the client group.

Role Expectations

The social environment should present role models which are relevant to the problem areas of the client and his family and which can be easily incorporated into the client's own learning. The client's role should be one which reinforces rather than decreases the client's self-respect and self-esteem.

Proportion of Clients and Non-Clients

Our experience suggests that the basic social environment should be structured so that clients are a minority rather than a majority of the individuals making up the social setting.

Emphasis on Client and Social System Strengths

The social environment should be structured to focus on and support strengths and areas of health of the client and his social system. Our experience is that an ongoing mechanism for identifying and reducing illness reinforcement patterns in the social environment is important.

A Number of Different Settings

Since different client and social system problems respond to different social environments, it is important that a variety of therapeutic environments be designed, each responsive to different treatment needs. In the ideal community treatment system, the social environment to be selected would be determined by a systematic evaluation, both of the client, and of his social environment in the real-life setting.

Our own experience suggests that an ideal system of different treatment environments would have a number of characteristics in common, such as warmth, open communication, and nonprofessional sponsors who are rich in life experience and sensitive to others. Such a network of small community-based social environments would differ systematically in a number of other variables, such as the degree of autonomy expected in the client role, the presence of children or teenagers and the facility to communicate in Spanish.

THE SOUTHWEST DENVER MODEL OF COMMUNITY TREATMENT

The southwest Denver community treatment system evolved through a combination of systematic design of social environments

and learning by trial and error. The present system has the following components:

Crisis Services

The majority of individuals or families who become clients at
mental health facilities do so at a state of crisis. Consequently,
it was decided to provide immediate crisis services at the point
of entry into treatment for all clients. Most requests for service
are evaluated within 24 hours and the staff member and/or volunteer involved in the initial crisis intervention is usually the
coordinator for all subsequent treatment activities.

Social Systems Intervention

Previous work indicated that social systems problems such as
family conflicts were often more potent determinants of requests
for mental health services than the problems of the individual
identified as the patient (Polak, 1967). As a result, all clinical
services at Southwest stress direct involvement with one or more
social systems whose problems are pertinent to the request for
service. The initial crisis-oriented evaluation procedure usually
occurs in the real-life setting of the social system involved, such
as at home or at work. Attention to crisis resolution and social
systems growth routinely coincides with work on the problems of
the individual identified as the client.

Crisis intervention and social systems intervention are a
central part of treatment even when the client is separated from
his real-life setting. If this separation is temporary, prepara-
tions for re-entry into the family setting begin on the day in
which the client is admitted to the inpatient alternative home.
Visits by the client's family members are encouraged during the
client's stay, and family members may participate in constant
observation procedures. Family problems pertinent to both the
symptoms of the client and the referral for treatment are focused
on intensively both during the client's stay and following discharge from the home. If separation from the family is to be long-
term or permanent, making the separation constructive becomes a
salient aspect of treatment.

The clinician who is involved in the initial crisis-oriented
evaluation in the client's home is the principal therapist for
social systems and family therapy procedures during the client's
stay in the community alternative home and continues to be the
primary coordinator after the client's discharge.

Rapid Tranquilization

The specific procedure of rapid tranquilization, which is an important component of total community care for acutely schizophrenic or psychotic clients, has been described elsewhere (Polak, 1971). By titrating hourly doses of one or more phenothiazines against the client's specific target symptoms of psychosis, an initial end point of significant attenuation of psychosis is reached in four to six hours. Although sleepiness may interfere with psychotherapy for the first two days, side effects usually improve rapidly on the third day, and the client typically is much more in touch with his own and his family's problems. This allows crisis intervention and direct social systems intervention, including the client, to begin on the day of admission and continue through the client's stay in the inpatient alternative home. After rapid tranquilization procedures are implemented in the first week, appropriate procedures for maintenance on phenothiazines are carefully worked out with the client and his family as an important part of treatment.

An acutely schizophrenic young man who is actively hallucinating may receive 500 mgs. of Thorazine in the first six hours to reach an initial tranquilization end point. He may then be placed on 1600 mgs. of Thorazine per day for the first three days; the dosage may be reduced to 1200 mgs. per day on the fourth day and further reduced to 800 mgs. on the sixth day, when the client may be discharged, and followed regularly for maintenance on Thorazine for at least six months.

Citizen Participation and Community Control

The Southwest Denver Mental Health Services has a citizen's board which is governing, not advisory. The board hires and fires the director, sets overall policy, and actively monitors ongoing programs. All fifteen board members live in Southwest Denver, eight representing specific neighborhoods and seven elected at large. Anyone who lives or works in Southwest Denver may register to vote in board elections, and center clients are encouraged both to vote and to run for election to the board. The community care system is, therefore, under the direct control of the community residents and consumers it serves.

Before hiring its first staff member, the board engaged in an active three-year planning process. The emphasis on providing immediate responsive service as close as possible to the home of the client is in accord with the board's statement of overall philosophy, which emerged from this planning process. Treating psychotic patients in residential community settings was vigorously

debated by the board before approval. With the success of the
initial program, the enthusiastic board support of the community
alternative system was crucial to its success. Board members
have recruited home sponsors and volunteers for the community care
system, and have been critical participants in the political and
funding process for community care.

Volunteer Involvement

From the outset, volunteers have played a major role in all
phases of center operations. The extent of volunteer involvement
is directly related to the high degree of involvement of community
members through the board. Volunteer hours total over a thousand
per month with the majority being directly involved in clinical
work with clients. Clients are encouraged to become volunteers
after their treatment and, in some instances, as part of their
treatment.

In the community care system, volunteers carry out a majority
of the "special constant observation" function for acutely psychotic,
suicidal, or potentially dangerous clients. When an acutely psychotic client requiring supervision and control is admitted to one
of the homes in the community, a 24-hour roster of volunteers and
staff members is organized so that one or two people remain with
the client until rapid tranquilization and other therapeutic procedures make constant observation unnecessary. Volunteers also
function as co-therapists for community care clients and their
families.

A Network of Small, Community-Based
Social Environments

Private Homes. Although techniques such as crisis and social
systems intervention enable us to treat the majority of clients who
otherwise might have been hospitalized at home, we believe that keeping a client in the real-life setting at all costs can sometimes be
destructive. When temporary or permanent separation is indicated,
we place the client in private homes.

We have contracted with six carefully screened and selected
families in southwest Denver to form the basis for our community-
based intensive care system. Each family accepts up to two clients
at one time for a base fee of $7.50 per day for room, board and
client care. Each family has a staff coordinator responsible for
family supervision and support, and home sponsors meet regularly
to learn from each other and from the staff. On a daily basis,
the clinical staff member following the client-guest visits the

home to conduct sessions with the client, involving whatever members
of the client's social system are relevant. In place of the 24-hour
nursing rotation on a hospital ward, our psychiatric nurses provide
24-hour nursing coverage to all the community treatment settings
using a bellboy paging system. They, in turn, are backed up by a
psychiatrist on call 24 hours a day. Care is taken to ensure that a
variety of different family environments are available and staff
members select the specific family that most closely fits each
client's needs.

Some family sponsors participate in formal treatment sessions,
while others do not. Clients participate in family chores and
activities. Meaningful personal relationships often develop between
family sponsors and clients, and clients frequently visit family
sponsors long after formal treatment has been terminated.

The decision to remove a client from his natural living situation rests upon an evaluation of the individual and system resources
and liabilities in the context of the following four guidelines:

(1) Temporary separation is indicated in the presence of an
imminent and serious threat to the life of self or others, if the
natural social system of other resources are insufficient to support
and handle the problem of impulse control.

(2) Temporary separation is indicated to provide rest and
respite in some instances where an acute crisis has overwhelmed the
resources of the natural support systems. For example, a five-day
admission for rapid tranquilization in our intensive observation
apartment may be indicated for the acutely psychotic young man who
has stayed up all night with his family for the last four days.

(3) Temporary placement may be indicated to provide a
supportive emotional climate for isolated, lonely, and withdrawn
persons essentially without natural social resources, so that they
can develop the trust and coping ability needed to construct their
own natural support system.

(4) Temporary and perhaps permanent separation may be needed
to break up extremely dysfunctional relationships where the potential
for changing those relationships for the better is minimal or
absent. In this situation, there is a careful cost/benefit examination of the probable consequence of separation versus no separation.
For example, we have seen several examples of sons, aged 20-30
living with their mothers under quite pathologically symbiotic
conditions where episodes of rage and upheaval of lethal proportions
alternate with quiet periods. After provision of substitute emotional resources for the mother, the son is often a constructive
candidate for permanent removal.

After the decision for separation is made, the client is placed in that home setting which most suitably matches his needs. To meet the wide range of client needs, a diversity of environments is essential. For example, the southwest Denver system includes:

(1) Settings employing Chicano sponsors for clients for whom a Spanish-speaking Chicano cultural setting is important;

(2) Settings with an emphasis on nurturing, meeting dependency needs and high levels of support;

(3) Settings conveying an atmosphere of practical goal setting and achievements;

(4) Settings where the client is expected to run his life with minimal sponsor support and input.

The role of the home sponsors highlights some of the advantages when carefully selected individuals without formal training take on responsibilities usually carried out by professional staff. The family sponsors tend to quite naturally treat clients in their homes as guests. They orient themselves more to the strengths and positive features of clients than to their pathology, and are much less likely than mental health professionals to view all client behavior in an illness framework. Home sponsors are warm, outgoing, healthy people, who are rich in life experience. We provide little in the way of formal mental health training, focusing instead on encouraging sponsor families to utilize their already existing skills.

We feel this system of small, specific, community-based social environments has a number of advantages over psychiatric hospitals:

(1) A number of specifically different community environments provide a more individually tailored and responsive system than the larger, less diversified social environment of the psychiatric hospital.

(2) Sponsor families provide a clear model of healthy individual and family behavior which can be generalized to the client's real-life setting more easily than learning which takes place in the artificial psychiatric hospital environment.

(3) In this "medium is the message" age, admission to a normal home rather than a hospital makes an immediate, clear statement to the client and his family. The client is expected to have higher self-esteem, feel less stigma, and assume greater responsibility for his own behavior than if he is hospitalized.

Intensive Observation Apartment. For clients requiring extremely close observation and supervision, we use an intensive
observation apartment. The apartment is staffed by a psychology
student and his wife, who are trained to provide constant observation for acutely psychotic or suicidal clients. Twenty-four hour
constant observation is provided when needed by a roster of volunteers backed up by nursing staff and the psychiatrist. Rapid
tranquilization in the intensive observation apartment is an
important procedure for acutely psychotic clients.

Home Day Care. It has been our clinical impression that the
system of private homes and the intensive observation apartment
have been most effective as replacements for acute psychiatric
hospitalization. For chronic clients, we have used, in addition
to the home and apartment system, a variety of socializing activities
such as a craft group, with long-term staff follow-up and selecting
boarding home and nursing home placement when required. A major
component of specialized services for chronic clients is the day
care program carried out in the home of one of the family sponsors.
This program focuses on cooking, homemaking, and social activities,
and works with 15 long-term female clients two times a week.

Back-Up Hospital Beds. As back-up to the home treatment
system, we have contracted services with psychiatric hospitals.
Experience to date indicates that over 80% of clients requiring
temporary or permanent separation from their natural-life setting
can be treated in the home system, thus avoiding hospital admission.
The use of adult psychiatric inpatient beds in southwest Denver
serving a population of 104,000, totaled 385 bed days in the 12
months from July 1, 1974, to June 30, 1975.

Under some conditions, treatment in community-based home
settings is insufficient or ineffective. We have found three
situations where admission to psychiatric hospitals as a back-up
to the home system appears constructive:

(1) Treatment of serious medical problems, either related or
unrelated to the mental health problems, concurrently with the
mental health problems;

(2) The immediate availability of sophisticated medical
diagnostic procedures is crucial to treatment;

(3) Brief treatment of behavior extremes requiring a more
controlled setting than a home structure.

RESEARCH EVALUATION OF THE SOUTHWEST DENVER
INPATIENT ALTERNATIVE PROGRAM

Three parallel forms of instruments were employed in our evaluation of the inpatient alternative program: client, clinical staff, and community informant, usually a relative of the client. Data from all three sources were collected at admission and at discharge; two sources, client and community informant, were interviewed at follow-up (four to five months post-discharge). In essence, this approach to evaluation does not view any one source of information about outcome, be it client, staff, or community informant, as necessarily more valid than other sources. Rather, all three perspectives have invaluable and distinctly different data to contribute to outcome assessment.

Table 1 contains discharge results of the inpatient alternative study. As can be seen, the home group showed more effective outcome in client ratings of satisfaction with the treatment results. This same scale was also significantly different for community informants, again in favor of the home group. No staff ratings differed for the two groups.

Table 2 presents similar outcome data for the follow-up study. Results obtained at discharge tended to maintain at follow-up. Four client measures reached significance: the total Treatment Effectiveness Scale, a subscale measuring satisfaction with Treatment outcome, mean goal attainment ratings, and the self-disclosure scale. No community informant and no staff ratings differed for the two groups. A modified self-disclosure scale (Jourard, 1971), which taps the degree to which the respondent opens up and reveals himself to others, did not differentiate between clients in the home and hospital groups at discharge, but a significant difference did emerge at follow-up; clients in the home group had significantly higher self-disclosure scores. This finding conformed precisely to our predictions and suggested that clients could use sponsor families as role models to improve communication with their own families.

DO HOMES REDUCE POWERLESSNESS AND DEPERSONALIZATION
EXPERIENCED IN PSYCHIATRIC HOSPITALS?

Rosenhan (1973), Goffman (1961), and others have described a number of characteristics of psychiatric hospitals that engender in patients intense feelings of powerlessness, loss of self-respect, and depersonalization.

To test for differences between the hospital and the home system on this dimension, an interviewer in the Southwest Denver Study asked both hospital and private home clients open-ended questions about

Table 1

Selected Staff, Client, and Community Informant
Discharge Outcome Scores* for Home (N = 37)
and Hospital (N = 38) Groups

Outcome Measure	Home Mean	Hospital Mean	t Value
Total Treatment Effectiveness Scale			
Staff	55.7	54.4	.5
Client	64.0	58.1	2.1 p <.001
Community Informant	64.2	58.5	1.9
TES Subscale:			
Satisfaction with Treatment Outcome			
Staff	16.6	16.0	.8
Client	19.3	16.5	4.0 p <.001
Community Informant	20.3	17.3	3.7 p <.001
Goal Attainment Ratings			
(across all goals set)			
Staff	24.2	23.3	.8
Client	25.3	22.8	1.8
Community Informant	20.5	22.8	.9
Total Self-Disclosure to			
3 Significant Others			
Client	41.6	37.6	.8

*For all measures in the Table, a higher score indicates better
outcome.

Table 2

Selected Client and Community Informant
Follow-up Outcome Scores* for Home (N = 30)
and Hospital (N = 32) Groups

Outcome Measure	Home Mean	Hospital Mean	t Value
Total Treatment Effectiveness Scale			
Client	61.0	55.3	2.0 $p < .05$
Community Informant	59.7	55.3	1.1
TES Subscales:			
Satisfaction with Treatment Outcome			
Client	17.8	15.5	3.0 $p < .01$
Community Informant	18.1	16.7	1.3
Goal Attainment Ratings			
(across all goals set)			
Client	26.9	23.5	2.9 $p < .01$
Community Informant	25.6	23.0	1.6
Total Self-Disclosure to			
3 Significant Others			
Client	49.9	34.3	2.15 $p < .05$

*For all measures in the Table, a higher score indicates better
outcome.

the treatment process at discharge and at follow-up four to five
months later. The verbatim responses of patients and community
informants were placed on separate cards with no identification as
to the name of the respondent or the treatment group.

Independent judges were asked to identify those responses
which mentioned a specific person by name, other than the client
himself. Responses mentioning one or more specific individuals by
name, even if critical, were interpreted as indicators that the
treatment environment had facilitated the development of a meaningful personal relationship. More general responses, such as references to the hospital, the treatment team, or the social worker,
were assumed to mean that the involvement experienced by the client
was more impersonal.

The results of this analysis are presented in Table 3. Treatment in private homes was more likely than psychiatric hospitalization to lead to the identification of a specific individual as
important in the treatment process. The difference approached
statistical significance for the client at discharge, and was
significant both for clients and informants at follow-up. The
proportion of clients treated in the hospital who named a specific
person when asked about the treatment process dropped from 18%
at discharge to 3% at follow-up, while the comparable percentage
of clients treated in a private home were 38% at discharge and 31%
at follow-up. It appears that personal relationships made by clients
in the homes remain more vivid over time than those made by hospitalized clients.

The implications of these data become clearer when the content
of these verbatim responses is compared (Tables 4 and 5). Clients
admitted to private homes often develop meaningful personal attach-
ments to one or more members of the sponsoring family. In several
instances, the client has adopted the sponsor family as part of
his own extended family. The private home system appears to eliminate some of the process of depersonalization and powerlessness
observed in psychiatric hospitals, and provides a social setting
which encourages the development of personal relationships.

Table 3

Proportion of Clients Who Identified a Specific

Individual When Asked About the Treatment Process

	Private Home Placement			Psychiatric Hospitalization			Significance Level (Chi Square)
	Specific Person Mentioned	No Specific Person Mentioned	Total	Specific Person Mentioned	No Specific Person Mentioned	Total	
Client at Discharge	14 (38%)	23 (62%)	37	7 (18%)	31 (82%)	38	p < .05
Client at Follow-up	8 (31%)	18 (69%)	26	1 (3%)	31 (97%)	32	p < .05
Informant at Discharge	5 (22%)	18 (78%)	23	6 (19%)	26 (81%)	32	
Informant at Follow-up	10 (38%)	16 (62%)	26	1 (3%)	34 (97%)	35	p < .01

Table 4

Total Sample of Verbatim Client Responses Identifying
Specific Individuals Important to the Treatment Process:

Psychiatric Hospital Group

At Discharge

Talking to Ben (staff psychiatrist). I had to communicate
with my husband and other people instead of sitting around like
a dope all the time. My husband realizes that he has to quit
talking for me. I now try to do it myself.

Walt (staff clinician, B.A. in history) pissed me off.
Their (staff) talking to me is something I already know, but they
make you stop and think. What you see is what you get.

Being in a mental hospital can scare the hell out of you, and
I think, I should say I know, that I'm not crazy, and with the
help from Bryan (staff clinician, social worker) and Ann (staff
clinician, psychiatric nurse), I've made a lot of changes for
myself that I might not have made if I didn't come here.

I feel Carol (staff clinician, mental health worker) helped
me a great deal, as did Stan (staff clinician, psychologist), by
really caring about me and trying to show me the way. Unfortunately, I had an awfully big head once I was released and didn't
face my own situations. Carol did try to help me but I was too
afraid.

Vicki, a patient at Fort Logan, helped me know the rules and
what to look for in the staff for help. She told me if I was
qualified for a home pass and how to get out.

Worker, Jane (staff clinician, psychiatric nurse), stuck by
me. She is the only one I am sure stuck by me.

More responsibility on me--being yelled at. Charlotte (staff
clinician, psychiatric nurse) was the best and helped me the most.

Bryan (staff clinician, psychiatric social worker).

Table 4--Continued

Psychiatric Hospital Group

At Follow-Up

Mary Lee (staff clinician, psychiatric nurse) is too young for that job and I found her partial--always taking the other side of a situation.

Table 5

Random Sample of Verbatim Client Responses Identifying Specific Individuals Important to the Treatment Process:

Private Home Group

At Discharge

Aunt Mary Puthoff (home sponsor) straightened me out like a plank.

Puthoffs (home sponsors) have made me realize I could live without going out and getting all bent out of shape. Puthoffs gave me a place to sleep and anything I wanted to get, clean clothes, free run of the house, and I could get a sandwich at 3:00 a.m. They were like a mother and father to me. They are the finest people I ever met.

My specific progress, I believe, came mostly from Barbara Soffa and family (home sponsors). I felt at ease with them, except for my not being accustomed to children and their never-ending spats, stingy attitudes, questions and affection. I was treated very good, fed well, given a nice atmosphere to be alone in if I so desired. You can't remain a recluse at their home! And thank heaven for that in my case, because I was.

Kay S. (staff clinician, psychiatric social worker) and Sister Gabriel (staff student placement nurse) are absolutely great. They treat one another very well. They go out of their way to be human and good to me. I lived with my husband like

Table 5--Continued

Private Home Group

---

cats and dogs. The tollards are good and I now feel some people care.

I learned how to work a washing machine and dryer. Pauline (staff clinician, psychiatric nurse) and Jackie (staff clinician, psychiatric nurse) made me feel at home there. The Tollards' (home sponsors) attitude. Clarence said he would pass me off as her daughter. I thought she really tried to satisfy me. Their daughter and son treated me like part of the family. She gave me responsibility after a while too.

At Follow-Up

Therapy and interest Ched (staff clinician, psychiatric social worker) showed in me.

Thanks to Mr. and Mrs. Puthoff (home sponsors), now my family respect me. Mary and Lee Puthoff helped me a very great deal by talking to me, taking me places and introducing me as one of their friends instead of a patient. If there were people here, I was part of the family. They never told me to stay in my room until the people left. I am very grateful to them.

I had help through the Soffas (home sponsors) and the clinic, and they got me to stop feeling sorry for myself and a new way to look at stuff, and I did, and now I am out.

The time I was at Tollards (home sponsors) made all the difference in the world. Kay S. (staff clinician, psychiatric social worker) and the Tollards.

Most progress due to treatment by team. I feel I am half way there. Ched (staff clinician, psychiatric social worker) was the therapist.

I was treated with great consideration and understanding by the Soffa family (home sponsors).

I feel I did improve and much of the improvement was made by and through the team and the Tollard family (home sponsors).

REFERENCES

Brook, Bryan D. Crisis hostel: an alternative to psychiatric hospitalization. Hospital and Community Psychiatry, Vol. 24, No. 9, September 1973, pp. 621-624.

Goffman, E. Asylums. Garden City, N. Y.: Doubleday, 1961.

Gump, P., Schoggen, R., and Redl, F. The camp milieu and its immediate effects. Journal of Social Issues, 13, 40-46, 1957.

Jourard, S. M. Self-disclosure: an experimental analysis of the transparent self. New York: Wylie, 1971.

Morrice, J. K. W. Emergency psychiatry. British Journal of Psychiatry, 114:485-491, 1968.

Polak, P. R. The crisis of admission. Social Psychiatry, Vol. 2, No. 4, 1967.

Polak, P. R. Rapid tranquilization. Am. J. Psychiat., 1971, 128, pp. 640-643.

Polak, P. R. Social systems intervention. Arch. Gen. Psychiat., Vol. 25, Aug. 1971, pp. 110-117.

Raush, H. L., Dittman, A. T., and Taylor, T. J. Person, setting and change in social interaction. Human Relations, 12, 361-378, 1959.

Rosenhan, D. L. On being sane in insane places. Science, 1973, 179, pp. 250-258.

THE IMPACT OF COMMUNITY LIVING AND COMMUNITY MEMBER INTERVENTION

ON THE ADJUSTMENT OF THE CHRONIC PSYCHOTIC PATIENT

Bernard Weinman* and Robert J. Kleiner**

*Philadelphia State Hospital, Philadelphia, Pennsylvania

**Temple University, Philadelphia, Pennsylvania

As one approach to the problem of chronicity and recidivism now facing psychiatric installations, the Philadelphia State Hospital established a community treatment program for chronic mental patients.[1] The purpose of the community treatment program was to enable chronic patients, heretofore considered to have poor potential for release, to gain direct and sustained experience in the community so as to enhance their level of adjustment and reduce their recidivism. For this purpose, indigenous community members were trained as social change agents by professional staff and were employed to assist patients in their daily life activities in the community.

The evaluation of the project included (1) assessing the effects of community treatment on the patients' release rate, readmission rate, and level of post-treatment community adjustment, (2) determining whether community members can serve in a major therapeutic capacity in influencing the behavior of patients, (3) delineating the type of living setting in which the community member can generate the most successful treatment outcome, and (4) identifying the characteristics of community member-patient interaction which relate to successful treatment outcome. The interactions that are dealt with are interpersonal cohesion and conflict.

METHOD

Description of the Community Treatment

Patients. The program focused on functional psychotic male
and female patients who had more than one year of accumulated
hospitalization, and could not be placed with relatives. They
generally manifested the symptoms of chronic psychoses--apathy,
isolation and dependency; many also suffered from delusions and
hallucinations. However, they showed sufficient control to respond
appropriately during some portion of a screening interview, and
were judged by the psychologist interviewer to have potential for
developing the social and coping skills necessary for at least a
minimal community adjustment. The average age was 48.9 years, and
the average duration of accumulated hospitalization was 13.2 years.
Of the 263 patients participating in the project, approximately
90 percent had been diagnosed as schizophrenic.

Those meeting the criteria of the program were transferred to
a special unit where they received a twelve week orientation to
prepare them to live in the community. During this period, each
patient was assigned to a counselor, usually a social worker or
psychologist, who worked with the patient in group and individual
counseling sessions, arranged for his financial support, and
placed him in the community with an appropriate community member
referred to as an enabler.

While in the community, the patient received the services of
his counselor and an enabler for approximately 12 months. The
first eight months were spent in a structured experimental community treatment program and the last four months were spent in
making the transition to a more independent or permanent situation:
some patients relocated to new quarters, some began assignments at
sheltered workshops or vocational training centers, and some found
full or part-time employment. After the 12 month period, project
services were discontinued and patients were left to their own
devices, although most continued to receive regular psychiatric
evaluations and medication at their local community mental health
center.

Enablers. Before working with patients, enablers took part
in several orientation sessions to the program. Although training
of enablers was an experimental variable, all enablers were exposed to some elements of training by professional staff during
the period in which they were assigned patients. Emphasis was
placed on influencing the social behavior of the patient and helping him adjust to and become part of the community. More specifically, enablers were expected to provide their patients with:
(1) training and assistance in social behavior and in the management

of daily life activities, e.g., personal grooming, housekeeping, food preparation and shopping, and (2) an orientation to a variety of community activities and resources which would facilitate community adjustment and integration.

The enablers' advantage in working as social change agents lay in their sharing of common socio-economic backgrounds with the patients, communicating with them in a down-to-earth manner, and spending long periods of time assisting them with daily life activities. Typically, the enablers were women with children who were either in school or grown up and out of the house. They had time on their hands, and a desire to be useful. They had a high school education or less with no particular training or experience in dealing with mental patients. Some had worked as nurses aides, and a few had an interest in people with mental problems because of mental illness in their own families.

Enablers View Their Role. Interviews were conducted with a number of enablers after the termination of the project to determine some of their specific experiences regarding their social influence role with patients.

Most enablers reported that patients, initially, required considerable instruction and daily reminding to keep themselves, their clothes, and their living areas clean. Many had to be shown how to take a bath and wash the tub, as well as how to make a bed, clean a sink, and sweep a floor. Patients also had to be taught how to cook and how to prepare a balanced meal, as well as basic eating etiquette. One patient of 30 years hospitalization had to be told not to put a whole hot dog into his mouth at once; many had to be urged to eat slowly instead of gulping their meal.

Enablers also spent considerable time teaching their patients how to handle money. Budgeting was taught by using envelopes marked "rent", "food", "utilities", etc., and by taking patients shopping to help them make economical and needed purchases. The problem usually was not in overcoming extravagance, but in convincing patients to buy even the most necessary items. A patient who has lived in an institution for decades finds it a shock when he discovers that he is expected to stock the kitchen of his apartment with utensils which he has rarely been permitted to use in the hospital. He must buy knives, forks, and some basic tools such as scissors, screwdriver and hammer.

The enablers also believed the time spent introducing their patients to services available in the community was extremely important. They escorted their patients to their local mental health clinic, to the dentist, the foot doctor, the druggist, and the laundromat, as well as to therapy sessions, social activities (e.g., picnics, parties, trips to parks, fairs and the shore) and occasionally a restaurant. They also ensured that patients were acquainted with such facilities as the post office, the "Y", the library, the movies, etc. Often the enabler's spouse helped with errands and driving.

As part of their daily contact with patients, enablers were often confronted with psychiatric symptoms and attendant inappropriate behaviors. Sometimes it was a matter of seeing that patients took their medication on time. However, on most occasions, professional staff would work with enablers toward seeking practical approaches to the problems posed by patient symptoms. Such was the case with a patient with a homosexual background who shared an apartment with two other men, but spent most of his time wandering the streets. It was decided that he was unable to adjust to living in close quarters with other men and that he could be helped to adjust if given more privacy in the apartment. The enabler helped the patients to screen off a corner of the apartment providing the problem patient with a substantial measure of privacy, and thereby resolving the crisis.

In most instances approaches for dealing with psychopathology suggested by professional staff had to coincide with the personality style of the enabler. Some enablers could confront their patient with his inappropriate behavior and "tell him that it will have to stop"; other enablers were more tolerant of psychopathology. Thus, one enabler who was faced with a chronic patient's tendency to lie in the street when she accompanied him on errands, viewed his behavior as "just resting" and continued to follow through with her services.

As an indigenous member of the community, the enabler was particularly valuable in serving as a spokesman for the patients and gaining the understanding and support of neighbors and local merchants. Indeed, one of the enablers took his complaint about some accusations made against his patients by a crossing guard to the mayor and borough council. The local newspaper covered the story dealing with the patients sympathetically, and the council resolved the issue in favor of the patients. Apparently, an individual such as the enabler, who is part of the local scene can be more effective than professional staff in dealing with emotionally loaded issues and prejudices.

The Independent Variables[2]

Focus of Professional Staff Services. To determine the more effective use of professional intervention and the viability of enabler services, the community treatment program was subdivided into two equivalent conditions: patient-centered and enabler-centered. Although patients in both conditions were assigned

enablers, in the patient-centered condition, professional staff
counselors worked directly with patients to modify their behavior;
in the enabler-centered condition, enablers were trained by counselors to assume a social influence role with their patients.

The essential components of both conditions consisted of
(1) individual counseling, (2) monthly group meetings to plan and
conduct community activities, and (3) biweekly group meetings to
discuss patient problems and their social adjustment. The professional staff counselors met with the enablers in the enabler-
centered condition and with the patients in the patient-centered
condition, (4) counselors also met regularly with all enablers and
patients for purpose of case review.

A fifth component of both conditions was the conjoint biweekly
group therapy meetings with enablers and patients which were held
to resolve problems in adjustment. These meetings were observed
through a one-way mirror by a second counselor who provided private
feedback through earphones to patients in the patient-centered
condition and to enablers in the enabler-centered condition. The
nature of the feedback centered on (a) prompting interaction--the
patient was prompted to interact with his fellow patients and his
enabler; the enabler was prompted to interact with her patients
and to influence them to interact with other group members,
(b) suggesting discussion of specific patient-patient and/or
enabler-patient conflict and problem areas, (c) providing clarification about the dynamics of interaction of the therapy group members, (d) giving verbal approval for desirable behaviors.

Living Setting. To delineate the type of living situation in
which the enabler could effect the more successful treatment outcome, two types of community living conditions for patients were
designed and investigated: (1) the live-in enabler condition in
which the patient lived in the enabler's home, usually with other
patients, and (2) the visiting enabler condition in which the
patient lived in an apartment with one or two other patients and
received regular visits from an enabler. Each visiting enabler
was expected to make daily two hour visits, five days a week to
each group of patients. The visiting enabler was paid for her
services through project funds and the live-in enabler was re-
imbursed by the patients themselves for room and board through
public assistance, social security allotments or other funds.

The live-in and visiting enablers shared a common social
influence role. They provided patients with training in social
behavior, assistance in daily living and introduced them to community resources. By the conclusion of the project, 71 enablers
had been employed in the community project--48 visiting enablers
and 23 live-in enablers. The former consisted of 7 men and 41
women, the latter were all women.

Each patient was assigned randomly to a given living condition[3] (i.e., the live-in or visiting enabler condition) and to either the patient-centered or the enabler-centered condition. Four community treatment conditions were thus established: (1) patient-centered focus within a live-in enabler setting, (2) patient-centered focus within a visiting enabler setting, (3) enabler-centered focus within a live-in enabler setting, and (4) enabler-centered focus within a visiting enabler setting. This design made it possible to study the effects of the two major project variables--staff focus and community setting--as well as the interaction between them.

Effectiveness of Community Treatment. The effectiveness of the community treatment programs was determined by comparing its results with that of two hospital based conditions: socioenvironmental therapy and traditional hospital treatment.

Socioenvironmental therapy (Sanders, Smith and Weinman, 1967) is a structured hospital social treatment program consisting of four major components: (1) a core of five weekly group activities designed to elicit social interaction and to develop the skills necessary for living in the community, (2) informal social activities to promote social contact, (3) group therapy and patient government to broaden and intensify interpersonal relationships, and (4) a staff trained to stimulate participation in the program.

The duration of treatment for individual patients undergoing socioenvironmental therapy was approximately the same as that allowed for community treatment--8 to 12 months. There were 253 patients in the socioenvironmental condition. Their average age was 48.6 years with an average of 15.5 years of hospitalization. Patients selected for the project were assigned randomly to the community treatment program and to the socioenvironmental therapy condition.

The second control group consisted of chronic schizophrenic patients who had been released from the hospital during the project period through traditional hospital ward programs. These programs included such activities as occupational and recreational therapy. The traditional ward treatment patients were selected on the basis of their comparability in age and length of hospitalization with patients completing community treatment. One hundred and nine patients were in this control condition. Their average age was 45.9 with an average of 10.8 years of hospitalization.

Practically all patients separated from the hospital, regardless of experimental condition, were routinely referred for aftercare services which consisted mainly of psychiatric evaluation and medication review.

The Intervening Variables: Cohesion and Conflict

The nature of the interaction that enablers had with their patients during the treatment program was viewed as a crucial determinant of treatment outcome. Of particular relevance to outcome were the cohesion building and conflict arousing behaviors which the enabler directed toward her patients.

The Measures

Hospital Separation and Return Rates. Community and socio-environmental treatments were compared on the proportion of patients who completed treatment successfully, i.e., remained in the community at completion of community treatment or attained placement in the community socioenvironmental treatment. The same psychiatrist made the disposition decision in both conditions. The patients in these two programs as well as those in the traditional ward program were also compared on their readmission rate after a 24 month post-treatment period. In addition, patients in the various community treatment conditions were compared on their readmission rates.

Self-Esteem Scale. The mean discrepancy scores between descriptions of actual and ideal behavior in seven different types of interpersonal situations constitute the measure of self-esteem (Parker and Kleiner, 1966). The larger the discrepancy score, the greater the self dissatisfaction, and the lower the self-esteem. Parker and Kleiner reported significant differences in discrepancy scale scores between a community and psychiatric sample. Significant differences were also found between a sample of project patients and a sample of enablers. The self-esteem scale was administered at the end of the eight month structured treatment period. Patients who failed to complete the initial eight month treatment period were not included.

Psychiatric Status Scale. This is a 15 interval rating scale with five behavioral descriptions of symptomatology which differentiate levels of psychiatric status--from essentially normal behavior to behavior which makes it inappropriate to live outside the hospital (Sanders, Smith and Weinman, 1967). The scale was administered at the end of the eight month treatment period; patients who failed to complete the initial eight month treatment period were not included.

Instrumental Performance Questionnaire. This is a nine-item questionnaire concerned with such issues as employment, shopping, use of public transportation, budgeting and managing funds (Weinman, Kleiner, Yu, and Tillson, 1974). It was administered

12 months after completion of treatment to patients who remained
in the community.

Social Performance Questionnaire. This is a five item
questionnaire concerned with the patient's social contacts with
neighbors, relatives and friends. It was administered concurrently
with the Instrumental Performance Questionnaire.

Enabler Cohesion and Conflict. The setting for the measurement of enabler cohesion and conflict was the conjoint patient-
enabler group therapy meetings described earlier. These meetings
were attended by several groups of patients who lived together and
their enablers. A counselor led the discussions and a second
counselor observed the group through a one way mirror to provide
private promptings and feedback to either patients or enablers as
determined by the experimental design. During a 15 minute segment,
starting at the halfway mark of each session, the discussion leader
and the counselor providing the private prompting remained silent,
and the interaction of the patients and enablers were observed and
recorded. Each therapy group met for an eight month period in biweekly sessions. The average number of sessions attended was 13.3
for patients and 12.8 for enablers.

Cohesion was defined as the expression by the enabler of
agreement with or enhancement of any member of her assigned group
of patients who lived together. The cohesion scores for each
enabler were derived by adding and combining the number of agreement and enhancement responses made by the enabler during each of
the group discussion sessions. The total score was then averaged
by the number of sessions attended by the enabler.

Conflict was defined as the expression of disagreement and
depreciation by the enabler toward any patient in her assigned
living group. The conflict scores for each enabler were derived
by adding and combining the number of disagreement and depreciation responses made by the enabler during each of the group discussion sessions. The total score was then divided by the number of
sessions attended by the enabler.

RESULTS

The Effectiveness of Community Treatment

The effectiveness of the community treatment program was determined by comparing the patient outcome measures in this program
with that of the two control programs--socioenvironmental therapy
and traditional ward treatment.

Hospital Separation and Return Rates.[4] A significantly greater number of patients in community treatment than in socioenvironmental therapy successfully completed their treatment program, i.e., 62 percent (N=242) and 50 percent (N=246), respectively (x^2 = 8.37, df = 1, p <.01).

Community Tenure. The findings indicate that community treatment generates somewhat fewer readmissions over a 24 month post-treatment period than socioenvironmental treatment, i.e., 16 percent (N=149) and 23 percent (N=122), respectively. However, this difference is not statistically significant.

The patients released from traditional wards incur by far the highest return rate. Forty-one percent (N=102) returned to the hospital within 24 months following release. This differs significantly from both the community (x^2 = 18.36, df = 1, p <.001) and socioenvironmental treatment programs (x^2 = 7.76, df = 1, p <.01).

Self-Esteem and Psychiatric Status. Community treatment patients show significantly greater improvement in self-esteem during treatment than socioenvironmental patients. The respective post-treatment mean discrepancy scores are .61 and .74 (t = 1.95, p <.05). There were no differences between the two treatment programs on self-esteem before initiation of treatment. Community treatment patients show a mean self-esteem score of .80 as compared to a mean score of .82 for socioenvironmental treatment patients.

There are no differences between community treatment and socioenvironmental treatment patients on post-treatment psychiatric status. The self-esteem scale and the psychiatric status scale were not administered to patients in the traditional ward program.

Instrumental and Social Performance. There are significant differences in instrumental performance scores among the three programs one year after completion of treatment (F = 3.92, df = 2/265, p <.02). Community treatment generates greater instrumental behavior than socioenvironmental treatment (t = 2.80, df = 204, p <.01), but not more than the traditional ward program. The respective means are 12.40, 11.00 and 11.77. There is no significant difference between the socioenvironmental and traditional ward treatment programs.

There are also differences among the three programs on social performance scores (F = 3.47, df = 2/265, p <.03). Both the community and traditional ward programs surpass the socioenvironmental treatment program in social performance (t = 1.64, df = 204, p <.05;[5] t = 2.65, df = 134, p <.01). There is no significant difference between the community treatment and traditional ward

treatment programs. The mean scores for the three programs
are as follows: community treatment 4.48, socioenvironmental
treatment 3.78, and traditional ward treatment 5.10.

The higher level of social performance generated by the
traditional ward program in comparison to the socioenvironmental
program is attributed to the higher attrition rate in the former
program. As a result of this attrition rate, only a rather select
group of traditional ward patients remained in the community. In
this context, it should be noted that the traditional ward
patients also exhibit a higher level of instrumental performance
than the socioenvironmental patients, although the difference is
not statistically significant.

It has been demonstrated that the community program is
superior to socioenvironmental therapy in generating a higher
separation rate from the hospital, in improving self-esteem, and
in producing superior levels of instrumental and social performance.
In comparison to traditional ward treatment, the community program
shows a much lower recidivism rate. The difference in return
rates make comparisons between the residual community samples of
the two programs, on the available outcome measures, tenuous.

Focus of Professional Staff Services and Patient Outcome.
The effects of this variable were determined by comparing the
results of the patient-centered and enabler-centered conditions.
In the former condition, professional staff worked as social change
agents with patients; in the latter condition, professional staff
trained enablers to serve in this capacity.

Table 1 shows the differential effects of these two conditions
on patient outcome. There is no difference in readmission rates.
The readmission rate for each condition was 16 percent following
the 24 month post-treatment period. There are also no differences
between the two conditions on self-esteem at completion of treatment. However, the patients in the enabler-centered condition
manifest significantly less psychiatric disability at completion
of treatment than their counterparts in the patient-centered
condition. The advantage of employing indigenous community members
for a service role with patients is demonstrated by the comparable
and even somewhat more favorable impact of enablers over professional staff on treatment outcome.

Living Setting and Patient Outcome. Table 2 shows that the
living situation in the community treatment program does influence
patient outcome. The recidivism rate following the two year post-
treatment period is significantly greater for the visiting enabler
condition than for the live-in enabler condition. Twenty-two
percent returned to the hospital from the former program as compared to only four percent from the latter.

Table 1

Effects of Focus of Professional Staff Services
on Patient Outcome: A Comparison of the Patient-
Centered (PC) and Enabler-Centered (EC) Conditions

Outcome Measure	PC	EC	Statistic
Return Rates (T_5)			
Number Returned	11	13	$x^2 = .00$
Number Remained Out	58	67	
Self Esteem[a] (T_3)			
Mean	.607	.612	$t = .07$
S.D.	.392	.418	
N	57	66	
Psychiatric Status[a] (T_3)			
Mean	7.85	6.22	$t = 2.38*$
S.D.	3.95	3.62	
N	54	68	
Instrumental Performance (T_4)			
Mean	12.33	12.53	$t = 35$
S.D.	3.39	3.13	
N	55	74	
Social Performance (T_4)			
Mean	4.22	4.68	$t = .90$
S.D.	2.86	3.01	
N	55	74	

Note - T_3: at completion of treatment; T_4: one year
following completion of treatment; T_5: two years following
completion of treatment.

[a]The lower the scores the more positive the status.

*$p < .02$

Table 2

Effects of Living Setting on Patient Outcome:

A comparison of the Live-In (LI) and

Visiting Enabler (VE) Conditions

Outcome Measure	LI	VE	Statistic
Return Rates (T_5)			
Number Returned	2	22	$x^2 = 6.87$***
Number Remained Out	48	77	
Self Esteem[a] (T_3)			
Mean	.502	.654	t = 1.92*
S.D.	.387	.405	
N	36	87	
Psychiatric Status[a] (T_3)			
Mean	8.18	6.47	t = 2.24**
S.D.	4.06	3.66	
N	34	88	
Instrumental Performance (T_4)			
Mean	10.91	13.21	t = 4.10****
S.D.	3.47	2.80	
N	46	86	
Social Performance (T_4)			
Mean	4.24	4.62	
S.D.	3.13	2.86	
N	46	86	

Note - T_3: at completion of treatment; T_4: one year follow-ing completion of treatment; T_5: two years following completion of treatment.

[a]The lower the scores the more positive the status.

*p <.06, **p <.03, ***p <.01, ****p <.001

With respect to the outcome measures administered to those ramaining in the community, no consistent pattern emerges. The patients in the live-in enabler condition tend to show a higher level of self-esteem at completion of treatment than their counterparts in the visiting enabler condition. However, the data for psychiatric status and instrumental performance indicate the superiority of the visiting enabler condition. The patients in the visiting enabler condition manifest significantly less psychiatric disability than the patients in the live-in condition at completion of treatment. They also show significantly greater instrumental behavior one year following completion of treatment. The two conditions do not differ in social performance. Thus, each of the two living settings of the community program has certain advantages and limitations for treatment.

The results have shown that patients in the enabler-centered condition are superior to their counterparts in the patient-centered condition in psychiatric status and comparable to them on the other outcome measures. Thus, enablers trained by professional staff can provide services to patients that generate even more favorable outcome than professional staff services.

With respect to the impact of living setting on outcome, living in the home of an enabler is more advantageous for community tenure and self-esteem. On the other hand, living in the more independent apartment situation and receiving the services of a visiting enabler has more beneficial effects on psychiatric status and instrumental performance.

Enabler Cohesion and Conflict and Patient Outcome

The final section of the results deals with the behaviors of the enabler which mediate change in the patients. Accordingly, the cohesion building and conflict arousing behaviors of the enabler are related to patient outcome in the overall community treatment program and in the four experimental conditions.

Overall Treatment Program. It is evident from Table 3 that the expression of cohesion by the enabler toward her patients is not associated with any of the measures of patient outcome. However, the expression of conflict is clearly associated with negative consequences. Thus, high enabler conflict during the community treatment program was associated significantly with low patient self-esteem at completion of treatment and with poor patient instrumental performance one year after completion of treatment.

Since conflict is a more powerful determinant of outcome than cohesion, it may obscure the effects of cohesion. For this

Table 3

Correlations Between Measures of Enablers'
Behavior and Patients' Outcome Measures

Outcome Measure	N	Enabler Cohesion	Enabler Conflict[a]
Community Tenure	122	.03	-.04
Self Esteem[b]	95	-.13	-.20*
Psychiatric Status[b]	94	-.12	-.03
Instrumental			
Performance	90	-.10	-.34**
Social Performance	90	.00	-.01

[a]Bi-serial correlations were used because of the relatively high number of zero scores.

[b]Signs reversed to adjust for lower scores equaling more positive status.

*p <.05, **p <.01

reason it was necessary to assess the effects of the relative amount of enabler cohesion (i.e., cohesion/cohesion + conflict). Correlations between percent enabler cohesion and the patient outcome measures reveal a positive association with community tenure ($r = 18$, $p < .05$) and with instrumental performance ($r = .28$, $p < .01$).

Experimental Conditions. Enabler cohesion in each of the four experimental conditions is not positively associated with any of the measures of patient outcome. When percent enabler cohesion is considered, the same pattern emerges that was found for the total population. Percent enabler cohesion is associated positively ($p < .10$) with community tenure and with instrumental performance on three of the four experimental conditions. The correlations for these conditions are as follows: (a) for the visiting enabler condition, .25 with community tenure and .31 with instrumental performance; (b) for the patient-centered condition, .22 with community tenure and .35 with instrumental performance, for the enabler-centered condition, .19 with community tenure and .27 with instrumental performance.

The effects of enabler conflict is apparent in all of the experimental conditions. When living setting is considered, enabler conflict was negatively associated with instrumental performance ($r = -.46$, $df = 28$, $p < .01$) in the live-in enabler condition and negatively associated with self-esteem ($r = -.25$, $df = 65$, $p < .05$) in the visiting enabler condition.

With respect to focus of professional staff services, enabler conflict was negatively associated with self-esteem ($r = .26$, $df = 40$, $p < .10$) and with instrumental performance ($r = -.43$, $df = 37$, $p < .01$) in the patient-centered condition and negatively associated with instrumental performance ($r = -.26$, $df = 51$, $p < .10$) in the enabler-centered condition. The greater negative consequences of enabler conflict in the patient-centered condition underscores the importance of professional staff concentrating their services on training enablers.

The negative impact of conflict expressed by tne relatively untrained enabler (i.e., those in the patient-centered condition) becomes more apparent when enabler conflict ratio scores[6] are examined. The ratio scores deal with the amount of conflict shown by the enabler toward her own group of patients relative to the total amount of conflict shown by the enabler to all members of the therapy group (i.e., her own group of patients as well as the other enabler(s) and patients). The greater the relative amount of conflict expressed by the enabler toward members of her own group of patients, the higher the ratio scores. Table 4 shows the relationship between this index of enabler conflict and the outcome measures. High conflict ratios obtained by relatively untrained enablers (i.e., those in the patient-centered condition) are associated significantly with deleterious consequences for their patients' self-esteem and instrumental performance. There is no significant relationship between conflict ratios and outcome for the trained enablers (i.e., those in the enabler-centered condition).

The results have shown that enabler cohesion does not mediate patient outcome either in the overall community treatment program or in the four experimental conditions. However, percent enabler cohesion (cohesion relative to conflict and cohesion combined) is associated with positive patient outcome in the overall community program and in three of the four experimental conditions.

Enabler conflict does mediate patient outcome in the overall community treatment program and in each of the experimental

Table 4

Correlations Between Enablers' Conflict Ratios
and Patient Outcome Measures in the Patient-
Centered (PC) and Enabler-Centered (EC) Conditions

Outcome Measure	PC	N	EC	N
Community Tenure	-.17	51	-.02	71
Self-Esteem[a]	-.34*	41	.15	54
Psychiatric Status[a]	-.13	38	-.07	56
Instrumental				
Performance	-.50**	38	-.19	52
Social Performance	-.01	38	-.04	52

[a]Sign reversed to adjust for lower scores equaling more
positive status.

*p <.05, **p <.01

conditions.   In all instances where significant relationships
were found, enabler conflict is negatively associated with patient
outcome.

The mediating effects of enabler cohesion and conflict are
most frequently reflected in the patient' instrumental performance
one year after completion of treatment.

DISCUSSION AND CONCLUSIONS

Influence of the Enabler

Perhaps the most important contribution of the project was
the role created for indigenous community members as social change
agents.   Unlike professional staff, the enablers can spend long
periods of time with patients, and they can be of particular value
in assisting patients to cope with the demands of daily living.
The behavior of the enablers during treatment influenced the

patients immediate response to treatment as well as their post-
treatment community adjustment. The cohesive building behavior
of the enabler was associated with positive treatment consequences
and their conflict generating behavior with negative consequences.
The latter behavior was a more powerful determinant of treatment
outcome.

Of the measures of patient outcome used, instrumental performance one year following treatment appeared to be most sensitive
to enabler behavior. It was associated positively with percent
cohesion and negatively with conflict. Self-esteem at completion
of treatment and community tenure during the two year period
following treatment were also influenced by enabler behavior. The
former was negatively associated with conflict and the latter was
positively associated with percent cohesion.

It was also demonstrated that the enabler can be at least as
effective as professional staff in changing patient behavior.
Thus, the enabler-centered condition generated a higher level of
psychiatric status than the patient-centered condition. In the
enabler-centered condition, the enablers were trained by professionals for a change agent role whereas, in the patient-centered
condition, the professional staff worked more directly as change
agents with patients. Both conditions were comparable in impact
on the other measures of patient outcome.

From a theoretical point of view, the superiority of the
enabler-centered condition is due to the close coordination by
the enabler in influencing the patient and preventing him from
being confused or overwhelmed by the conflicting or incompatible
expectancies of the significant others. In the enabler-centered
condition, the enabler had the major responsibility for coordinating the patient's activities. She expressed both her own
demands as well as those suggested by the professional staff. In
the patient-centered condition, coordination was diluted because
demands on the patient were made by both the professional staff
and the enabler. Thus, the probability of conflicting demands
was increased and the potential for professional staff or enabler
influence on the patient's behavior was diminished.

Another reason for the greater effectiveness of the enabler-
centered condition was the effect of training upon the enabler.
The findings regarding the differential effects or enabler conflict on patient outcome suggest that the quality of the enabler-
patient relationship was generally more positive in the enabler-
centered condition.

Therapeutic Features of the Living Setting

The type of expectations and demands made of patients in the community appear to generate different consequences. The most striking differences were found in return rates and level of psychiatric adjustment. Living in the home of an enabler was associated with greater community tenure and poorer psychiatric status than living in an apartment and receiving visits from an enabler. Apparently, the care and supervision received in the enabler's home was paramount to maintaining patients in the community who otherwise would have returned to the hospital. Obviously, their counterparts living in the more independent and demanding apartment situation were required, more often, to return to the hospital when they manifested agitated or regressed behavior. Hence, the patients placed in apartments showed a higher readmission rate and less psychopathology while living in the community than patients placed in the homes of enablers.

One might expect patients who had experienced the live-in enabler condition to exhibit a high recidivism rate after their 12 months in the program, when they are left to their own devices. However, this was not the case primarily because 67 percent of those remaining in the community continued to reside with their enabler for the 24 months subsequent to completion of treatment. In the visiting enabler condition, 78 percent remained in their original apartments, but, of course, without the services of an enabler.

It is postulated that a salient factor motivating the enablers to retain patients in their home after treatment, in spite of the many difficulties encountered, was the friendship bond established between the enabler and the patient. Evidence for this is found in the attitudinal differences toward mental patients which occur as a consequence of the enablers having patients in their homes. Attitudes toward mental illness were assessed prior to assigning patients to enablers, and at the completion of their patient's community treatment program. From these attitudinal items it was possible to construct a nine item scale relating to the desirability and undersirability of living and associating with a "mentally ill person." More specifically, tne items dealt with whether obscene and/or insulting language was characteristic of mental patients, whether they neglected their personal appearance, whether they were dangerous, knew right from wrong, were more prone to engage in angry arguments and/or disagreements with those living around them, and whether they would make relatives and/or neighbors uneasy.

The initial assessment showed no attitudinal differences between prospective live-in and visiting enablers. However, at the completion of their patients' treatment program, live-in

enablers viewed mental patients significantly more positively than
visiting enablers (x^2 = 6.91, p < .01). This difference was due
to a significant shift in the attitudes of the live-in enabler.

The more positive attitudes toward mental patients shown by
the live-in enablers may also account for the different changes
in the self-esteem of patients in the two conditions. It should
be recalled that the patients completing the live-in enabler condition tended to have greater self-esteem than patients experiencing the visiting enabler condition. No doubt the enhancement
of self-esteem in the live-in enabler condition derived from the
enabler perceiving and presumably relating to patients as persons
rather than as individuals with traits which make them undesirable
to associate with or to have in one's home.

Neither of the community living settings is offered as an
elixir for chronic psychoses. However, each can be applied
judiciously in accord with individualized treatment goals. Living
in the home of an enabler who provides assistance with the activities of daily living is highly advantageous for preventing readmission. Although commercial boarding homes are as sheltered
and tolerant of psychopathology as the live-in enabler setting,
the latter generated fewer readmissions. Patients in the live-in
enabler condition showed significantly greater community tenure
during the two year post-treatment period than those placed in
boarding home settings from socioenvironmental treatment
(x^2 = 6.60, df = 1, p < .02). The return rate was four percent
for the enabler living setting and 22 percent for the boarding
home setting. The live-in enabler condition was also significantly
more effective than commercial boarding homes in engendering
instrumental performance. The respective means were 10.96 and
9.39 (t = 2.16, p < .03).

The companion community condition which assists patients to
live in their own apartments has other advantages. Although showing a higher post-treatment return rate than the live-in enabler
condition, the visiting enabler condition develops higher levels
of instrumental performance. It also generates significantly
lower return rates than traditional ward treatment programs. Perhaps of greatest importance is the fact that this type of program
is more feasible because of the availability of community members
to serve as visiting enablers. By continuing the services of the
community member for a longer time period, it may be possible to
reduce further the recidivism rate of this type of program.

A New Role for Professional Staff

The effective utilization of indigenous community members requires that professional staff assume a training function. They
should train the community member to overcome the social deficits
of chronic patients and to help them deal with the requirements
of daily living. Management of psychopathology remains in the
purview of the professional staff. The role of the community
member is to exert a significant influence on the social behavior
of chronic patients so that it more closely approximates standards
which are acceptable to the community. To help them perform this
role effectively, professional staff should focus on helping the
enablers establish interpersonal relationships with patients that
enhance cohesion and resolve conflict.

Because this paper has concentrated on the role of the enabler,
the data dealing with the impact on treatment outcome of the
cohesion and conflict of the individual patient as well as that of
his living group have not been included. Also of interest are the
results regarding sex differences, particularly with respect to
the differential treatment afforded by the enabler to men and
women patients on the basis of the degree of their psychiatric impairment. These findings will be reported in future publications.

Footnotes

1. This project was supported by an NIMH Hospital Improvement
Project Grant entitled, Community treatment of hospitalized chronic
patients, 03-R-000, 803, 4-1-65 to 3-31-72; and a companion Research
Grant entitled, Treatment deployment for chronic psychotics,
MHI5U08, 5-1-67 to 8-31-74. It was conducted at the Philadelphia
State Hospital from 1965 to 1972.

The authors gratefully acknowledge the assistance of Jin Yu,
Jim Wilson and Minot Tillson in the collection and/or analysis of
the data.

2. The theoretical basis for the independent and intervening
variables used in this investigation have been presented in the
original research proposal and in Weinman, Sanders, Kleiner and
Wilson (1968, 1970).

3. Once patients were assigned to a living setting, efforts were
made to pair them so that a patient functioning at a low level was
placed with a more competent patient.

4.   Thirty-five patients were lost from the project sample as follows: Community Treatment--12 did not attend their prescribed treatment meetings and/or moved to a different living setting; three died during the 12 month community treatment period; and six died during the 24 month follow-up phase. Socioenvironmental Treatment--two died during their year of hospital treatment and five died during the 24 month follow-up phase. Traditional Ward Treatment--one died during the 24 month follow-up phase and six could not be located.

5.   One failed test.

6.   Enabler conflict ratio scores were computed as follows:
$$\frac{IG}{IG + OG}$$
In-group (IG) refers to conflict expressed by the enabler toward her assigned patient group. Out-group (OG) refers to conflict expressed by the enabler toward other enabler(s) and their assigned patients who also attended the group therapy sessions.

REFERENCES

Parker, S., & Kleiner, R.J.   Mental health in the urban Negro community. New York: The Free Press, 1966.

Sanders, R., Smith, R. S., & Weinman, B.   Chronic psychoses and recovery. San Francisco: Jossey Bass, 1967.

Weinman, B., Sanders, R., Kleiner, R., & Wilson, S.   The community as a focal point in treatment of the chronic psychotic patient. Symposium presented at the meeting of the American Psychological Association, San Francisco, 1968.

Weinman, B., Sanders, R., Kleiner, R., & Wilson, S.   Community based treatment of the chronic psychotic. Community Mental Health Journal, 6, 1970, 13-21.

Weinman, B., Kleiner, R., Yu, J., & Tillson, V. A.   Social treatment of the chronic psychotic patient in the community. Journal of Community Psychology, 1974, 2, 358-365.

Part III

EXAMPLES OF SYSTEMS OF

ALTERNATIVES TO MENTAL

HOSPITAL TREATMENT

ALTERNATIVES TO HOSPITALIZATION--

THE SACRAMENTO STORY

Donald G. Langsley* and Richard M. Yarvis**

*Department of Psychiatry
University of Cincinnati Medical Center
Cincinnati, Ohio
**Sacramento Medical Center
Sacramento, California

The past decade has seen a dramatic reduction in the use of state mental hospitals. In a large part, this has been a result of mental health treatment programs in the community. The professional literature and regional conferences have focused on specific treatment programs designed to avoid admission to a mental hospital. In many parts of the United States one can find crisis intervention, halfway houses, partial hospitalization programs, outpatient programs and other facilities designed to treat the mentally ill individual (and/or his family) without admission to a mental hospital. Community programs have demonstrated direct relationships between the development of new treatment services in the community and the diminution of state mental hospital admissions (see Figure 1). But this does not explain all of the reasons for the decrease in state hospital populations. In addition to preventing admissions by community treatment, mental hospitals have drastically reduced average lengths of stay and discharged large numbers of patients. In some instances this has happened as a result of mutual planning by community and state hospital staff leading to the development of a community treatment program prior to discharge. In other instances (far too many of them) there have been wholesale discharges to communities unprepared to treat

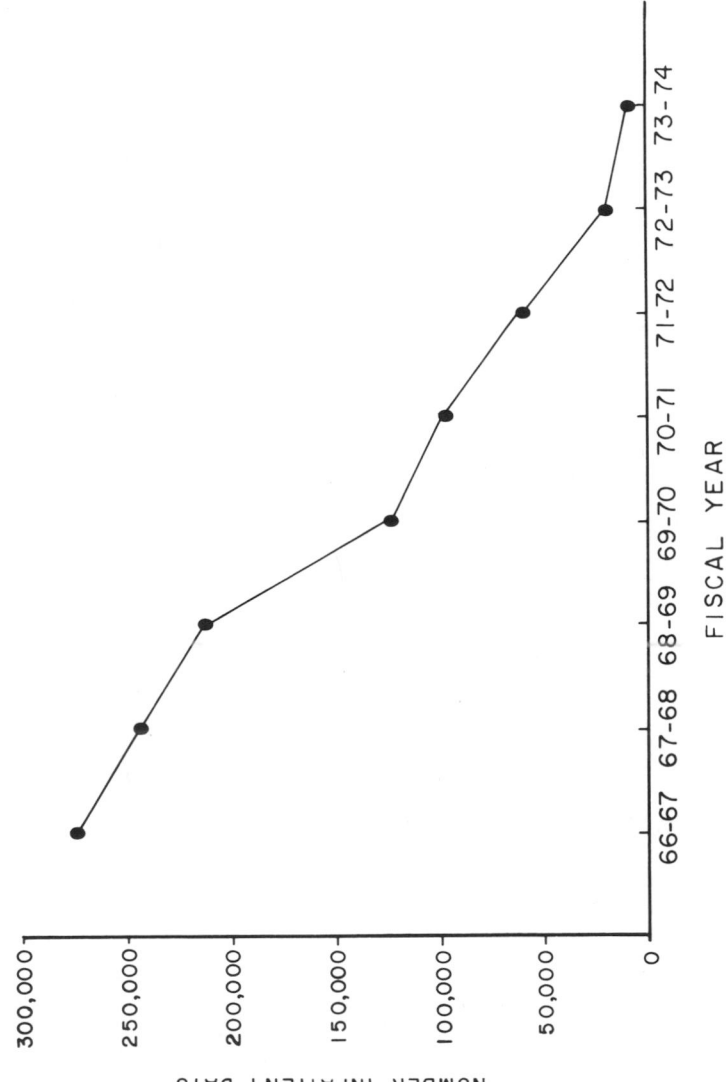

Figure 1. Sacramento County Hospital inpatient days from 1966–1974.

the former state hospital patient. In such cases the consequences
have been a removal of the "back ward" patient to the "back alley"
of the community. This has resulted in neglect of patients who
have had to live in physical squalor. Deep-seated community fears
about "mental patients" have relegated some such individuals to
the worst section of town. Some have suffered for lack of food and
clothing. Some have vegetated in front of a television set. In
regions close to state mental hospitals, ghettos for the mentally
ill have arisen. It is not surprising that there have been a
number of exposes in the media. Some have been motivated by state
hospital employee associations--groups obviously interested in
maintaining jobs. Despite occasional exaggeration and the fact
that the media have focused on the worst cases of neglect without
a balanced presentation of the positive programs, it must be acknowledged that some patients have been treated poorly.

The consequences of long-term institutionalization have been
well documented. The induced dependency, the progressive regression,
the development of the "sick role" and the alienation of and from
family which results from long absences has affected a large number
of individuals. There is reason to hope that avoiding hospitalization from the beginning will diminish or eliminate these sequelae
of hospitalism. Perhaps a future generation will see very few
problems of this type. Can we simply neglect the current generation of chronically ill patients who do suffer from the consequences
of institutionalization because we expect the disease to disappear?
Humanitarian concern and the fact that some who suffer from hospitalism have been rehabilitated will not permit such neglect.

Many reports have focused on a single demonstration project or
an innovative approach to this population. The range of programs
reported in this volume suggests that many approaches work and
that the common denominator is an enthusiastic and dedicated staff.
Some programs have been carefully evaluated with close attention
to research design including attention to sampling, control groups,
and multiple outcome measures. Others have relied on anecdotal
reports. The report of the Sacramento program focuses on the thesis
that treatment and rehabilitation of the former mental hospital
patient must be part of a total system of mental health services
for a defined population. It must be part of the system which
includes attention to children, adults and families who become
acutely disturbed as well as rehabilitation programs for those
who are chronically ill. We suggest that the basic requirement is
a commitment to mental health treatment and prevention for a defined
population. Such a commitment means that all of the mental health
service needs of that population are the responsibility of the
agency assuming such a responsibility. Such a commitment makes it
far more likely that no group will be neglected.

THE COMMUNITY

Sacramento County includes the Capitol of California. Located
in the agriculturally rich central valley of California, it is 90
miles east of San Francisco. Sacramento is bisected by the major
East-West Highway (Interstate 80) and Interstate Route 5 running
North and South. The 1975 population is 680,000, an increase
of 48,502 since 1970 and 177,222 since 1960. The largest minority
group includes Spanish-Americans (9%), Blacks (6%), Asian-Americans
(3%), and there is a smattering of Native Americans and other
minority groups. The principle sources of income are government
employment and agriculture. In addition to the State Capitol and
associated offices, there are two air force bases and an army
depot. There is in addition one large aerospace firm. Agriculture is the major source of income and the central valley is famous
for its rice, fruit orchards, tomatoes, nuts and grapes.

The climate is pleasant with warm but dry summer weather.
Those who drive through Sacramento on a warm summer afternoon do
not always realize that the temperature drops 40 degrees each
night. Rainfall is almost entirely limited to the winter months.
Freezing temperatures and snow are almost nonexistent.

Although Sacramento is not totally free of urban problems,
it is clearly one of the more pleasant communities of this country.
In a recent survey of large, medium and small size cities to rate
quality of life, Sacramento was rated number two in the nation
among cities over 500,000 in population. It is a community which
has been sensitive to human needs and which has been willing to
support and fund health services. The governing body is a Board
of Supervisors consisting of five elective officials.

HISTORY OF MENTAL HEALTH SERVICES IN SACRAMENTO

Before 1968 Sacramento had little or no public funded mental
health treatment programs. Those who became acutely ill were
brought to the county hospital and admitted to one of two locked
wards for evaluation--one for men and one for women. Half of
those admitted were sent to state mental hospitals on indefinite
commitments. The other half were sent home. State hospital
inpatient residents from Sacramento exceeded 600. At that time
the average length of stay for first admissions in the state mental
hospital was more than 60 days. Locally there was one small county
mental health clinic located in a building which previously had
been used as a juvenile detention center. It did not advertise
the availability of treatment out of fear of being overwhelmed by
demand. There was a waiting list for outpatient treatment and the

clinic reported eight or nine thousand outpatient visits per year.
There were no mental health services for children. Mental health
consultation or other approaches to prevention did not exist.
There were no crisis or emergency services. An individual brought
to the emergency room on Friday evening would be admitted to the
hospital by an intern but would not be seen by a mental health
professional until Monday.

The private sector of mental health professionals included
approximately 35 psychiatrists, and an equal number of clinical
psychologists and social workers. Many of these were in part-time
practice. There were no free-standing psychiatric hospitals but
two general hospitals did have psychiatric inpatient units for
private patients. A group of social agencies did serve certain
segments of the community but there was no coordination or plan
for comprehensive services. One of the community hospitals that
expressed some interest in developing a mental health center
(Sutter) was in the process of organizing a program. They had
received federal community mental health center construction funds.

Alcoholics were taken to the county jail. Approximately 30
such individuals per day were "admitted" to the drunk tank. There
were no special services for drug abusers although that problem
was very much in the public eye by 1968. Some of the patients who
were returned from state mental hospitals were housed in family
care homes but there was no organized aftercare program or easy
way of obtaining maintenance medication and psychological support.
As required by law, there was a County Mental Health Advisory Board
but it met infrequently and did not have a close association with
mental health professionals. The local mental health association
was interested in helping and did begin a social rehabilitation
program for ex-patients but it was an isolated service and not part
of a coordinated county plan. The Advisory Board and Mental Health
Association both had recommended the construction of an improved
psychiatric inpatient service.

SPECIAL CIRCUMSTANCES FOR CHANGE

A number of special circumstances in the year 1968 made it
possible to undertake a comprehensive mental health program in
Sacramento. Three major factors must be taken into account. The
first of these factors is the fact that a new medical school was
opened by the University of California, in Davis and in Sacramento.
The new school provided an opportunity for the development of
innovative programs and for the establishment of community mental
health programs as the locus for education in medicine, psychiatry,
and other mental health professions. The school was undertaken

with the specific plan of developing educational programs in
Sacramento. The individual appointed as chairman of the department of psychiatry (the senior author) was also asked to take on
the additional responsibility of mental health director for
Sacramento County. In part, this was due to the lack of existing
leadership in mental health services and in part it represented
an awareness of the potential for collaboration between the county
and the medical school. The position of County Mental Health
Director in the California system is one which permits (and
requires) the incumbent to develop and implement mental health
programs. This merger of functions turned out to be a fortunate
turn of events. The second factor was the passage of the California
mental health statute (Laterman-Petris-Short Act). This was a far-
reaching piece of legislation which has turned out to be a model
for many other states. It eliminated indefinite commitment to
state mental hospitals, encouraged (and funded) the development
of community mental health services on a 90/10 matching fund
basis (state support 90%, local matching support 10%). Also
included were provisions for annual planning and for community
involvement in planning. It placed the responsibility for mental
health planning and services at the county level--a logical unit
of government for this task since the county had been all along
providing health services to the indigent and other residents.
The third fortuitous factor encouraging the development of this
program was related to a firm commitment by the county to develop
a modern community mental health program. This meant cooperation
both from county government and from important citizen and professional groups. This degree of cooperation has been a major
factor in the success of the Sacramento program.

There were undoubtedly other factors at work. The new department chairman--mental health director--was an individual interested
in community mental health programs and dedicated to the development of alternatives to hospitalization. His experience in the use
of family crisis therapy as a result of a five year project in
Denver had convinced him of the feasibility of the community
approach. This point of view was shared by the initial faculty
recruited for the department. Yet another element in the development of this program was the fact that it was the only community
mental health and educational institution in the area. Sacramento
County is predominately urban but it is the tertiary care resource
for a large number of rural and semi-rural counties in northeastern
California.

GOALS AND BASIC STRUCTURE

The goals of the program as agreed upon by the professionals, the citizens groups and the government officials involved can be listed as follows:

1.   Quality Service--all concerned are devoted to devising that treatment program which best approximates the needs of each patient and which represents the best clinically available treatment.   The staff, although basically psychodynamic in orientation, was dedicated to an eclectic point of view rejecting no treatment which was clinically appropriate.

2.   Accessibility--mental health services, both direct and preventative, were to be located as close as possible to those being served.   The catchment area concept was adopted and it turned out that federally defined catchment areas made some sense in terms of geography, population, natural units of government and transportation.   It was decided to have a principle mental health center within each catchment area but to centralize a very limited number of services which are especially expensive or limited in terms of need.   Thus each catchment area was to have a mental health center which minimally had daytime emergency services, outpatient services, partial hospitalization, and consultation-education for adults, children, and families.   Night and weekend emergency services and inpatient services were to be centralized for the three catchment areas to be served by the University and were to be located at the existing inpatient services in the two other catchment areas.   No new inpatient beds were to be developed in Sacramento County.   In addition to the basic mental health center, each catchment area could establish satellite clinics on a part-time or full-time basis. These were to be located in various neighborhoods of the catchment area so as to increase accessibility.

3.   A Mix of Direct and Preventative Services--each mental health center was to establish direct treatment services for patients needing them.   In addition, programs of mental health consultation and other mental health prevention services were to be an important part of the program.   The mix of direct and community services is to be determined in each catchment area based on the needs and plans for that particular population. Services for alcoholics, drug abusers, and the aged were to be developed either directly in each catchment area or through some type of cooperative county program.

4.   Emphasis on Avoidance of Hospitalization--the goals of the program included an emphasis on avoiding unnecessary hospitalization.   Crisis intervention and emergency services were to be given the highest priority in the development of the programs.

It was recognized that immediate intervention could help avoid unnecessary admission to the hospital. It should also be remembered that those who undertook the program had come from a project which had conclusively demonstrated that family-oriented crisis inter- vention could keep people out of the hospital and that the follow- up results were as good or better than hospital treatment.

5.   Emphasis on Children and Families--recognizing that children are the most neglected group in terms of available mental health needs, this program has devoted a great deal of effort and emphasis to direct and preventative services for children. It has long been felt that effective children's services must be family oriented--another concept which fit very well with the philosophy of those who planned and undertook the Sacramento program.

6.   Commitment to Evaluation--since University personnel participated in the original planning of the program it should not be surprising that there was a commitment to the evaluation of mental health services. Some of those who were recruited in the initial staffing showed an equal dedication to program evalua- tion--at least two had backgrounds in public health as well as mental health. The program director had built a systematic evaluation component into the demonstration project at Denver. In this age of "accountability" this point of view fitted in well. It represented an opportunity for University personnel to demon- strate the usefulness of clinical and applied research techniques.

7.   Commitment to Total Community--the county mental health director and the mental health centers' chiefs (or team leaders) have determined from the beginning that they have a commitment to the total population within their geographic areas. This may be the most important factor in the development of these programs. A commitment to the total population means that the mental health needs of all citizens--the chronic as well as the acute, children as well as adults, alcoholics, drug abusers, aged people, minority groups as well as middle class neurotics--all of these citizens were to be served by the program. Clearly, the availability of funds and other resources would place some limits on the program but priorities were to be set with a view towards this sense of responsibility.

8.   Multidisciplinary Team Approach--each catchment area was to be served by a mental health center staff consisting of a team of mental health professionals, paraprofessionals and volunteers. The team approach permitted a dedication to continuity of care. It also permitted the highest possible quality of service at a time when doctoral level professionals were few in number and expensive. The team approach trains a large number of people to

be primary therapists and uses a physician back-up in all appropriate cases where medical responsibility is required. It also
provides for the use of the most experienced professionals as
supervisors and teachers as well as their use in the role of
clinicians.

The Sacramento County mental health program consists of a
series of contractual services. In California the county is the
level of government responsible for planning and implementing
mental health services. It is encouraged to do so either by direct
county employees or through a contract mechanism. In order to
involve all existing mental health services and the private sector
of mental health professionals, Sacramento County has chosen to
use a large number of contract services. The county mental health
director has a small staff designed to produce the annual mental
health plan and to monitor the contractual services. The only
direct services operated by the county are an alcohol traffic
safety project, and a drug alternatives program operated under
various contracts. These constitute the largest portion of the
Sacramento County program.

The basic geographic unit of the mental health program is
the catchment area. Each of the three catchment areas served by
the University have a population varying from 130,000 to 150,000.
The two catchment areas served by the community hospitals, which
have expanded their private inpatient services into full service
mental health centers, have a population of 110,000 and 130,000
respectively. Each mental health team consists of approximately
sixty staff members. This includes four or five psychiatrists
(one of whom is a child psychiatrist), four clinical psychologists,
ten to twelve psychiatric social workers, fifteen nursing staff and
psychiatric technicians (including some mental health nurses trained
in the Master's level), five to ten mental health aides (paraprofessionals) and supporting clerical staff. A fourth mental
health team, the "crisis team" based at the Sacramento Medical
Center (the University hospital), provides round-the-clock emergency
services nights and weekends. It also operates a 27-bed inpatient
service. These 27 beds constitute the only psychiatric inpatient
service for the three University-served catchment areas totaling
more than 450,000 in population. The crisis team is staffed by
five psychiatrists, two clinical psychologists, eight psychiatric
social workers, and a large group of nurses and psychiatric
technicians (who function both in the crisis and the inpatient
units). The inpatient unit is operated as a program available to
each of the three catchment area teams but patients admitted to the
inpatient service continue to be the responsibility of the primary
therapists on the mental health team serving the catchment area
where the patient lives. The primary therapist comes to the inpatient service daily and works with the inpatient staff around

the treatment of that patient. By maintaining this structure and
responsibility, temptation to hospitalize patients because they
are difficult or demanding is avoided. Hospitalization is used
to accomplish specific goals and to deal with identified retarded
or potentially destructive behaviors.

DIRECT TREATMENT SERVICES

Each catchment area offers a range of direct treatment
services for adults and families as well as specialized services
for children. The direct treatment programs for the general
population include crisis intervention services. Outpatient
treatment, including aftercare-medication clinics, is found at
each of the three mental health centers operated by the University
as well as at the other two Sacramento County mental health centers.
Outpatient treatment programs are also offered at satellite clinics
within each catchment area. The satellite clinics, as mentioned
above, are generally part-time clinics designed to provide service
as close as possible to individuals within the catchment area.
Each mental health center has a partial hospitalization program
featuring day hospital treatment. Night hospital and weekend
hospital services have not been in demand. Two of the catchment
areas operate a methadone maintenance program for the entire county.
Each program has approximately 150 addicts on methadone maintenance.
It is part of an overall drug abuse program which includes general
mental health services, preventative and educational services and
inpatient programs where necessary. As noted above, inpatient
services for the three University catchment areas are centralized
at the Sacramento Medical Center. This includes short term inpatient treatment for adults and adolescents and medical detoxification for drug abusers and alcoholics.

For children there are also a series of programs designed to
meet the specific needs of children and families. This includes
crisis intervention and outpatient evaluation and treatment in
each of the mental health centers and their satellites. There is
a partial hospitalization program for adolescents and another
partial hospitalization for pre-adolescent children which is
operated for all three of the University catchment areas. Hospitalization for children is avoided whenever possible but when
necessary children may be admitted to the pediatric ward at the
Sacramento Medical Center or to the psychiatric ward at the same
institution or to a child psychiatry unit at Sutter Memorial
Hospital--one of the two non-University mental health centers in
Sacramento County. Other direct treatment services include a
therapeutic classroom program operated jointly with a school
district in one catchment area. This is a specialized psycho-
educational program designed for children with learning and

behavioral disorders. Space and educational facilities are provided by the school and special education teachers and other mental
health staff are provided by the mental health program. In addition, other early intervention programs are under development.
These include a well baby clinic and other health care services
designed to identify family crises before they develop into full-
blown mental illness or behavioral disorders.

    In addition to all of these services operated by the University
Mental Health Centers, various rehabilitation programs and other
specialized services are available as part of the total county
mental health program. These include a detoxification unit in
the central city area which admits the 30 individuals daily who
previously would have been sent to the drunk tank at the jail.
These are backed up by several recovery homes, a county-operated
alcoholism center, and alcoholism programs for minority groups.
For children who require residential treatment there are three
centers in the county which operate as part of the county mental
health program. For drug abuse there is a self-help group called
Aquarian Effort. Other facilities include a special residential
setting for single men of the central city area, mental health
aide services, a suicide prevention center and specialized services
for patients requiring longer term hospitalization at three convalescent hospitals within the county. A special contractual
arrangement offers an active treatment program beyond the type of
custodial care often found in such institutions. This arrangement
provides sub-acute 24-hour treatment for certain types of chronic
patients.

COMMUNITY-PREVENTIVE SERVICES

    The Sacramento County program strives for a balance of direct
and community services. Realizing that mental health consultation
has not yet been firmly proved to prevent mental illness, we nevertheless commit a fair amount of staff time to this effort. The
indirect services for adults and families include consultation to
courts, probation, welfare, churches, residential care centers
and nursing homes. Two of the University mental health teams have
a full-time Coordinator of Pastoral Services who is responsible
for relationships with community churches and religious groups,
who supervises and teaches pastoral counseling and who involves
the churches of the community in the county mental health program.
There is also consultation to the criminal justice system--one
University psychiatrist spends half his time doing consultation
and patient evaluation in the two county jails and working with
other elements of the criminal justice system including adult
probation. Another University psychiatrist spends part of his

time in doing consultation with the various geriatric programs in
Sacramento County. The crisis team at the University hospital has
developed a psychiatric liaison-consultation service so as to
provide consultation to the other departments at the medical center.
Other consultation services have been developed specifically to
meet the needs of children. These include consultation services
to many schools in each catchment area served by the University.
The two non-university centers do school consultations as well.
There is also a special consultation service for the county's
Juvenile Center. This facility sees several thousand youngsters
each year who have committed no crime but who represent the end
product of serious family disorganization or personal disorganization. Mental health professionals are available for program as
well as case-oriented consultation. There is also consultation
to child abuse services, to the child probation service, to the
welfare department and other agencies serving children. A
specialized consultation program works closely with the pediatric
clinics and pediatric inpatient service at the University hospital.
The child mental health professionals participate in a county-wide
council for planning and coordinating children services. There
are also school staff development programs designed to provide
mental health consultation and information to the teachers and
administrative staffs of primary and secondary schools in Sacramento
County.

SPECIAL PROGRAMS FOR CHRONIC MENTAL PATIENTS

Mental health services are incomplete unless they recognize
that those who suffer from chronic mental illness or who have been
long-term patients in a state mental hospital have special problems
and needs. This group often suffers from the "Social Breakdown
Syndrome" associated with long-term institutionalization. They
have often been extruded from families simply because of their long-
term absences in institutions far from home. The self-image of
such individuals is that of persons unable to function in society.
This is reinforced by the social stigma associated with being a
state hospital patient. The dramatic reduction of patients resident
in state hospitals in the past decade and the return of such patients
to their communities has been accompanied by charges of neglect in
this particular population. It must be candidly admitted that these
charges are sometimes justified. On the other hand, it is possible
to develop community mental health programs specifically designed
to meet the needs of this population.

In the Sacramento County program the catchment area mental
health teams have taken seriously the charge to respond to the
mental health needs of all elements of the population. This includes the chronically mentally ill--those who have been in state

mental hospitals and those who suffer from a chronic social problem
associated with psychotic disorders. For that group a continuum
of mental health services is necessary. This ranges from emergency
services (crisis intervention) and admission for short-term acute
intensive treatment to sub-acute treatment, partial hospitalization,
supervised living within the community, training for independent
living and independent living itself. The crisis services are
provided either at a mental health center or if necessary via a
traveling mental health team able to respond to the acute emer-
gencies often associated with this population. The patient who
has decompensated and requires immediate hospitalization may be
admitted to one of the three intensive treatment units (psychiatric
inpatient service) within the county program. The purpose of such
an admission is generally for acute treatment and recompensation.
Some of these patients often require more than the 10 or 15 days
of hospitalization associated with an acute illness. The Sacramento
program has contracted with three convalescent hospitals in the
county to develop sub-acute treatment for the mentally ill. A
certain number of beds are set aside for patients referred by the
five catchment areas. The contract permits convalescent hospitals
to hire additional staff such as social workers or activity
therapists in order to carry on a treatment program. Patients
may be treated in such a setting for several weeks if necessary.
Those patients who do not live in a family are frequently then
placed in a residential care home for supervised living. They
then participate in one of the three programs called the "community
interaction program" (CIP). This is a daytime rehabilitation program specifically designed for the chronically ill. Patients are
transported to the program until they have learned to use public
transportation. The programs are operated under contract with the
Community Services Section of the Department of Health and are
staffed by professional social workers, activity therapists and
others. The programs have often chosen their own name such as
"The Fair Shake Committee" or the "Warm Hands Company" or "Cross
Roads." Patients participate in this program all day long and
receive their lunch in the same manner as they would at a partial
hospitalization or day hospital program. The community interaction
programs feature various types of activities therapy and social
group activities. The staff of these units also consult regularly
with the operators of the board and care homes or residential
centers where the patients live. Patients are often taken on field
trips into various locations in the community to familiarize them
with traveling unassisted and to renew their social contacts with
community facilities. Patients often put on "bake sales" or wash
cars or undertake other activities in order to raise small amounts
of money for therapeutic activities. Each CIP staff also transports
its patients to the medication clinics of the aftercare programs
sponsored by each of the three University mental health centers.

CIP patients are registered with the mental health clinic and the staff of the mental health clinics work with CIP staff to provide consultation as necessary. This series of three CIP programs presently has five to six hundred patients in active rehabilitation programs. They have provided a vivid demonstration of the need for and utility of specialized services for the chronic patient. More importantly, they demonstrate the fact that such programs must be tied into a panoply of mental health programs for acute and chronic patients, for children and adults, featuring direct treatment and preventive services. By themselves, these community interaction programs would be able to deal with only a limited aspect of the needs of the chronic patient. Tied into a mental health system, they make some sense and represent an economical, humane and effective program directed at this population.

Within the mental health center special attention is paid to this group by establishing aftercare-medication clinics. Many of the patients are on maintenance medication and are brought to the centers by professional staffs of the Community Interaction Program or other social workers from the Community Services Section who are funded by the county mental health service. There are more than 500 such patients registered in the aftercare clinics operated by the three University mental health centers. These clinics provide more than a brief 10-minute interview and prescription renewal. They operated in conjunction with therapeutic groups and activity groups designed to enhance socialization and contact within this population. Each patient is assigned a primary therapist who maintains continuity of contact. When the primary therapist is not a physician there is always medical-psychiatric involvement relative to prescription of drugs. Primary therapists also work with CSS social workers or other elements of the total program designed for the chronic patients. Records are kept of all patients for follow-up when patients miss appointments. Since the patients in the three University centers and in the two other mental health centers in Sacramento County use a unit numbering system, it is possible to track any patient receiving public funded mental health services through the system. It is a system designed to keep patients from "falling between the cracks."

CITIZEN INVOLVEMENT

Community mental health programs call for a working relation-ship between the professionals and the community in order to define needs, develop programs, interpret the programs to the community, and to provide ongoing evaluation and determination of priorities. The California law calls for each county to have a mental health advisory board of 14 members representing the public, certain

professional groups and government groups. This board approves
the annual county mental health plan and advises the mental health
director as well as the county board of supervisors on mental health
issues. Recognizing that the county board cannot possibly represent all of the diverse interests and ethnic groups in each catchment area, Sacramento County has established an advisory committee
for each catchment area. The catchment area advisory committee
includes one member from the county-wide board and six to ten
other individuals. The others are all required to be residents
of the catchment area. Every effort is made to make the advisory
committee representative of the residents of the catchment area
including ethnic minorities, women, etc. These catchment area
committees meet at least monthly and work closely with the staff
of the mental health center. A committee understands its role as
an advisory and participatory role--not as a governing board. The
governing board responsible for the total mental health program
is the County Board of Supervisors. However, the effective interaction between government, mental health professionals, and these
committees had permitted realistic definitions of need and mutual
establishment of priorities. It is also enabling professionals
to have contact with community people and to obtain community
input in the planning process. The catchment area committees have
been valuable in interpreting the programs to the citizens of each
catchment area.

EDUCATIONAL PROGRAMS

The reason for the University's involvement in this extensive
mental health service program is that it represents a realistic
setting for the education of mental health professionals and paraprofessionals. The three University centers are staffed by
faculty. All of the psychiatrists, psychologists, supervising
social workers and supervising nurses are members of the full-time
faculty of the Department of Psychiatry and Division of Mental
Health. Having faculty staff, such centers permit the establishment of educational programs for physicians and other mental health
professionals. The University operates a three-year psychiatric
residency program in which all of the first and some of the second
and third year residents receive their training in the three
community mental health centers and the crisis team at the
Sacramento Medical Center. The residency also includes integrated
programs with the San Joaquin County Mental Health Service in
Stockton and with the V. A. program at Martinez and Sacramento.
There is also a fellowship program in child psychiatry with four
first and four second year child fellows. Here, too, the clinical
base is the community mental health center. There is a clerkship
for medical students which is carried on at the mental health

centers and at any given time there may be four to six Junior
medical students at a mental health center. There is also an
internship in clinical psychology with two interns in each of the
three centers. A Ph.D. program in clinical psychology is sponsored
by a Graduate Group made up entirely of faculty of the Division
of Mental Health in the UCD School of Medicine. Seven students
are accepted per year and when the program is in full maturity
this will include a total of approximately 30 graduate students.
Social work students from California State University, Sacramento,
and other graduate schools of social work receive their field
placement in the centers as do nursing students, occupational
therapy students and students from a local community college
which has a Human Services program. There are also three to five
pastoral counseling interns each year and a number of new graduate
university students, as well as first, second and fourth year
medical students taking additional elective time in psychiatry.
The large number of students may seem surprising to most community
mental health centers but give evidence to the fact that community
mental health centers can be the locus of quality educational programs as well as service programs.

EVALUATION

Another essential element of a community mental health program
relates to evaluation. The area of program evaluation is one in
which the UC Davis-Sacramento group have a major commitment. Since
the University operates three mental health centers for Sacramento
County it will not be surprising that there is a high degree of
interest in evaluation of the program itself as well as of the
treatment systems within the program. The program evaluation staff
of the University includes two professionals at the doctoral level,
one at the master's level and nine staff assistants. The resources
of the University including the computer center and consultation
around machine processing of data have made it possible to mount
a program evaluation section which has been very active. Program
evaluation includes the development of data for management purposes,
for planning mental health programs and changes in those programs
as well as specific research projects designed to evaluate the outcome of patient treatment and educational programs.

In terms of management statistics it may give the reader some
idea about the size of the program to realize that during 1974-75
there were approximately 12,000 new admissions to the various mental
health programs operated by the University. Since some of those
were represented by patients who were admitted to more than one
service element, the unduplicated count may be more valuable.
There were 7,515 unduplicated admissions--that is the number of

different persons seen in the program. This included 877 inpatient
admissions and a total of 7,177 inpatient days. Crisis clinic
visits (6,536), outpatient clinic visits (47,938) and methadone
program visits (65,125) bring the total outpatient visits to
nearly 120,000 visits per year. In addition to the outpatient
visits there were 7,539 partial hospitalization days of care and
37,328 hours of mental health consultation carried on by the staff
of the three centers.

The program evaluation unit is preparing a manual for program
evaluation in community mental health centers for use in other
centers. For the evaluation of individual patient outcome it has
developed the Davis Outcome Assessment System. DOAS obtains data
from patients and therapists at intake and at subsequent periods
until the termination of treatment. Information obtained includes
a listing of treatment goals (for Goal Attainment Scaling), a
checklist of life events and various measurements of impairment and
well-being. Therapists also provide measurements of impairment and
of improvement over time.

CONCLUSIONS

Alternatives to hospitalizing the long-term or "chronic"
patient can be developed within a system of community mental
health programs when that system makes a commitment to a total
population and develops a variety of direct and indirect services
for chronic as well as acute patients. The special needs of
chronically ill must be identified and kept within an overall
system rather than as a single project. When that system includes
an evaluative component it is possible to define needs, develop
programs and assess the outcome of programs in a manner which
permits modification and further planning.

REFERENCES

Langsley, D. G. and Barter, J. T. Community alternatives to
   state hospital treatment. Psychiatric Annals, 5:163-170,
   1975.

RESCUE AND REHABILITATION

Werner M. Mendel and Robert E. Allen

University of Southern California

Los Angeles, California

In 1966, a number of us got together (Roberts, Greenfield, & Miller, 1968) to discuss alternatives to hospitalization. We envisioned a world in which the hospital would no longer hold a central position in health care delivery for the mental patient. Services which for the past several hundred years had been administered to mentally ill patients in hospitals were found to be better and more economically delivered with fewer side effects in settings other than the hospital (Mendel, 1968).

During the past decade there has been much experimentation with alternatives to hospitalization and a considerable amount of follow-up data has been collected (Taylor and Torrey, 1973). Yet despite overwhelming evidence that hospitals are not the location of choice for the treatment of mental illness, hospitals have not been abolished. In fact, the few attempts at closing hospitals have been hampered by a lack of development of alternate resources in the community. A backlash to the proposal of alternative treatment has developed by the public, funding agencies, and the professions. In 1977 it can be agreed that models for alternatives to hospitalization can work. These alternatives are not practical at this time because there are not enough of them in the community. There is no major effort by the public or the professions to create such alternative facilities at this time.

In spite of very adequate and tested models for alternatives such as the one demonstrated in Wisconsin's Training for Community Living (Stein, Test, and Marx, 1975), or the models of family crisis intervention (Langsley, 1968), day treatment (Herz, Endicott, Spitzer, and Mesnikoff, 1971), crisis centers (Glasscote,

Cumming, Hammersley, et al., 1966), hospitals continue to exist.
Psychiatric units in county hospitals and private facilities continue to build beds. Beds are still the prime arena for mental
health care delivery. Health insurance companies reimburse primarily for hospitalization and refuse to reimburse for alternatives
(Scheidemandel, Kanno, and Glasscote, 1968). Only 14 state hospitals have been closed throughout the United States (Greenblatt,
1974). Thoughtful professionals still continue to advocate the
use of state hospitals (Rieder, 1974). Thus, the abolition movement, although based on sound research and carefully evaluated
treatment outcome, has run into serious difficulty. We have
proposed an explanation elsewhere (Mendel, 1974). It has become
perfectly clear that professional comfort, economic forces, and
social and cultural resistances have much more to do with the
continuation of the hospital as the central health care delivery
system than does science or considerations of patient care.

     Ten years after ample demonstration and testing of alterna-
tives, the hospital remains the professional center of the health
care world. It is viewed as the doctor's indispensable workshop;
it remains the largest and most rapidly rising expenditure of the
health care dollar. Hospital prices have risen 300% between 1965
and 1975. For the nation as a whole, health expenditures rose from
thirteen billion in 1950 to 57 billion in 1968. The proportion of
the gross national product spent on health care rose from 4.5% to
6.6%, an increase of 47%. It is estimated that the bill for health
care will exceed 100 billion dollars within a few years and will
approach 8% to 10% of the gross national product. Along with the
rise has come a substantial shift in the distribution of expenditures
for services reflecting the technology of health care. In 1968 hospitals took 40% of the health care dollar. The share of the health
care dollar going for hospital cost is increasing steadily while
the share going for professional fees and services is decreasing.
Hospitals are an expensive way of delivering health care (Somers,
1971).

     Health care is a powerful economic force in the nation. It
is an economic channel through which much of the nation's politics,
policy debate and concerns flow. Such a large industry, through
which 100 billion dollars flow each year, is easily buffeted by
the changing political, social, economic and human rights concerns.
We can no longer look at medicine as simply a scientific concern
managed by a technical community; nor is it primarily a humanitarian
health care delivery system. Rather, it is a large political force
with huge expenditures, with legions of employees who are highly
unionized and who maneuver for political, economic and social

position. Pressures are brought by consumers (patients, providers,
physicians, therapists, hospitals, clinics, corporations), government regulations, third party payers, insurance companies, employees unions, and reimbursement schemes, etc. Demonstrating
that a technique exists which is effective in getting the task of
treating patients done, which can be implemented much less expensively than the present system and which has few side effects, is
not enough. Just as the railroads had to carry firemen long after
locomotives were automatically fueled, so medicine is tradition-
bound and unionized with traditional roles played by the various
professions and paraprofessions. Unfortunately, just as railroads
were put out of business so medicine is putting itself out of
business by its particular form of featherbedding. Hospitals
which are designed to be crisis centers providing equipment and
resources for acutely physically ill patients are in fact used for
housing and isolation of the chronically physically and mentally
ill.

   The medical model is locked into the concept of the central
position of the hospital. The medical model has served us well as
the most benevolent form of intervention in mental illness. Now,
like a religion, it has become a set of rituals and procedures,
traditions and laws which must be followed by all who function
within its influence, even when these rituals and laws are entirely
anachronistic and in no way applicable to the situation at hand.
Organized hospitals, organized medicine, organized nursing, as well
as government regulations are all designed to not change anything.
Reimbursement supports the status quo and punishes innovation.
Public attitudes and prejudices insist that doctors, hospitals and
nurses function in traditional ways. They insist, for example,
that the hospital is a place of rest where the patient goes to bed.
Yet for psychiatric patients, going to bed is the worst possible
treatment. Patients should not be in bed. They do not benefit
from physical rest when they need to be trained for life.

   Thus, we have reluctantly come to the conclusion that the
medical model has outlived its usefulness even though for centuries
it has been the vehicle for the delivery of health care to the
mentally ill. For years other models of intervention have been
available and were practiced. In part, how society managed
aberrant behavior depended on the accident of who did the intervening and where the patient happened to live. These alternate
models include the legal model, where aberrant behavior is treated
as a crime, the individual is seen as a criminal, restitution is
made through punishment. There is the educational model where the
aberrant behavior is seen as a lack of proper knowledge, the place
of restitution is the school administered by teachers and the

process is called learning. There is the theological model in which
the aberrant behavior is seen as a sin, the individual is a sinner,
restitution is made to God and administered by the priest. All of
these models work in 1975 and all of them, in fact, are functioning
in various aspects in society. Like these other models, the medical
model is a highly traditional system in a major industry.

Besides the theological, legal, educational and medical models,
it is also possible to conceive of intervention by society within
the model of rescue and work rehabilitation. Such a model makes
much sense and has many advantages. It is designed for helpful
and benign intervention, it permits the client to take an increasingly active part in the management of his own destiny. It fits
the ethics of our society which proposes that each person should
be responsible for himself and for his own destiny. Also, the
rehabilitation model does not seem to pose enough of a political,
economic, or civil rights threat to any group to mobilize significant reaction.

The process of rehabilitation begins with defining the person
as having a defect. Thus rehabilitation fills the need of society
to define a group as alienated, different, defective, inferior,
mysterious and dangerous. It allows the potential client to have
"insight," that is, to admit that he is in need of rehabilitation.
In this way the client reaffirms society. The rehabilitation model
also meets the missionary needs of society by proposing that the
defective client should join the majority culture through some
process, in this case, called rehabilitation. The problem in the
client then is seen as a defect which is identified and which
prevents his functioning. It does not require a cure as if it
were treatment in the medical model. It does not insist on nurses
and doctors as the central providers of the process. The rehabilitation model does not demand that the individual be in a hospital at $160 a day for room and board and it does not insist that
he rest or medicate his way to health. Rather it allows the individual to be identified as being in crisis, a crisis in which he
cannot support himself, and in which he cannot manage the social
space of his life. He needs rescue from crisis. This rescue
operation may be carried out in a variety of settings. It may be
carried out in the family (Langsley, 1968), in the hospital
(Mendel, 1966), with an outpatient psychiatric emergency team
(Gittelman, 1972), or in any number of ways devised already or
yet to be devised. All of these techniques of crisis intervention
are equally effective since crises resolve themselves. By definition
no one ever stays in a crisis. The important aspect of the crisis
is that the individual who is in crisis is particularly vulnerable
to changing the path of his existence in a major way. The type of

crisis intervention defines the future of the person and the vocabulary to be used in the next crisis. Thus, if in his crisis he is
taken into the hospital and defined as a patient, he will tend to
define himself as sick and future problems in living will be handled
in a similar way. Other systems each have their own form of crisis
intervention and each result in defining the subsequent course of
interaction between the individual and society within the metaphor
of the particular transaction.

We propose that an individual usually first comes for help
for a crisis in living, crisis in work, crisis in interpersonal
relationships, crisis in managing psychosocial space, crisis in
handling his feelings. During this crisis a relationship can be
established with a representative of the helping agency allowing
the rehabilitation process to begin. In the crisis the client is
comforted, his pain is relieved, and his defect is repaired as much
and as quickly as possible.

Rescue thus begins with the alleviation of pain and discomfort.
Next the client and his psychosocial space is carefully evaluated
and a program is designed to help him to restitute for his defect,
to live with substitute functions and to find other ways of getting
what he needs. He is helped to acquire different and new skills
with which to manage the things which he cannot manage.

All of this, although bearing some similarity to other interventions, is entirely outside of the medical and treatment model.
In rehabilitation we use medical skills for assessment and relief
of suffering. We also use educational techniques for training and
retraining; we call on psychosocial techniques for providing support
during the rehabilitation process. In the rescue and rehabilitation
activity we set specific goals and we measure progress against these
goals.

DESCRIPTION OF CLIENT POPULATION

The clients with whom we are concerned come from the population
of chronic mental patients. Many of these individuals in the past
and in the medical model have been diagnosed as chronic schizophrenic
patients. This is probably the most correct diagnosis. These same
patients have also been called chronic character disorders, particularly "narcissistic" and "inadequate" characters. They have
also been labeled as chronically dependent and they certainly include
some patients who are mentally retarded. In short, they include
all of the patients who are unable to manage their life. Regard-

less of clinical label, the persons are well-described (Stein,
Test, and Marx, 1975) as "having a limited repertoire of instrumental and problem-solving behaviors to meet the goals and demands
of life leading to persisting difficulties with work habits,
socialization, leisure time activities, etc., and as having a
powerful dependency need, frequently expressed as an aggressive
dependency on family and institutions."

The clients diagnosed by us as schizophrenic we describe as
having failed in three areas of life (Mendel, 1975b). They manage
anxiety ineffectively and expensively. Interpersonal relationships
always fail, the desired results are never obtained and always
leave the person feeling a little bit worse about himself. And
they demonstrate failure of historicity, that is, an inability to
use their own personal lived history as a basis for making decisions,
planning their life or managing anxiety or interpersonal relationships. These defects for which the person must be rehabilitated
represent the core of the population of clients who require what
we have called in the past supportive care in the medical model
and what we now call a program of long-term rehabilitation.

The rehabilitation process must provide training for the individual to help him to develop skills with which to manage his
anxiety, his dependency, his interpersonal relationships and with
which to make up for the defect of historicity. When he is supplied
with techniques and tools that help to either overcome or restitute
for the consequences of these defects, his life improves. As his
ability to function improves, the client becomes more able to work,
to play and to engage in satisfying interpersonal relationships.
The techniques of rehabilitation are carried out within the context
of the relationship of the client to an agency or to an individual
representative of an agency.

Out client population is unable to hold jobs, they are unable
to care for themselves. Often they are defined as mentally ill and
become the chronic hospital population because no one can cope with
their inappropriately expressed aggressive dependency needs. These
same people are also chronic law breakers and make up much of the
chronic jail population presenting with problems of alcoholism,
vagrancy, etc. It is also these people who tend to be on welfare.
In other words, they do not have the tools with which to function
in our society. In times past it was possible for these individuals
to function somewhat more effectively, particularly in a nondemand-
ing rural environment. Their differences were tolerated and they
were able to function enough to pay their own keep. Now this population requires special training, special help to get along in
society. They need rescue during crisis, and then training and
retraining to give them the tools with which to function in society.

It is this technique of rescue from crisis and rehabilitation for
living in an urban technological community which we propose to
use as a replacement for hospitalization and outpatient treatment.

In our society one of the most important aspects of self-hood
is the ability to earn a living and to be productive. This ability
is closely tied to self-esteem for the individual. Our client population consists of individuals who cannot make it in society, who
cannot support themselves, who resort to "going crazy" as a way of
getting help. We train these clients to work and get a job in the
competitive real world. The metaphor of treatment is rescue from
crisis and rehabilitation for work. This approach must be clearly
differentiated from the techniques previously used in which the
individual engaged in tasks occupying his time while in the hospital (occupational therapy, and industrial therapy, patient labor,
the farm, etc.). It must also be distinguished from the use of
work as a primary therapeutic instrument where the value of the
activity is understood in terms of psychodynamic content. We are
interested in helping the individual who has not been able to
work to assess his skills and knowledge and to develop new ones.
We help him to focus on available or possibly available jobs and
then we help him to get work. We then do whatever is necessary to
keep him working. By giving the client these new tools, a new
hook into the majority culture, he will no longer need to be defined
or define himself as helpless, hopeless, and inadequate. We rescue
him from the crisis, we rehabilitate him, and we support him once
he is working. This is real work, not make do work or busy work.
This is work which is paid for with real money and is really productive. The process is in sequence and begins in the form of a
token economy in the hospital (except money is used--not tokens),
a sheltered workshop, then on-the-job training programs and finally
a rehabilitation placement in a real community job when this is
possible.

PROFESSIONAL ROLES

Before describing the practical application of the rehabilitation process, we should discuss the change in professional role
models necessitated by the shift to a new philosophy replacing the
usual concepts of psychiatric care. Indeed, much of the initial
work done in developing the project dealt with those who delivered
rather than those who received services. After two years most of
the new roles are well-defined.

Although common practice and the forces of tradition make it
no easy task, it is possible to carry out the first step in this
program of rehabilitation by the usual staff of a psychiatric hospital if this is the only type of facility available. With the

expedient use of existing members of a system of psychiatric care delivery, this model can be applied in most psychiatric facilities. Of course, if the hospital has to be used for a program of rescue and rehabilitation then costs will be 200% to 300% more than if the program were carried out in a setting specifically designed for such a program.

Of the many role changes necessitated in shifting to the rehabilitation model, none requires more scrutiny and attention than that of the person most wedded to the medical model, the psychiatrist. Much difficulty is encountered in convincing many psychiatrists to practice in a model which does not seek a cure, which emphasizes such psychiatrically mundane matters as being able to work six hours a day in an assembly line and requires skills of shaping behavior rather than causing psychological reorganization. There are, however, three major areas which are important in both medical and rehabilitation models and which are both centrally important and illustrative of the major differences in the two models. These areas are diagnosis, treatment, and the assessment of psychological strengths.

Diagnosis, of course, is a cornerstone of any psychiatric treatment. But while diagnosis in the medical model tends to be the end point, in the rehabilitation model it is only the necessary beginning. For example, a diagnosis of schizophrenia in the medical model often connotes a pessimistic outlook and a tendency to offer little treatment. In the rehabilitation model diagnosis is the indication that a prescribed and definite approach to intervention must be instituted to insure the possibility of favorable outcome. It is vitally important to correctly diagnose so that rehabilitation may be accurately planned and undertaken. This is done much in the same manner that one would evaluate nerve and tendon injury after an industrial accident, so that the correct repair can be made and the program of learning to cope with deficits in function can begin.

Just as diagnosis is only the beginning, medical treatment is the enabling factor in a rehabilitation model rather than a self-justifying end. In using schizophrenia as a model, it is too often the case that merely keeping a person in therapy or on medication becomes the goal. Proper medical intervention, i.e., medication, is generally necessary to resolve the acute symptoms and rescue the individual from disorganizing influences of hallucinations and delusions. However, such treatment does little to correct the deficits of chronic interpersonal and cognitive impairments (Bockoven and Solomon, 1975).

While the medical model places a different emphasis on diagnosis and treatment, it does prepare a psychiatrist to make use of these

tools. The new diagnostic thrust which the psychiatrist must
develop is the skill to assess <u>strengths</u> and <u>abilities</u> necessary
in a rehabilitation model. Examples taken from traditional
psychiatry show that we speak of "the schizophrenic" instead of
an individual with schizophrenia. We seek pathology and its
manifestations rather than skills and strengths. We form problem
lists rather than goal plans. If we accept the fact that diagnosis
and treatment are merely the necessary first steps, it is obvious
that the traditional psychiatric role has little further to offer.
There must be a shift in emphasis so that the psychiatrist can
deal with those qualities which allow an individual to reach the
best adjustment and highest possible level of functioning. The
skills a psychiatrist can bring to the rehabilitation model have
been described elsewhere (Mendel, 1975a). The psychiatrists'
understanding of the rehabilitation process determines whether he
can carry out his part of rehabilitation procedures.

     Just as the role of the psychiatrist shifts from concentrating
on insight and cure to getting the best possible adaptation, the
role of the psychologist shifts from one who furthers psychological
understanding to one who evaluates ability to function. The
psychologists' new role places little emphasis on projective and
subjective evaluation and a great deal on determining cognitive
functioning. Plans for work, school, or a structured workshop
must be grounded in a clear assessment of individual potential.
Since failure in many areas is one of the hallmarks of schizophrenia
in an individual's life, successful rehabilitation must guard
against failure. This is done by planning around deficits, not
ignoring them.

     The role of the social worker focuses on the real and over-
whelming problems the chronically disabled have in dealing with an
urban environment. These problems consist of such deceptively
simple matters as arranging a living situation so that someone can
get to work without a three-hour bus ride. When we deal with
people who are without economic, social and interpersonal resources,
then such problems require great effort and attention. Because the
social workers focus on problems in the community, their role also
requires skillful consultation with existing community agencies
and living facilities. The rehabilitation plans and goals established in the initial crisis rescue phase must be constantly
reassessed and redefined as the client faces adjustment to living
in the community.

     The role of occupational and recreational therapy in the
rescue and rehabilitation model of intervention differs markedly
when compared to that found in the usual medical model. Although
occupational therapy is firmly based on assessing strengths,
planning rehabilitation procedures, and teaching new skills, in

the acute hospital treatment model the talent of such therapists
is not fully used. In our setting, the occupational therapist is
the central person for work evaluation and the early work rehabilitation process carried out in the hospital. Theirs is a
formally structured approach, devised to separate actual work
abilities and attitudes from the disorganization accompanying an
acute exacerbation of the disorder. Levels of work are clearly
identified so that individuals will not be asked to perform tasks
which are cognitively beyond their abilities. As the cognitive
disorganization improves, skills also increase. The occupational
therapist is able to accurately predict at any one point whether
the individual can most benefit from a structured work situation,
further training or is in fact able to cope with the demands of
competitive employment in the community. Through the information
available from the occupational therapy assessments, the therapist
is able to provide information to the appropriate agencies so that
the patient's strengths and skills can be used. With careful evaluation and planning, it is even possible for clients who are still
subject to hallucinations to handle a work situation quite adequately.

     Traditional recreational therapy is often relegated to filling
time and making the hospital more fun. In our project, recreational
therapy addresses itself to a wide variety of social skills which
need to be taught so that the chronically disabled can make better
life adjustments in the real world. These include grooming, personal hygiene, how to act during a job interview, or how to ask
someone for a date. The functions of the recreational therapist
also involve much community consultation.

     We found that the profession which has had the most difficulty
in adopting new role models has been nursing. This may be explained
because nursing has been committed to the model of acute medical
illness. By the nature of usual nursing hierarchies and nursing
administration, the nurse on a given ward is less able to be independent and adjust to the needs of the clinical situations. A
nurse is required to follow a prescribed model of behavior which
is established by administrative superiors who are not related to
direct patient care. In a project such as ours where the role of
the hospital is deemphasized, nursing must become actively involved
in the community. It is clear that a new model for nursing needs
to be developed. In our project this has not yet happened and is
actively resisted by nursing administration.

     There are other role definitions which are not specific to
any profession but are necessary to the rehabilitation process.
With the deemphasis on primary therapy, all members of the staff
must be skilled in crisis intervention, supportive psychotherapy,
and they must possess skills in shaping behavior.

The rehabilitation model requires continuity of care.   The
concepts of hospital care and aftercare are no longer operant in
such a model. Any member of the staff may be the person with whom
any individual client forms his most lasting attachment.   It is a
fact that the project as a whole will be the permanent treating
agency providing continuity of care.   All staff must be willing
and able to offer all aspects of supportive care.

DESCRIPTION OF THE REHABILITATION PROJECT

The project is housed[1] and uses the staff of a traditional 20-
bed acute psychiatric inpatient ward at the Los Angeles County-USC
Medical Center Psychiatric Hospital.   The staff consists of a part-
time psychiatrist ward chief, an occupational therapist, three
psychiatric social workers, a clinical psychologist, a medical
case worker, a recreational therapist, and two vocational counselors
from the California State Department of Vocational Rehabilitation
who were assigned to the project. With the exception of the third
social worker and the two rehabilitation counselors this is the
usual staffing pattern at the hospital except that the usual ward
has two full-time psychiatrists and three or four residents in
training in psychiatry assigned to it.   Others who, because of
their interest, provide services to the project but who are not
formally assigned to the staff include a clinical pharmacologist,
a teacher in adult education programs assigned to the Medical Center,
a variety of volunteers and several third year medical students.

Clients of the project are drawn from routine admissions to
the acute psychiatric facility. Although all diagnostic categories
are treated, the prime focus is on individuals who have been diagnosed as schizophrenic and have had multiple prior psychiatric
admissions. Except for readmissions of patients already involved
in the project, we do not determine whether an individual should
or should not be hospitalized. The only criteria applied in
screening is that the client be between the ages of 18 and 55 and
that he or she is willing to come to a ward where the emphasis will
be on work and rehabilitation. Most of the clients reflect the
demographic groups that one would expect in an urban county hospital.   They are relatively lacking in formal education, have poor
work histories and work skills, and are in the lower socioeconomic
classes. Approximately half of our clients are on welfare or disability, and approximately half have either no family in the
immediate area or they have family which wants to have nothing
further to do with them.

The majority of clients are acutely psychotic when they enter
the program. We focus on rapid diagnostic assessment (although we
select clients who have been previously diagnosed as having schizophrenia; some in fact do not) and treatment intervention.   The

emphasis is placed on appropriate medication and quick symptom removal. The third part of the initial evaluation is a detailed work history and assessment of potential work skills. There is also an attempt to establish with the client definite goals and the beginning of a rehabilitation plan, although this obviously must be reassessed and changed many times.

Work is the metaphor by which we deliver supportive and rehabilitation psychiatric services. Although we call ourselves the work ward and the work activities take up a good portion of the client's time, we do not value work merely in itself. Work does provide structured activity beneficial to individuals with disordered cognition. It also provides a route for the accurate and quick appraisal of work skills and social and cognitive abilities. Work becomes the vehicle to reach normal adaptation.

The clients are assigned to a level of functioning rather than specific jobs. For example, clerical tasks such as assembling, collating, and organizing a hospital chart can be defined in such a manner that it takes only minimal or relatively advanced cognitive function. The work stations are correlated to a model of cognitive development based on Piaget's model for the development of formal thought. As schizophrenic disorganization clears, cognitive skills improve, and the clients are assigned increasingly more demanding jobs. They are paid for their work. The amount of pay depends on both the difficulty of the job and the client's level of performance.

After a period of two to five days, it is generally possible to make an initial assessment of job skills, work habits, social adjustment, and ability to function so that some goals can be tentatively planned. It is at this point that the vocational counselor, using information obtained by the psychiatrist, psychologist, social worker and occupational therapist, can develop and plan for the next phase of rehabilitation. All of the assessments of function and planning is done with the client's active participation (see Figure 1). As the client and the rehabilitation counselor complete the plan, the social worker begins to help the client to find a place to live in the community. Because of the economic problems faced by most clients, choices are relatively few and often are limited to large rooming houses known euphemistically as board and care institutions.

After the client visits several boarding facilities or returns to his own home and has decided upon a job or school or training situation, he leaves the hospital. On an average, the total process takes about three weeks and is probably somewhat lengthened by the complications of arranging the living situation

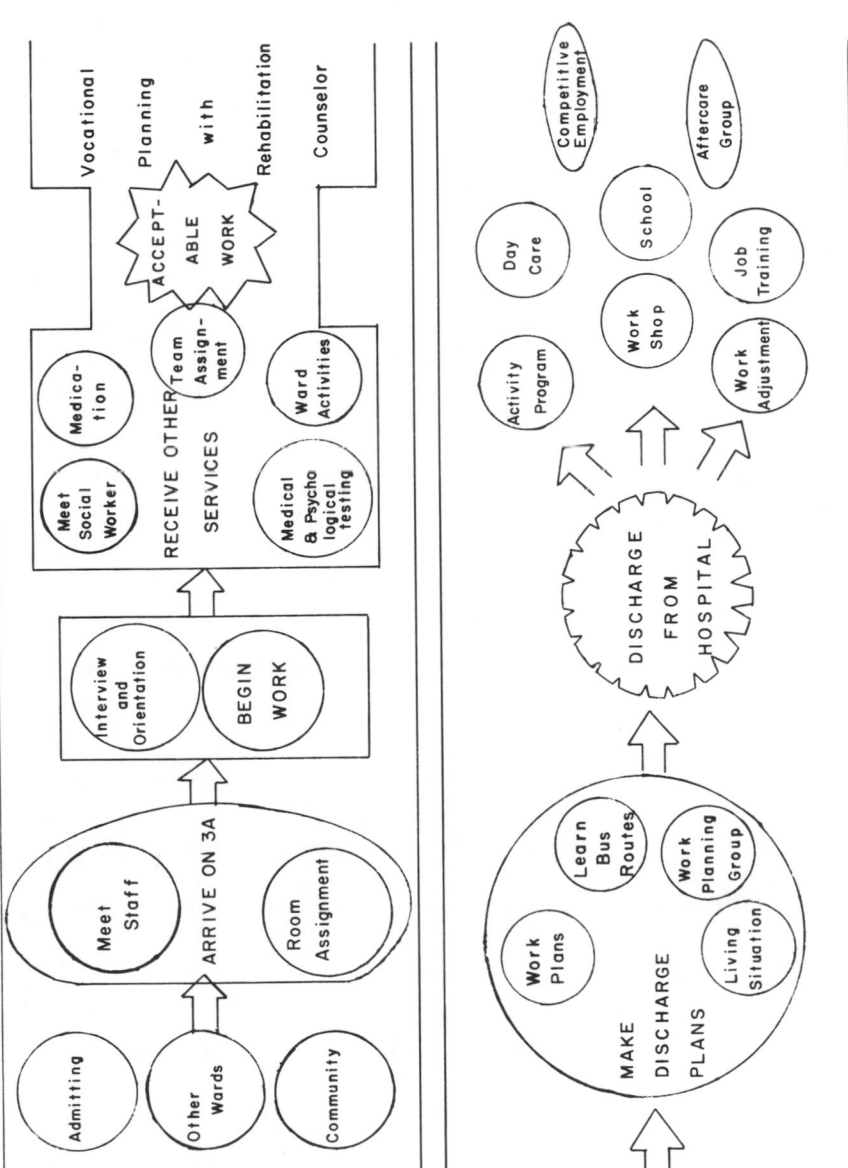

Figure 1.   Flow of a client through the work/rehabilitation program.

in some reasonable proximity to work or school. As an alternative, the clients who are still in need of more structure
after discharge sometimes return for daily work training.

There is no discontinuity between the period the individual
spends in the hospital and his discharge. In most cases he has
already been attending whichever rehabilitation program has been
established for a few days while still in the hospital. After
discharge from the hospital there are a variety of follow-up
contacts possible for the client. These include groups run by
the rehabilitation counselors, the invitation to stop in on the
ward at any time for any problem, and formal follow-up groups in
the community managed by the social workers but attended by a
wide variety of staff including the recreational therapist,
medical case worker, and clinical pharmacologist. Formal group
meetings are on a weekly basis and are modeled on peer group
support, discussion of common problems, and social activities.
When crises occur, the staff members often with community liaison
go into the field to handle the situation. In such crises we deal
primarily with employers, teachers, workshop evaluators, and
board and care operators.

If psychiatric crisis intervention is ever necessary, attempts
are made to interfere as little as possible with school or work.
It has been our experience that readmission to a unit where the
client is well-known to the staff need not markedly interfere with
the adjustment the individual is making in the community. For
example, someone may be able to return to work after a day or two
in the hospital and continue to function on the job even though
he is somewhat symptomatic and may have to return to the hospital
each night for several days.

Our expectations as to the degree of rehabilitation which
should be achieved depend on the assessment of the individual's
potential. Some clients do very well in a structured workshop
situation, yet lack enough ability to succeed at competitive
employment. For these clients a job in such a sheltered workshop
is often the appropriate level of rehabilitation which allows them
to function in the community and to make some contributions to
society for which they get money and feel self-value. For others,
the workshop situation may be only the first step toward full
competitive employment. Although competitive employment is the
goal, success at a job does not mean to us that the client has no
further need for our services. It only means that work rehabilitation has been successful. The client still requires all of the
support resources and rehabilitation skills so that he can continue
to function.

PRELIMINARY RESULTS

The outcome of a controlled study for the rescue and rehabilitation model of intervention in mental illness is not yet available.
Our research is only in the second year of a five-year study. Any
reasonable outcome study for intervention in chronic problems must
cover periods much longer than the one or two years usually reported
in the literature. However, we have assembled preliminary data
which seems to indicate the feasibility of the rehabilitation model.
Two trends are emerging. The first is that such a model is not
acceptable to many individuals who could probably benefit by it.
The second observation is that for those who do find it acceptable,
it is a highly successful method.

Of all those individuals diagnosed as having schizophrenia
who made initial contact with the project (by virtue of being in
the county hospital and agreeing to participate), 47% elected not
to participate by the time they left the hospital. Seventy-two of
152 clients chose other options than participating in the work-
rehabilitation program. These options included leaving the hospital
(the ward connected with the project is truly open), moving out of
the area, wanting to rest, getting intensive psychotherapy, or
declaring themselves "cured." Of those 80 people who at the time
of leaving the hospital were committed to a plan based on rehabilitation, 81% are still in the plan after follow-up intervals
of six months to two years. Twenty-three percent (15 clients) are
functioning in jobs at a competitive level, others are in job training programs, sheltered workshops, school, or they actively seek
jobs. Twenty-three percent (15 clients) have been briefly hospitalized under the rescue and rehabilitation model, with the rehospitalization not markedly interfering with their plans and ongoing
programs.

The criticism which can be applied to such figures is that we
are somehow selecting only those people who are well enough to
successfully participate in a work program. However, we have been
unable to find any significant clinical difference between those
who will not accept the program from those who do. Also of those
clients whose clinical picture is compatible with the Feighner
criteria for "hard-core" or nuclear schizophrenia (Feighner, 1972),
44% opted out and 56% agreed to participate in the work program at
the end of hospitalization. Of those, 80% (41 clients) are still
in plan one to two years after leaving the hospital. Similarly
to the first group, 29% have been briefly rehospitalized without
interruption of the rehabilitation process.

These data are preliminary and not controlled. Our controlled
comparison is with those treated in a traditional medical model to

evaluate final outcome. We are also evaluating so-called prognostic factors to see if they reflect the disability itself or the model used for intervention.

THE FUTURE OF THE NON-MEDICAL MODEL

The medical model which views disorganized and disordered behavior as sickness and which presupposes that help is treatment leading to cure, fits the field of psychiatry only by a considerable leap of logic. Psychiatry for the past hundred years has built its theories on a basic faith that behavior can be understood in terms of the anatomy, physiology, and biochemistry. Perhaps some day much more of it will be understood. Through an accident of history for the past few hundred years the care of individuals who are disordered in their behavior and thinking have been the concern of the medical profession. Even though there is a biological substrate for behavior, we also know that behavior is complex. The medical model does not particularly fit our explorations of interventions in psychiatric disorders. Biology changes behavior but also behavior changes biology. Since the medical model introduces serious difficulty to the psychiatric treatment transaction, it behooves us to develop other models for intervention One such model is proposed here. The advantage of the work rehabilitation model is that it allows us to take as given certain facts of society. One of these facts is that our majority middle-class culture expects every individual who is an adult to support himself and to work. Quite apart from whether this makes sense in terms of national economics or political philosophy, it is a fact of our time that the work ethic persists and each individual has to live within that ethic. We have outlined the many social, economic and professional difficulties which make it impossible within the medical model to change the traditional mental health intervention from treatment in the hospital to treatment in the community.

It is unfortunate that many of our colleagues, frustrated in their scientific proposals, resort to attacking society. These colleagues feel they have discharged their duty to their patients by finding fault with society and lamenting the economic and social forces which are "reactionary," that is, which do not go along with "liberal" ideas (Davis, Dinitz, and Pasamanick, 1974). Such a response to frustration is a grave error. Scientists who succumb to the temptation of scapegoating society do a great disservice to themselves, their patients, and their science. Politically, it is always the far left which suspects the conspiracy of the establishment. It is the far right which fears the conspiracy of the far left. Both of these views take a conspiratorial position to explain their own inability to have things the way they want them (Mark Harris, 1975). They choose to completely overlook human

nature. Neither the far left nor the far right is dealing with
anything other than human nature. The far left must finally face
the fact that people like to be well-off, comfortable, safe, and
secure; at least they want the hope that some day it can happen to
them. People are not willing to make revolutions for the good of
mankind if they themselves are cold, wet and hungry. Similarly,
the far right must realize that there are always those who are
out of power who want to get to power. There are the young who
want to get rid of the old. This is human nature since the beginning of mankind. These are not conspiracies, unless it makes
sense to talk about human nature as a conspiracy. The limits of
human nature are the conspiracy.

Our colleagues who 15 years ago helped to design programs of
nonhospital treatment and who demonstrated that patients do better
in the community, are puzzled by the fact that society has not
changed the treatment of the mentally ill. They blame politicians
and taxpayers and community planners accusing them of backwardness,
reactionary thinking, lack of concern for patient welfare, lack of
understanding of cost accounting, etc. What our colleagues do not
recognize is that they are railing against human nature. The
people who are in power do not want to give up power; groups do not
want to change their behavior; professionals who are comfortable
do not want to become uncomfortable; society which has found a way
of coping with an unpleasant situation (mental illness) does not
want to explore other ways of coping.

Because human nature is as it is, because medicine and the
medical model is a firmly established ritual in the majority culture
which is not about to change, we propose that a different model be
developed for the care of those individuals who cannot manage in
society and who have traditionally been labeled as mentally ill.
We propose that the mentally ill individual should be rescued
during the moment of crisis and that this rescue be carried out in
a humanitarian way. In the rescue, a relationship can be established with the representative of the helping situation. The
subsequent long-term rehabilitation intervention should be directed
to help the individual to function in society. It should give the
client tools with which to work productively and to benefit from
this productive position in society.

Footnote

[1]We wish to emphasize that the only reason for housing the
project on an acute psychiatric inpatient ward is because the ward
is there and available while other facilities are not. This does
increase the cost tremendously (costs in the hospital are $168 per
day while costs of providing a similar program in the community are
$54 per day), and also create problems with personnel having to
function in ways not consistent with traditional role models.

REFERENCES

Bockover, J. S., Solomon, H. G. Comparison of two five-year
  follow-up studies: 1947 to 1952 and 1967 to 1972. Amer. J.
  Psychiat., 132:796-801, 1975.

Davis, A. E., Dinitz, S., and Pasamanick, G. Schizophrenics in
  the new custodial community. Columbus: Ohio State University
  Press, 1974.

Feighner, J. P., Robins, E., Guze, S. B., et al. Diagnostic
  criteria for use in psychiatric research. Arch. Gen. Psychiat.,
  26:57-63, 1972.

Gittelman, M. Sectorization: the quiet revolution in European
  mental health care. Amer. J. Orthopsychiat., 42:159-167, 1972.

Glasscote, R. M., Cumming, E., Hammersley, D., et al. The
  psychiatric emergency. Washington, D. C.: Joint Information
  Service of the American Psychiatric Association, 1966.

Greenblatt, M. Historical forces affecting the closing of mental
  hospitals. In: Proceedings of a Conference on the Closing of
  State Mental Hospitals "Where is My Home?". Encino: Plog
  Research, Inc., April 1974, pp. 3-17.

Harris, M. Conspiracy to the left of us! Paranoia to the right
  of us! The New York Times Magazine, August 24, 1975, p. 12.

Herz, M., Endicott, J., Spitzer, R., and Mesnikoff, A. Day versus
  inpatient hospitalization: a controlled study. Amer. J.
  Psychiat., 127:1371-1380, 1971.

Langsley, D., Kaplan, D., Pittman, F., et al. The treatment of
  families in crisis. New York: Grune & Stratton, Inc., 1968.

Mendel, W. Brief hospitalization techniques. Chapter in: Current
  Psychiatric Therapies, Masserman, J. (Ed.). New York: Grune
  & Stratton, Inc., 4:310-316, 1966.

Mendel, W. On the abolition of the psychiatric hospital. Chapter
  11, in: Comprehensive Mental Health. Madison: The University
  of Wisconsin Press, 1968. Pages 237-247, Roberts, L. M.,
  Greenfield, N. S., and Miller, M. (Eds.).

Mendel, W. Lepers, madmen--who's next? NIMH Schizophrenia
  Bulletin, 11:5-8, 1974.

Mendel, W. Supportive care. Los Angeles: Mara Books, Inc., 1975a.

Mendel, W. A flexible and responsive non-hospital patient care
    program. Chapter in: The Changing Mental Health Scene,
    Hirschowitz, R. (Ed.). To be published by Spectrum Publications,
    Fall 1975b.

Rieder, R. O. Hospitals, patients, and politics. NIMH Schizo-
    phrenia Bulletin, 11:9-15, 1974.

Roberts, L. M., Greenfield, N. S., and Miller, M. H. Comprehensive
    Mental Health. Madison: The University of Wisconsin Press, 1968.

Scheidemandel, P., Kanno, C., and Glasscote, R. Health insurance
    for mental illness. Joint Information Service of the American
    Psychiatric Association, Washington, D. C., 1968.

Somers, A. R. Health care in transition: directions for the
    future. Chicago: Hospital Research and Educational Trust, 1971.

Stein, L. I., Test, M. A., and Marx, A. J. Alternative to the
    hospital: a controlled study. Amer. J. Psychiat., 132:517-522,
    1975.

Taylor, R. and Torrey, E. Mental health coverage under a
    national health insurance plan. Presented at the Annual
    Meeting of the American Psychiatric Association, Honolulu,
    Hawaii, May 1973.

THE REHABILITATION SERVICES OF FOUNTAIN HOUSE

John H. Beard

Fountain House, Inc.

New York, New York

A CLUBHOUSE ENVIRONMENT

If today is a typical day at Fountain House, and I hope that
it is, the front door of our clubhouse on West 47th Street, just a
few blocks from Times Square, will open and close many, many times.
By noon today, some 200 of our members will have arrived, and by
late afternoon, our attendance will reach close to 400 men and
women, ranging in age from 16 to 78, who are demographically representative of the population of New York City and share in common a
history of mental illness, often with multiple or long-term hospitalizations. By the end of the evening, another 200 members will
have arrived at the clubhouse for our social programs, and in a
period of a month, over 1,000 individuals will have participated
in the day, evening and weekend programs of Fountain House, for a
total of over 10,000 visits.

In the course of just one day and one evening, I believe that
almost everything that ever happens at Fountain House will probably
happen, and during the course of our Conference today, Fountain
House will be a very busy place. And it is the kind of busyness
which is apparent and visible to all. Our members greet everyone
at the front door, help with the daily signing in at the reception
desk, and the checking of coats. They go out with pushcarts to the
A & P Store, prepare the food for the noonday lunch, provide table
service to fellow members, and then do a good job cleaning up.
They go around the house and get the news of the day, type the
stencils, run the mimeograph machine, and give everyone their daily
newspaper.

They man our busy switchboard, make hospital visits to fellow members, and make home visits to those who may be withdrawing and isolating themselves in the community. They run calculators, punch IBM cards and do card sorting. They keep careful track of daily attendance records, prepare and modify their own individual rehabilitation plans by talking into a tape recorder, and they serve as tutors for their fellow members who are trying to secure their high school equivalency or continue their college education.

Members help fix up our 52 apartments, conduct tours throughout the house for some 3,000 visitors each year, and they greet every new member, showing them the clubhouse and explaining to them what Fountain House is all about. They go to work on either individual or group job placements in commerce and industry, as part of their rehabilitation, serve as faculty in our National Training Program, made possible through support from the National Institute of Mental Health, and many of our older members, in their late 50's, 60's, and 70's, like to help in our nearby Thrift Shop.

Our members operate our Snack Bar in the new sixth floor Youth Area, prepare the daily TV newscast which is viewed in the six basic activity areas of the clubhouse every morning, and almost all members attend the closing meeting at 3:30 each day in the dining room. And some of our members, for various reasons, tend to sit more often in the living room, play cards in the game room, or watch TV, being not yet able to assume more active, participatory roles in the activities of Fountain House.

Today, I am sure there will be some arguments between members and also between some members and staff. There will be good news, such as getting out of the hospital, getting a full-time job, or receiving one's first paycheck through transitional employment. And there will be some bad or upsetting news--feelings of not being liked, of being made fun of, of being misunderstood, of being treated unfairly, of losing a job or failing on a transitional job placement, or having to go back to the hospital.

Most such transactions occur, without appointment, and are simply a normal, accepted part of the daily routine in each of the six rehabilitation areas of the clubhouse: The kitchen-dining room, the clerical office, the Snack Bar, our Education and Research Center, the diversified first floor unit, and the Thrift Shop.

As both staff and members participate together in all clubhouse activities, including daily cleaning functions, all of us tend to blend and merge with each other, being not easily distinguishable to most of our visitors or to new members when they first arrive. It is clear, I think, that a non-traditional role is played most of

the time, by most of the staff, which consists of individuals pro-
fessionally trained in psychology, social work, rehabilitation and
vocational counseling, as well as mental health workers trained at
Fountain House, including members who have achieved through their
rehabilitation a successful social and vocational adjustment.

In brief, what we are trying to do in the daytime hours at
Fountain House is to serve more adequately the increasing numbers
of people leaving our mental institutions who are obviously not
needed by the community to which they are returning. A contributing
or participating role is simply not available to them, and this may
well illustrate how we are successfully transferring into the
community a disability process which was so often inherent in
large mental institutions providing long-term hospitalization.

In our day program at Fountain House, we are trying to create
a community of people where the individual patient, as a club member,
can make a genuine contribution, can be clearly needed, authentically
appreciated and recognized. We would like our environment to be one
which expects individuals to arrive, and is aware of their absence.
In many ways we are a kind of family, a large extended family, where
disappointments occur, aspirations emerge, and opportunities of many
kinds are available. Our relationships to each other reflect, we
hope, a continuity and personal relevance to whatever is happening
in one's life, and the range of such experiences is indeed broad
and diverse.

THE BUSINESS COMMUNITY

A major vocational opportunity, known as "transitional employment," is available to all of our members, and through the years
this program has proven to be extremely popular. Currently, some 41
New York City and New Jersey business firms make it possible for 130
of our members to go to work each day, on a half-time basis, as an
integral part of their vocational evaluation and rehabilitation.
Receiving the normal rate of pay, from $2.35 to $4.00 an hour, their
earnings now approximate $350,000 a year.

By design, the transitional employment program circumvents or
removes certain barriers which all too often prevent the psychiatric
patient from both the seeking and the securing of employment. At
Fountain House the opportunity to go to work on a half-time basis
in a normal place of business, on either an individual or a group
placement, is guaranteed to all, irrespective of an appropriate
job reference, a successful vocational history, the ability to pass
a job interview and a history of mental illness and psychiatric
hospitalization.

Such barriers, of course, help explain why so many psychiatric patients are not motivated even to seek work opportunities when such factors are used to deny employment on the basis of being significant indicators of an individual's inability to do a specific job, particularly entry-level employment.

In the past year programs of transitional employment have been established in over twenty other mental health facilities elsewhere in the nation. A total of 122 employers are now making it possible for over 360 psychiatric patients to go to work each day with earnings well over a million dollars a year.

A keen and growing interest exists in utilizing the role of commerce and industry in facilitating the work adjustment of the vocationally disabled, and a major emphasis of our current national training effort at Fountain House is to be helpful in the fuller utilization of the business community in the rehabilitation process.

A PLACE TO LIVE

In the fall of 1958 we leased our first apartment, a one-room studio located directly across the street from our clubhouse. Today we lease some 53 apartments in New York City so that our members, many of whom are just returning to the community, can pool their resources and have a more adequate and attractive place to live.

The more severely disabled individuals seeking assistance at Fountain House are typically unemployed, financially dependent on S.S.I. or public welfare, are lacking the capacity to negotiate with landlords and are unable to provide the required deposit of at least one month's rent in advance.

In brief, our population is simply not lease-oriented. Our agency, however, as a mental health facility, has the skills to serve as a housing agent and can eliminate those barriers which prevent so many patients from securing more decent housing. We can locate apartments, sign leases and bring together compatible individuals who, through their combined income, can secure a bedroom of their own, living room, a kitchen and bath, rather than reside alone in single room occupancy hotels, for example.

Modest but attractive furnishings are regularly available to us through our Thrift Shop, and the fixing up and maintaining of apartments has provided meaningful activities for members in our day program. Such skills as sewing, decorating and painting are sorely needed and much appreciated.

Our apartments are located in four of the five boroughs of New York City, but many are located within walking distance of our clubhouse, including a cluster of some 16 apartments in a 19-unit building directly across the street from Fountain House. Typically, two members occupy each apartment, but in some instances apartments accommodate from three to four members.

As to the therapeutic or rehabilitative purpose of the apartment program, as a service in itself, our objective has been simply to provide a more attractive housing alternative. Our members can stay in their apartments as long as they like and can take over the lease from Fountain House if they wish to. We do not want to foster the sense of having to move on, but rather support a feeling of stability with respect to where one lives.

Through group meetings at the clubhouse, residents can discuss problems of mutual concern, such as disagreements, a desire to change roommates, and miscellaneous housekeeping responsibilities and problems. A significant rehabilitative function is performed by residents when they can express their concern for any marked emotional changes or physical problems which may occur with a fellow resident. Also, many of our residents enjoy and seek out the opportunity to provide overnight accommodations or a weekend visit for patients requiring a more gradual transition from mental hospital to the community.

With increased numbers of psychiatric patients returning to the community it is essential to prevent, if possible, the transfer of the disability process from custodial institutions to patient care systems emerging in the community. Of necessity, housing accommodations must be provided, and a variety of patterns are emerging--rooming houses, half-way houses, nursing homes, single room occupancy hotels, group residences, foster homes and various types of apartment programs. The providing of decent housing, however, whatever its form, is not in itself equivalent to meeting the social and vocational needs of the disabled who are being returned from mental institutions. Where a person lives, sleeps at night, and has breakfast in the morning is not an appropriate substitute for an environment within the community where the disabled individual is genuinely expected on a daily basis, has a contribution to make, is appreciated and recognized, and wants to go.

In providing apartment accommodations generally typical of the community at large, a great deal of housing can be secured for a relatively low expenditure of charitable dollars. Our 53 apartments cost $123,000 a year for rents and utilities, and each year we incur a deficit of about 10%, due largely to vacancies which occur from time to time, and when we are unable to collect a rental which is due from an individual resident.

EDUCATION AND RESEARCH

In earlier years our research efforts were confined largely to demonstration projects supported mainly by the Rehabilitation Administration and by grants from private foundations. Our transitional employment program of job placements in commerce and industry, as well as our apartment program, are examples of this earlier work. More recently we have conducted a five-year project of programmatic research, also supported by the Rehabilitation Services Administration, the major findings of which are now emerging and some of which can be briefly summarized.

First, it was found that the deaf mental patient participated to the same degree as the non-deaf in the four major programs of Fountain House--the pre-vocational day program, transitional employment, apartment living, and our evening social-recreational program. Their participation was welcomed by our members, many of whom became skilled in signing and enjoyed, for example, living with the deaf members in our apartments.

A ten-year study of 4,575 applicants to Fountain House well documented the high drop-out rate following intake. Some 28% failed to return beyond one visit, and a further 19% failed to make more than five visits to the clubhouse.

In settings elsehwere in the nation it has been documented that the availability of services is not equivalent to their utilization, and it was demonstrated in two of our studies that significant reductions in the drop-out rate can be secured through the use of audio-visual presentations at intake, as well as through the use of reaching out visiting teams composed of selected members interested and skilled in conducting such visits.

Other studies relate to equally significant aspects of the rehabilitation process, and the extent to which the availability and use of such services can affect rehospitalization rates over longer time periods, as well as the duration of hospitalizations when they occur. While it was demonstrated that no significant reductions were obtained in rehospitalization rates over a nine-year period between a control and experimental population, the duration of such hospitalizations were significantly reduced, as well as the rehospitalization rates, when related to the variable of reasonable exposure to the rehabilitation environment.

Of special interest to us at this time is the rehabilitative effect of group placements in industry in facilitating the work adjustment of the vocationally disabled psychiatric patient. A two-year follow-up has been completed on 224 individuals, commencing with the day they first went to work on a part-time basis on one of

our group placements. It was found that the study population
spent 24% of the two-year time period on group placements, an
additional 12% on individual placements in commerce and industry,
and just under 13% on full-time, independent employment. Almost
one-half, therefore, of the two-year time period was spent either
at work on transitional employment placements or on an independent
job of one's own.

When these clients were not able to maintain work adjustment
in the business community, they resumed participation in the pre-
vocational day program at Fountain House. Some 27% of the two-
year time period was spent in the day program, and another 6% was
spent in other rehabilitation or educational facilities. From
our perspective we view the rehabilitation of the severely disabled
mental patient as a longer-term process, rather than one which is
short and time-limited.

Some 83% of the two-year follow-up period was therefore spent
either working in industry (49.3%) or pursuing further rehabilitation educational efforts (33.2%). The balance of the two-year time
span (16.8%) related to other, less work-oriented categories of
community adjustment. Only 7.6% of the time period was spent on a
withdrawn, isolated basis in the community, 3.1% in psychiatric
hospitals, 2.1% relating to inactivity due to physical illness, 1.4%
due to miscellaneous reasons such as home responsibilities, etc.,
and less than 1% for decreased time. In securing the follow-up
data, we were fortunate to have the dedicated assistance of various
members of Fountain House which enabled us to account for 97.6% of
the two-year time period for the 224 subjects.

It is clear that we have not yet documented that transitional
employment significantly returns the vocationally disabled individual to independent employment in the community. We do know, however,
that through transitional employment, and through easy and often
frequent easy re-entry into pre-vocational services, a large majority of the disabled population remains active in the rehabilitation
process (83%), with half of the two-year time period being spent
successfully at work, and increasing amounts of time spent on
independent employment, some 5% in the first year to 17% in the
second year. It is reassuring that the severely disabled do not
withdraw into the community from a work-oriented rehabilitation
process nor, to a significant degree, spend much time rehospitalized.

As to our educational efforts, we welcome some 3,000 visitors
each year at Fountain House from elsewhere in the nation and from
many foreign countries. We believe this is helpful in the establishment or development of facilities elsewhere, not only in the
United States but in such countries as Australia, Pakistan and

Poland where close collaborative relationships have been established, including the training of foreign staff at Fountain House.

Like other facilities, we have served the traditional function of providing field placements for graduate students in social work, vocational counseling, psychiatric nursing, community psychiatry, as well as other mental health disciplines.

Our major educational effort in the past few years, however, has been to assist in the replication elsewhere of transitional employment. At the present time through the support of the National Institute of Mental Health we are conducting a training program for mental health facilities elsewhere in the nation. These include community mental health centers, sheltered workshops, psychosocial rehabilitation facilities, and state mental hospitals who wish to establish or develop community-based rehabilitation services to facilitate the social and vocational adjustment of the more severely disabled psychiatric patient.

A three-week training period is provided at Fountain House, as well as site visits and field consultation to individual facilities. We are now in the first year of our training program and have had a most rewarding experience in working with visiting colleagues from such facilities as the Green Door in Washington, D.C.; the Dallas County Community Mental Health Center; Hedwig House in Norristown, Pa.; Brookline Mental Health Association in Boston; Lincoln Community Mental Health Center here in New York City; the Comprehensive Community Mental Health Center of Savannah, Georgia; and the Dumont Mental Health Center in New Jersey.

Our major concern, of course, is that the training experience be reflected in the development of new and needed services within the visiting facility. The program staff of Fountain House, who perform the primary training function, have already found it extremely rewarding to see the clear and documented relationship between training efforts and the establishment elsewhere of new, essential rehabilitation services such as apartment living, transitional employment, social programs, and other services so crucial to the adjustment process of the more disabled patient in the community.

I think all of us at Fountain House look forward with eager-ness and excitement, and also appreciation, to the training opportunities which have been extended to us, and we feel much the same way about certain research issues which can enable us to organize, restructure, or strengthen the delivery of our reha-bilitation services to those whose need is so obviously great. As elsewhere, all of the parts of Fountain House inter-relate, and we appreciate the presenting to you of this brief review or glimpse of what we are trying to do at Fountain House.

ALTERNATIVES TO CHRONIC HOSPITALIZATION -

THE BOSTON STATE HOSPITAL EXPERIENCE

Jonathan O. Cole,* George Gardos,* and
Michael Nelson**

*Boston State Hospital
Boston Massachusetts
**Massachusetts General Hospital
Boston, Massachusetts

This paper grows out of the experiences of the three authors
with Boston State Hospital and its chronic patients over the past
nine years. The hospital has served the City of Boston for over
a century. By the late 1940's it was seriously overcrowded,
despite wholesale relocations of patients to other "newer" hospitals
(e.g., Metropolitan and Gardner State Hospitals), and a policy was
then adopted to have all newly admitted patients resident in Boston
less than 13 years transferred to Grafton State Hospital--a rural
facility south of Worcester. Despite these stunts, the hospital
was overcrowded with a census of about 3,000 at peak. It began
to decline a little during Dr. Barton's tenure when family care
and home treatment programs were instituted. With the advent of
antipsychotic drugs, the census decline was continued. By the
time Dr. Milton Greenblatt took over the Superintendency (1963),
the census was about 2,000.

When Dr. Cole arrived to take over the Superintendency, the
census was about 1,350. Six years later it had shrunk to a little
over 600 when Dr. Nelson replaced him. Now the census of in-patients
is either 230 or about 350, depending on what is included in the
tally.

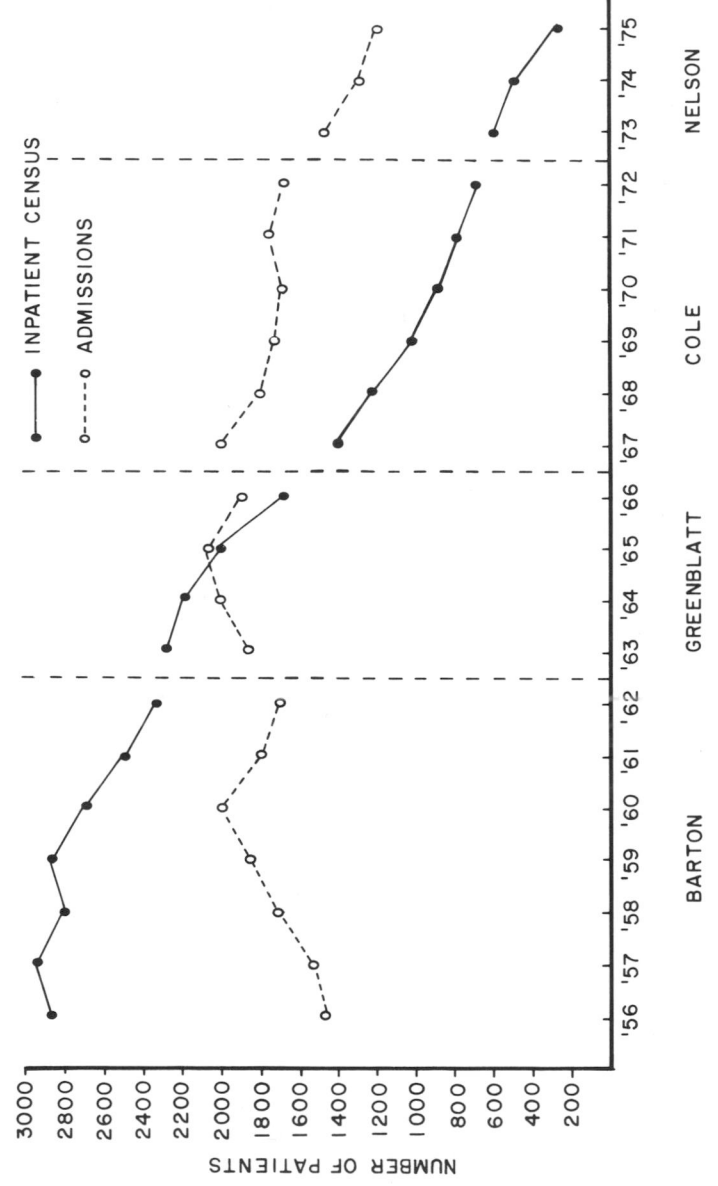

Figure 1. Admissions and inpatient census of Boston State Hospital over time
and under four superintendents.

The scope of this paper will be to consider the various pressures and programs leading to this drastic decline in in-patient census--where and how did the patients go?--and to consider the desirability of the changes which have occurred. To the casual observer, it is apparent that the in-patient hospital has declined in census under four consecutive superintendents (Figure 1). The programs involved will be considered in sequence.

Under Walter Barton, his emphasis on the admission service, then a single building serving all of Boston, may have helped reduce the census by discouraging the creation of too many new chronic patients. The use of antipsychotic drugs had a major effect as well. The other major innovation was the creation of the Home Treatment Service, a specialized crisis intervention program covering only a fraction of the hospital's catchment area, which demonstrated that many psychotic patients could be treated in their homes without hospital admission.

Under Milton Greenblatt many new programs of a psychosocial nature were added. A sheltered workshop, run by a non-profit foundation (PROP), was created within the hospital and provided vocational rehabilitation to many patients. The Family Care Program for placing chronic in-patients with foster parents in community residences was greatly expanded from its 20 slots under Dr. Barton. The old Superintendent's house was used as a halfway house, with the Protestant chaplain and his wife serving as house parents. Pre-placement wards for patients being prepared for nursing homes were created as was an "apartment" in the hospital where a small group of patients could be prepared for joint placement in a community apartment. The shift of welfare budgets from the local communities to the state and the arrival of Medicare and Medicaid programs made community and nursing home placements of indigent patients in large numbers fiscally feasible for the first time. An old employee's residence was also used to prepare chronic female patients for community placement.

A fervor for community placement ran through the chronic services. A vigorous nursing supervisor had a dramatic flair and would throw beds out of second story windows when a patient was discharged to symbolically prevent the bed ever being filled again. It was said that Dr. Greenblatt would stride up and down before a physically deteriorating chronic building with 100 occupants and declare that it should be closed and, lo and behold, nine months

later it would be empty and would be closed or become available
for community programs.

At the same time the hospital's catchment area of 1,000,000
was divided into five community mental health center areas,
Massachusetts Mental Health Center, Boston University Medical
School, Tufts Medical School, the Lindemann Center (next to
Massachusetts General Hospital) and Boston State Hospital, each
being assigned an area.

Under Cole, Family Care and Nursing Home placement continued
and expanded. Other community facilities (e.g., the Center Club,
an ex-patients' club in downtown Boston and Well Met, a halfway
house complex in Cambridge) as well as out-patient and aftercare
facilities to handle patients were used increasingly in lieu of
hospitalization. In addition community consultation programs to
nursing homes, welfare offices and the Visiting Nurses Association
were expanded to help maintain psychotic patients outside the
hospital.

The practice of sending all patients resident in Boston less
than 13 years to Grafton State Hospital was stopped and a large
number of chronic patients were reabsorbed from Bridgewater State
Hospital (of Titticutt Follies fame), Medfield State Hospital,
Grafton State Hospital--which was closed entirely--and Monson State
School, about 250 patients in all. The census, however, continued
to decline. The Cooperative Apartment Program was invented by
Chien (Landlord supervised Cooperative Apartments: A New Modality
for Community-based Treatment by Cole and Chien) and extensively
used. During this period, the Lindemann Mental Health Center
opened and took over all admissions from 1/5 of the hospital's
catchment area using only 40 beds plus community programs and the
Massachusetts Mental Health Center began to handle all admissions
and chronic patients from its fifth of the old catchment area with
its 120 beds.

Under Nelson, the movement of chronic patients into the community continued. Day programs, a thrift shop, two residential
houses and workshop facilities emulating New York's Fountain House
were begun physically in the community on a shoe string and have
continued even under fiscal adversity. The buildings housing the
Boston University and Tufts in-patients plus their associated
staffs were transferred fully to their respective mental health
centers, causing the head counting problem noted above. Are these
in-patients (about 120 in all) to be counted in the Boston State
Hospital census? The Boston University patients will shortly be
moved to their newly constructed mental health center next to the
medical school in Roxbury.

Under Cole, the Boston State Hospital catchment area was divided into two mental health centers, the West-Ros-Park and Dorchester centers but all chronic patients were kept in a separate service. Now, finally, the mental health centers are all fully responsible for their own chronic patients and the residual 90 geriatric and bed-ridden patients (from our original 1,200 patients of this sort in the late 1950's) will probably soon be transferred to the Lemuel Shattuck, a state Public Health hospital. The West-Ros-Park center will soon be getting its in-patient beds transferred to a community general hospital.

Our current guess is that only about 40 chronic non-placeable non-geriatric patients plus about 30 acute beds for Dorchester Mental Health Center patients may remain at Boston State Hospital as the irreducible hard core if no major change in staff or funding occurs.

There were two factors in the Boston State Hospital experience which run counter even to the policy of the Massachusetts Department of Mental Health.

(1) Although chronic wards have, from phase to phase, been attached to acute wards or to community mental health centers, the shrinking of the chronic in-patient population--1,000 even in 1967--to its current low of 250 was done almost entirely by chronic unit staffs working out ways of moving chronic patients into the community. And almost all of it was accomplished without unitizing the chronic patients into geographic units, a move which has only been forcibly consummated recently. Whether it's better to do it this way, we can't say, but it has certainly been effective. At least in Boston, staff who like to work with acute patients really fight getting involved with residual chronic patients--they'll only handle their own newer chronics while staff members on chronic units often develop unsuspected skills at formulating both individual patient treatment plans and ingenious programs for larger patient groups. Only in the last couple of years when the chronic patient groups became quite small and manageable have the acute programs been willing, even under pressure, to assume full responsibility.

(2) For many years we assumed that most chronic patients had no catchment area. The fact that Danny P. was born in East Boston in 1909 seemed to us irrelevant since he had had 50 years in Boston State and had no known relatives. Thus the hospital, despite being given its own mental health center catchment area of 200,000 Bostonian souls (North Dorchester, Mattapan, West Roxbury, Hyde Park and Roslindale) has tended till recently to place chronic patients in sheltered environments near the hospital, keeping many in day hospital programs.

A recurring phenomenon as the hospital shrank was the "cream rising to the top." In any group of very chronic patients--even after many had been placed--there always seemed to be two or three who looked better adjusted and less psychotic and thus, "placeable." When these were placed, lo and behold two others looked better. Whether patients always improve a bit in waves, whether our criteria or "placeability" kept stretching or whether removal of a ward's "best" patients leave a sociotherapeutic gap eliciting improvement in other patients is unclear.

Despite a chronic Zeitgeist favoring placement of patients out in the community so we could free up staff for better and richer programs for community and hospital patients, we believe we avoided inconsiderate dumping and have tried hard to match patients to particular nursing homes and to evaluate the patient, the community setting and the future support needs before each individual place- ment. At most we have started new cooperative apartments with a clutch of 4 - 7 patients being placed de novo together. As viewed from the levels we three authors have occupied, we believe that the lower level staffs really tried their best to make good placements for their patients.

It is all very well to muse on the social milieu surrounding this great patient exodus, but where did they go and was it a good idea to send them there?

WHERE DID THEY GO

Assuming that at least 2,500 of the 3,000 inpatients at Boston State Hospital in 1950 were chronic in the sense of being hospital- ized for more than two years fairly steadily and the Boston State Hospital has absorbed 250 equally chronic transfers from Bridgewater (the state facility for the criminally insane), the state schools for the retarded and other state hospitals and also assuming that out of 1,500 admissions a year at least 50 become chronic and stay at least two years, about 4,000 chronic patients have gone some- where other than Boston State Hospital.

Some of them were cured or made very much better by the anti- psychotic drugs and went home or back to their jobs. This may have been a large number in the mid 1950's, but probably not more than 500.

A large number have probably died--in or out of the hospital --of natural causes. In 1965, 45% of the 1,900 in-patients were over 60. If this was true of even 1/3 of the original 3,000 in 1950, then 1,000 would be over 80 if they were still alive and probably another 500 of the more recent chronic patients were over 60 when initially admitted.

Halfway houses are probably not a major factor, at least in the earlier phases at Boston State Hospital. The older superintendent's house was a halfway house for seven years (till the sewer collapsed) and was a show place and generally well run, but it housed at most eight patients with an average stay of six months-- generally attractive, responsive, verbal younger patients--and couldn't have accounted for more than 60 discharged patients. About 1/3 of its patients relapsed in the halfway house and were returned to the hospital.

Zoning rules and relative lack of state funds to support the operating costs of halfway houses suppressed their use, though two other houses acquired free from the city of Boston have been run for about two years and account for perhaps another 30 patients.

Wel Met, a free standing halfway house network in Cambridge handled some of our patients. Under their aegis 20 college students took 20 chronic patients to Cape Cod to an old poor house farm one summer and kept most of the patients out for several years--the hospital lent Well Met two attendant positions for three years in partial compensation. The whole scheme was a wild idea that worked. The college kids even got course credit from Harvard for the summer! But it was a one-shot event, not a master plan for chronic patients.

Family Care was a larger contributor. Under Mrs. Lilleskare, a group of highly motivated nurses established a network of foster families who took in chronic patients at $5.50/patient/day. Usually a family would care for 4 - 6 patients in a big old house, but some were smaller. The homes were visited twice a week and the nurses were available to go out and cope with emergenices. The hospital provided a clinic set up where the family care patients came for medical or psychiatric evaluation. Most homes were near the hospital, but a couple were in exurbia. This program has handled 150 patients at a time for almost 10 years with a miniscule annual readmission rate (2 - 3%) and with 20 - 30 patients leaving the program because they've become employed or have moved in with their families each year. Lack of state funds to pay the per diem--a special fund set up at the Department of Mental Health--limited further expansion of this program. It's annual Christmas party for all staff, "foster parents", and patients is a marvel to behold! The settings vary from very close supportive family-type environments to quiet but distant settings for quiet chronic patients. Probably 600 patients were taken out of the hospital by this route.

The most fiscally and administratively ingenious device for placing psychiatric patients into the community was the "Coopertive" or "Coop" apartment program, developed entirely by Dr. Ching-piao Chien (Chien and Cole, 1973) with the fitful cooperation of the local Public Welfare Office. The general plan was to find a

cooperative landlord who was willing to rent an apartment in his
residence to a group of psychiatric patients on welfare and to
assume responsibility for teaching the patients how to keep house
and adapt in the community in cooperation with Dr. Chien and his
staff (generally a Licensed Practical Nurse and an Occupational
Therapy Assistant). Almost all the apartments were in "three-
deckers"--old buildings with three apartments, one above the other,
with the landlord living in one of the apartments. The apartments
did not require the special zoning changes and the elaborate safety
and sanitation codes governing halfway houses or boarding houses
and fell under the more reasonable requirements of the Welfare
Department for all apartments rented by its clients. For the first
two years of the program, the landlord received a small extra fee
--about $10.00 per patient per month for his supervisory duties--
but this was abolished by fiat later as part of a general abolition
of special rates on a State-wide basis. The landlord was, however,
able to charge a somewhat higher rent for these furnished apartments than he might have received on the open market.

Interestingly, almost all landlords were black small property
owners living within a mile or two of the hospital in Mattapan or
North Dorchester. Generally they had no prior contact with
psychiatry or mental health and entered the program, which they
generally heard about by word-of-mouth out of a mixture of humanitarian and financial interests. They were screened during a brief,
several session, training program and were visited twice a week
thereafter by a member of the hospital's team. For quite a while
a member of the Welfare Department staff was loaned to the program
and was very helpful in getting patients onto the welfare rolls,
an obvious requirement for participation in the program.

The hospital provided monitoring, a 24-hour emergency number
for landlords' assistance with practical or vocational or family
problems. The program at its peak has carried about 140 patients
in 20 - 25 apartments supervised by a full-time staff of six (one
RN, two LPN's, an OT assistant, an attendant nurse and a secretary)
plus about 1/3 of Dr. Chien's psychiatric time.

The program differed from Family Care in the following ways:

Family Care	Coop Apartments
Still on hospital books	Discharged from hospital
Had no income	Handled own welfare check
All medical services from Boston State Hospital	Eligible for City Hospital or local Medicaid funded medical services

Family Care	Coop Apartments
All costs borne by Department of Mental Health	All subsistence costs borne by Welfare Department
Patients relatively more dependent	Patients relatively more independent
Run by psychiatric nurses	Run by a psychiatrist using lower level personnel

As with many innovative programs, the originator left for a better job elsewhere and, in one of the hospital's many reorganizations about a year ago the two programs (Cooperative Apartments and Family Care) were merged under a single leadership in a single geographic area in the hospital. Most recently, these programs have been dispersed.

The Cooperative Apartment Program had two interesting problems. The first was the amazing slowness with which the mechanism was adopted by other Massachusetts state hospitals. After it had been running four years at Boston State, Medfield State Hospital finally opened a single cooperative apartment in Quincy.

The other problem was racial. Boston State never succeeded in getting a white landlord to take part in the program, even though similar three-deckers existed in adjacent white areas. At one point some spokesman for the black community complained that we were dumping psychotic whites on their turf, which tended to make their area less attractive and was dangerous for the patients (about 80% of whom were white), mostly because Mattapan and Dorchester were high crime areas. Somehow these accusations, both relatively true, were never pushed with enough intensity to seriously jeopardize the program though they may have contributed to a plateauing of the program at about 130 patients.

With both Family Care and Cooperative Apartments, the programs combined only handled about 300 patients at any one time. Both had surprisingly low readmission rates (under 4% per year) but some patients were transferred to nursing homes because of increasing age and physical weakness or because of apathetic withdrawal without florid psychosis. Others went on to jobs and became self-supporting or worked out arrangements for living with relatives or friends. About 20% per year turnover from such causes would allow about 300 patients to exit from the hospital via the cooperative apartment program over its six years of operation.

As can be deduced from the above program descriptions a good part of the Boston State Hospital census reduction could not have resulted from innovative community placement programs of the sort

described. One suspects nursing home placement and death, for
neither of which we have adequate data, contributed significantly.
If Stotsky's 1966 figure of 165 nursing home placements is extended
and corrected for the subsequent nine years, perhaps 1,200 patients
were placed in nursing homes.

    We do have one piece of follow-up data of a cohort of patients.
In 1963, Boston State Hospital was one of seven public mental
hospitals which took part in a collaborative study of the efficacy
of high dosage chlorpromazine therapy in chronic schizophrenia.
To be included in the study, patients had to be between 18 and 55
years of age, continuously hospitalized more than two years,
diagnosed schizophrenic without mental retardation or organic
brain dysfunction. The 123 patients included in the study at
Boston State Hospital constituted almost all the patients eligible
for the study and can thus be viewed as representative of the
younger chronic schizophrenics then in the hospital (average age
about 45 at the time of the study). We've done a chart survey of
their disposition--"last known location"--about a year ago. At
that time of the 110 patients with available records, eight were
dead, 27 still hospitalized, 29 in nursing homes, 10 in Family
Care, 12 in Cooperative Apartments, 13 in a parent's or relative's
home and 11 in their own or a conjugal home.

    Obviously, one can view this data in many ways. One can say
"Hooray! Only 1/4 of the patients are still in the hospital!" or
one can say "Terrible! Only 10%, at most, are truly independent
and living on their own!" The data partially support the senior
author's chronic suspicion that much of the drop in hospital
census was a sleight-of-hand trick in which unprotesting chronic
patients were moved from the back wards of state hospitals to
nursing homes, a distinction possibly lacking a difference.
Actually his fears were somewhat mollified since only a bit over
a quarter of the patients were so treated--though it is the largest
single category and the nursing home disposition was probably used
much more frequently for patients too old for the collaborative
study.

    Some statements about the nursing home solution to the problem
of the public mental hospital need to be made. It has never shared
the limelight with sexier and more humanistic approaches to the
release of chronic patients--one hesitates to call it "de-institu-
tionalization" but we bet that it has been very widely used. In
part, its use is a fiscal consequence of the Medicaid law (psychiatric patients have never benefitted much from Medicare's Extended
Care Facility provisions--they are too brief for most patients);
The financial factor is that (1) patients transferred to nursing
homes stop being supported by the Department of Mental Health and
are fiscally transferred to the Department of Public Welfare, and

(2) for some period the state collected 50% of its costs as
federal reimbursement for patients under 65 in nursing homes under
Medicaid but collected no reimbursement for such patients in state
psychiatric hospitals. Even the 50% federal reimbursement for
patients in state hospitals over age 65 was of no direct benefit
to the hospitals in Massachusetts; this money disappeared into the
State's General Fund and had no direct effect on hospital programs.
This whole ploy made a fiscal profit for the state and indirectly
was a great boon for the mental hospital. Until very recently
Boston State Hospital's employee census remained around 1200 while
its in-patient census dropped and dropped. This has meant better
ward staffing and transfer of many staff to community programs--
about half the clinical staff are now so deployed--and has probably
benefitted lots of patients and has expanded programs for kids and
adolescents. The whole move has raised the welfare budget though
it has been remarkable how little notice has been taken of this
consequence in Massachusetts at least.

The crucial question which should be answered is "are the
patients better off in nursing homes?" This can be an extraordi-
narily complex problem. At the superficial level it's certain
that nursing home toilet facilities are "better", since Boston
State's facilities approach the medieval in some buildings where
there are no seats in any of the buildings. The linen supplies
are probably more reliable. On the other hand, Boston State's
Medical-Surgical Building--now down to three mixed medical-geriatric
wards--does a first class job with demented incontinent patients
who require feeding; patients nursing homes avoid like the plague.
But if the hospital were still overcrowded, these "total care"
patients could not be well treated. The problem is complex.

Asking the patient how he likes his current domicile is very
unsatisfactory, since chronic patients often appear to fear change
or to give bland empty answers or to be mute, making it hard to
use the patient's response as the ultimate criterion. The "good-
ness" of the setting is probably a function of many things--the
patient's level of functioning, the nursing home's staff attitude,
the local resources, the patient's access to activities in the
home, the neighborhood or in the hospital. On the other hand the
state hospital has many assets for the stable chronic patients
with ground privileges--canteen access, hospital stores, movies,
sleeping under the trees in summer, occasional access to illicit
sex and alcohol, hospital jobs--paid or unpaid and the opportunity
to observe the multitudinous minor events in a large hospital's
day. One can guess that nursing homes may be more monotonous though
somewhat more comfortable.

It's occasionally suggested that nursing homes have less
"stigma" than state hospitals; we doubt that this is an important
issue for chronic patients though it is sometimes (but not always)
important to families.

Perhaps a study should be done in which a skilled unbiased clinician (if one exists), who knows the patient reasonably well, should assess his/her status prior to placement and again afterward. We know of no such studies of nursing home placements alone.

However, one study approximating this was carried out by Drs. Gardos and Nelson last year (Gardos and Nelson, 1976). From the four chronic non-geriatric wards remaining in the hospital (total census = 150 patients) 57 patients were identified as suitable for discharge to a community residence. They were all rated by a psychiatrist, a social worker and a nurse, each on an appropriate scale (the MSIS Periodic Evaluation Record, the Linn Social Dysfunction Rating Scale and a newly designed simple 10-item nurses' observation scale). Forty-eight of these patients were available for evaluation a year later. Of these 28 had been placed in the community (12 in cooperative apartments, 2 in Family Care, 1 in a halfway house, 3 in their own homes and 10 in nursing or rest homes). The placed and unplaced patients were equivalent on all measures at baseline. A year later a psychiatrist, nurse and social worker judged the community-placed patients to be less severely ill. They required less antipsychotic medication and had shown significant improvement in "uncooperativeness" and "delusions"; they were also observed to be neater. Trends on other items almost all favored the community group. The community patients showed more goal directed activities and showed less dissatisfaction (Factor 3 on the Linn Scale). There was some increase in speech productivity. Some patients who had worked on hospital jobs before nursing home placement were no longer working a year later, however.

Generally, this study is consistent with the presumption that community placement is good for chronic patients. We believe that the Boston State Hospital's programs, which emphasize close monitoring of community placements, are responsible for this result which is somewhat more positive than some other studies in the literature. It's clear that our study does not have random assignment to placement and non-placement. Though many patients were not placed for reasons irrelevant to their clinical condition (e.g., family resistance) others may have not been placed because of intercurrent worsening or because their associated mental retardation required placements with more support and supervision than those available at this time.

To recapitulate our very gross guesstimates of the fates of chronic patients released from Boston State Hospital since the 1950's, probably 4,000 such patients have left the hospital. Probably 1,500 have died of old age or other medical causes in the hospital or after placement in various settings. Perhaps another 800 have been placed and are living in nursing homes. About 100 have left via halfway houses and about 600 through family care and 300 through cooperative apartments. This accounts for 3,300 of

the patients. If 15% or 600 left to return to their own homes or
to independent living situations of one sort or another, most of
the patients are accounted for. Probably 200 chronic patients are
still hospitalized either chronically or recurrently at one of the
five mental health centers now operating in the original Boston
State Hospital catchment area. These figures almost balance our
approximate books and may not be too far from the truth. We have
long wished that NIMH would fund a full cohort follow-up study of
all patients resident in hospitals like Boston State Hospital at
some point 10 - 15 years ago to give a clear and accurate answer
to the question "Where _did_ the patients go?"

CURRENT STATUS

        Recent programs, principally initiated by Dr. Nelson, have
emphasized the need to have staff and facilities for day care,
aftercare and social and vocational rehabilitation follow--or move
with--the chronic patients into the community. Earlier programs
moved the patient's living space into community homes, apartments
or nursing homes but brought many patients back to the hospital
during the day for work, rehabilitation or day activity programs.

        Under Dr. Nelson a small ($5,000) grant from the local
Epilepsy Foundation, plus four hospital staff positions, some
$1,000 in other hospital money and local contributions of space,
three houses, a church basement, and a store have led to the
establishment of five programs:

(1)   A community rehabilitation center where community and
      some hospital patients come for vocational and social
      rehabilitation activities (in the church basement);

(2)   A three decker apartment building with three apartments
      houses 12 ex-patients and a house mother. All 12 patients
      now have full or part-time jobs (after two years in the
      community) and the program is patient run and self-
      sustaining financially and socially;

(3)   A thrift shop has been established by an occupational
      therapist with the initial rent being paid by the hospital.
      It is also now self-sustaining and mainly patient-run.

(4)   A house has been set up for day and evening social club
      activities for long term chronic patients. It has a non-
      hospital community board with input from the Epilepsy
      Society. (In passing, lest one wonders at the role of
      an Epilepsy group in all this, about 1/3 of our chronic
      patients have epileptic histories and others have organic
      brain defects or developmental disabilities.)

(5) A second activity house has been created after the first
      was allocated to Boston University since it happened to
      be located in the catchment area.

Finally, it needs to be clearly and strongly stated that all
of these programs for moving chronic patients to the community
could not have succeeded in markedly reducing the hospital's census
if the acute treatment programs had not very successfully prevented
the development of large new cohorts of chronic patients each year.
We may now have "revolving door" patients but we don't have masses
of demented denudative incontinent patients of the sort that filled
many wards at Boston State Hospital in the old days.

To review what we believe we have learned at Boston State
Hospital about chronic patients:

(1) Most chronic patients, given drugs, staff attention,
      structure, remotivation and activities or occupations,
      can be placed in the community in one of a range of
      settings.

(2) The cost in psychiatric staff is small compared to in-
      patient beds, probably one lower-level staff member for
      each 30 chronic patients with some nursing and psychiatric
      back-up and some type of twenty-four hour emergency
      service available.

(3) Some activity and rehabilitation programs are needed for
      all patients who are not in ordinary jobs. These may be
      best provided in community settings, but hospital set-
      tings are often easier to arrange initially.

(4) Elements of ingenuity, "scrounging" and fund raising are
      essential to augment the harder funds coming through
      state agencies, but more narrowly restricted.

(5) Patients, given good carefully monitored and active com-
      munity programs, tend to improve in social competence
      the longer they stay in the community.

(6) In special placements of the sort we have used, the stress
      on the community is small. We cannot speak to the stress
      on families of having a recurrently psychotic member in
      their midst.

(7) Much of what has been done recently has been done on a
      larger scale in New York by Fountain House and has been
      parallelled with some differences by the Center Club in
      Boston. We believe the model is exportable, but can't
      really judge the impact of state-to-state differences in

funding and regulations and community differences in
tolerance for the chronically psychotic and the availability of residential and activity space for ex-patients.

Lastly, let us pray that current pressures on state budgets
do not lead to massive slashes in support for psychiatric patient
programs and land us all back into another snake pit era after all
our efforts to improve our treatment programs for both acute and
chronic patients.

REFERENCES

Chien, C. and Cole, J. O. Landlord-supervised cooperative apartments: A new modality for community-based treatment. American
Journal of Psychiatry, 1973, 130, 156-159.

Gardos, G. and Nelson, M.H. A controlled follow-up of discharged
chronic patients. Paper presented at the 129th Annual Meeting
of the American Psychiatric Association, Miami Beach, Florida,
May, 1976.

Part IV

THE BRITISH EXPERIENCE

PLANNING AND EVALUATING SERVICES FOR CHRONICALLY

HANDICAPPED PSYCHIATRIC PATIENTS IN THE UNITED KINGDOM

John K. Wing

Institute of Psychiatry

London, England

THE ORGANIZATION OF HEALTH AND

SOCIAL SERVICES IN ENGLAND

The English National Health Service (NHS) is a pyramidal organization with a government department and cabinet minister at the top, and an infrastructure of 14 regional and 90 area author-ities. Each area consists of one to three geographical districts with approximately 100-400,000 population.

A District Management Team - comprising district community physician, district administrator, district finance officer, a nurse and two elected representatives of local general and hospital practitioners - has the duty of planning and administering local health services. This team is responsible, within the limits of a budget laid down from above, for meeting the health needs of the district. To help them remember their responsibility, there is a consumer organization in each district, called a Community Health Council, which has the specific task of keeping a check on the quality of health services and commenting on it critically in an annual report.

Four main principles underlie the National Health Service:

1. Health service authorities should accept responsibility for the whole of a geographical area, coterminous so far as possible with that of a local government authority. Everyone needing treat-ment should be able to obtain it. Services should be geographically accessible from all parts of the area and should usually be sited

227

within it.   There must, however, be freedom of choice within reason, so that services should not be completely area-bound.

2.   Health services should be comprehensive and varied, including for example in-patient and partial hospitalization units, out-patient clinics, domiciliary and other consultation, and an emergency service.   The number of places should be adequate.   The staff should be well trained and have reasonable time to devote to their clients.   The health services should overlap with those concerned with the provision of social and welfare services, vocational guidance, and protected environments of various kinds, including hostels and workshops for the permanently handicapped.

3.   These area health services should not only be comprehensive, they should be integrated.   This principle assumes that there should be no delays in transfer and no sudden changes in the level of social performance demanded.   Communications should be free so that staff in each part of the service know what is available elsewhere and can readily take over when a patient is transferred.

4.   The chief aim of the health services is to decrease or contain morbidity, first in the patient, second in the patient's immediate family, third in the community at large.   Each agency has a combination of diagnostic, therapeutic, rehabilitative, and preventive functions.   Prevention is better than cure.   Primary, secondary, and tertiary preventive methods should be used to stop disease occurring in the first place, to detect illness at an early stage, to limit development of chronic disabilities following an acute illness, and to prevent the accumulation of secondary handicaps if clinical disabilities are unavoidable.   This is what is meant by the "containment" of morbidity.   Since much psychiatric handicap is chronic, many patients are likely to remain in contact with services for a long time.   Fairly large numbers will therefore accumulate and the development of secondary handicaps will need special attention.

     If fully put into practice, these principles should ensure that morbidity is reduced as much as it can be, but the aims have not, of course, been fully realized.   Our services for the elderly, for the disabled, for the mentally ill and retarded "have failed to attract the attention and indeed the resources which they need" and "the domiciliary and community services are under-developed." The minister responsible for the recent re-organization, Sir Keith Joseph, pointed out that these gaps and deficiencies occurred because the responsibility for providing adequately for each geographical area had never been specifically invested in any one identifiable body.   This was why the government introduced the new organization, with a simple management structure.   "Real needs must be identified and decisions must be taken and periodically reviewed as to the order of priorities among them.   Plans must be

worked out to meet these needs and management and drive must be
continually applied to put the plans into action, assess their
effectiveness and modify them as needs change or as ways are found
to make the plans more effective" (Joseph, 1972).

The English social services are organized in rather a different
way. The same government department is in overall charge but responsibility is carried by local government authorities - the
counties and boroughs - each of which has a social service department. The NHS is financed through central taxes; the social service
departments are financed by local taxes together with a substantial
central grant, particularly to the poorer areas.

This administrative separation of the health and social
services is the result of a long series of political compromises.
It has obvious disadvantages, notably in leading the medical and
paramedical professions on the one hand, and the social work professions on the other, to underrate each other's theoretical and
practical expertise and to behave, to some extent, as though the
medical and social components in assessment, treatment and care
are more separable than is in fact the case. This has sometimes
meant that social elements in etiology and treatment have been
overlooked or even denied, in medical practice, while the client's
disabilities and specific vulnerabilities have been overlooked or
even denied in social practice.

The consequences of such tendencies are particularly obvious
when we consider the provision of alternatives to the large comprehensive psychiatric hospitals. In England, most of the alternatives - day centers, hostels, group homes, boarding out schemes,
sheltered housing, and domiciliary support and welfare - are provided by local social service departments. The main exception is
vocational rehabilitation and sheltered employment which are the
responsibility of the government Department of Employment. There
are also voluntary bodies of various kinds, filling in the gaps,
pioneering new services and acting as watch-dogs and critics.

Thus, although we do have a fairly comprehensive network of
health and welfare services, based on need rather than on the individual's capacity to pay, the opportunities for lack of coordination are numerous. The problem of finance should also be mentioned,
since it is clear that spending on health and social services has
to be restricted, not only in times of economic difficulty such as
we are facing at present, but even when the economy is booming.
The question of priorities is paramount. Should we spend our money
and resources on a new renal dialysis unit or on a center for behaviorally disturbed mentally retarded adolescents?

Such questions are particularly likely to arise during a discussion of alternatives to mental hospital treatment, because many
of the people under consideration are chronically handicapped. In
this paper, I shall review the evaluative work carried out in
England during the past twenty years and then try to come to some
tentative conclusions concerning likely future trends.

RECENT TRENDS IN THE PSYCHIATRIC HOSPITAL POPULATION

The number of people in hospitals for the mentally ill in
England and Wales reached a peak in 1954 (344 per 100,000 population). This was by no means as high as in some European countries
and the figures in Eire and Scotland were considerably higher
(e.g., for Scotland the figure was 410 per 100,000 in 1954). However, there has been a marked decline during the past twenty years,
the latest figure for England and Wales being 220 per 100,000 at
the end of 1972. In the United States, the peak occurred earlier
and reached a higher level than in England. Nevertheless the subsequent decline has been a good deal more rapid so that fewer
hospital beds are now used in the U.S. than in England.

Brooke (1972) pointed out that countries with fewer than 200
beds per 100,000 population fell into two groups, "one comprising
some less economically favored countries and the other a group of
Eastern countries with the dispensary system and socialized
medicine." Although we have not consciously based ourselves on the
Russian model the plans for the English mental health services
definitely envisage that the number of beds will continue to fall
to a point at which the major hospital need will be for short-stay
beds, which could be accommodated in district general hospitals
(50 beds per 100,000), while the need for long-term places would
be met partly by special units for people with dementia (30 beds
per 100,000) and other special needs (e.g., security, addiction,
etc.), and partly by extra residential, day and domiciliary
facilities provided by local authority social service departments.
The large comprehensive psychiatric hospital would then no longer
be needed (DHSS, 1975).

There are three components in this computation: the old long-
stay, the new long-stay and the short-stay. ("Long-stay" means
more than one year in residence). Table 1 shows the rates of
short-stay and long-stay beds used in two areas - Camberwell in
south-east London and Salford, Lancashire - where case-registers
have been in operation for several years (Wing and Fryers, 1976).
Both are segments of conurbations, with the declining populations
characteristic of such areas, and the long-stay rates per 100,000
are not therefore comparable with national figures. They do, however, illustrate the steady decrease in numbers of long-stay beds.
Salford is fairly characteristic of the NHS, in that a large

Table 1

Beds used by short-stay and long-stay patients

on annual census days

Camberwell and Salford Registers

(Rates per 100,000 total population)

| | In-patients | | | |
| | Less than 1 year | | More than 1 year | |
	Camberwell	Salford	Camberwell	Salford
31 December 1964	89	-	240	-
31 December 1965	75	-	240	-
31 December 1966	77	-	234	-
31 December 1967	88	56	224	292
31 December 1968	104	54	215	280
31 December 1969	106	55	207	272
31 December 1970	110	59	197	260
31 December 1971	125	58	183	259
31 December 1972	108	48	185	255
31 December 1973	105	51	179	245
31 December 1974	116	68	173	234

(from: Wing and Fryers, 1976)

proportion of short-stay patients remain for less than a month in hospital, whereas in Camberwell there is a rather leisurely approach more characteristic, perhaps, of teaching hospitals.

Table 2 gives more detail concerning the long-stay patients from Camberwell and Salford who were in hospital on 31st December 1974. In the case of Camberwell, where the case-register began with a census of all psychiatric contacts on the last day of 1964, it is possible to separate the present long-stay figures according

Table 2

Patients in hospital for more than one year on 31 December 1974
by diagnosis: Camberwell and Salford Registers

Cohorts beginning 31 December 1964 and 31 December 1967

| | Cohort beginning 31 Dec. 1964 | | Cohort beginning 31 Dec. 1967 | | | |
| | Camberwell | | Camberwell | | Salford | |
	No.	Rate/100,000	No.	Rate/100,000	No.	Rate/100,000
Old long-stay	150	105	159	112	219	180
Dementia	5	3	6	4	7	6
Other diagnosis	145	102	153	107	212	175
New long-stay	96	67	87	61	65	53
Dementia	32	22	31	22	7	6
Other diagnoses	64	45	56	39	58	48
Total long-stay	246	173	246	173	284	234
Dementia	37	26	37	26	14	11
Other diagnoses	209	147	209	147	270	222
	(10 year accumulation)		(7 year accumulation)			

to who were long-stay on that date and who have become long-stay since. The "old long-stay", in this computation, comprise the 150 individuals who were long-stay on 31 December 1964 and have remained in hospital throughout the following ten years.   Only five of them remain who were diagnosed as suffering from dementia ten years ago, reflecting the high death rate associated with this condition.   The commonest diagnosis among the remainder is schizophrenia. During the past ten years, another 96 "new long-stay" patients have accumulated - 67 per 100,000 total population. About one-third of these are suffering from dementia; schizophrenia accounts for another one-third.

Table 2 also shows the long-stay group on 31 December 1974 split up according to their status seven years earlier, in order to make comparison with Salford, where the case-register began operating with a census on 31 December 1967. It is clear that a new long-stay group of patients suffering from conditions other than Dementia is accumulating at approximately the same rates in the two areas.

Figure 1 shows in detail the build-up of a new long-stay group of Camberwell patients (omitting those with dementia). The three curves indicate the number of people who have become long-stay since the three given starting dates and are still in hospital at the end of each subsequent year. The hazards of predicting the future from curves of this kind are well-known (Fryers, 1973; Hailey, 1974) and the U.S. National Institute of Mental Health has been laudably wary of engaging in statistically-based speculation. There are several new case-registers in England, however, in rather different types of area (Nottingham, Oxford, Southampton and Worcester) and when data have been collected for five or ten years, it should be possible to make useful statements concerning the factors associated with a high or a low rate of accumulation of patients in psychiatric hospitals.

Meanwhile it is already clear from the Camberwell register that the accumulation of new long-stay patients is occurring not only in psychiatric hospitals but in alternative forms of accommodation such as day hospitals, day centers, sheltered workshops, hostels and group homes as well (Wing and Hailey, 1972).   Hassell et al (1972) have shown the same thing for psychiatric day centers in Birmingham, England.

It is therefore clear, both that the old long-stay group is not declining as fast as was expected and that a new long-stay group is still accumulating, though much less slowly than in former days. A very substantial part of the problem of providing alternatives to the mental hospital is concerned with the question as to whether it is possible to try to care for people who are at risk of becoming long-stay in some other way. Statistics are not

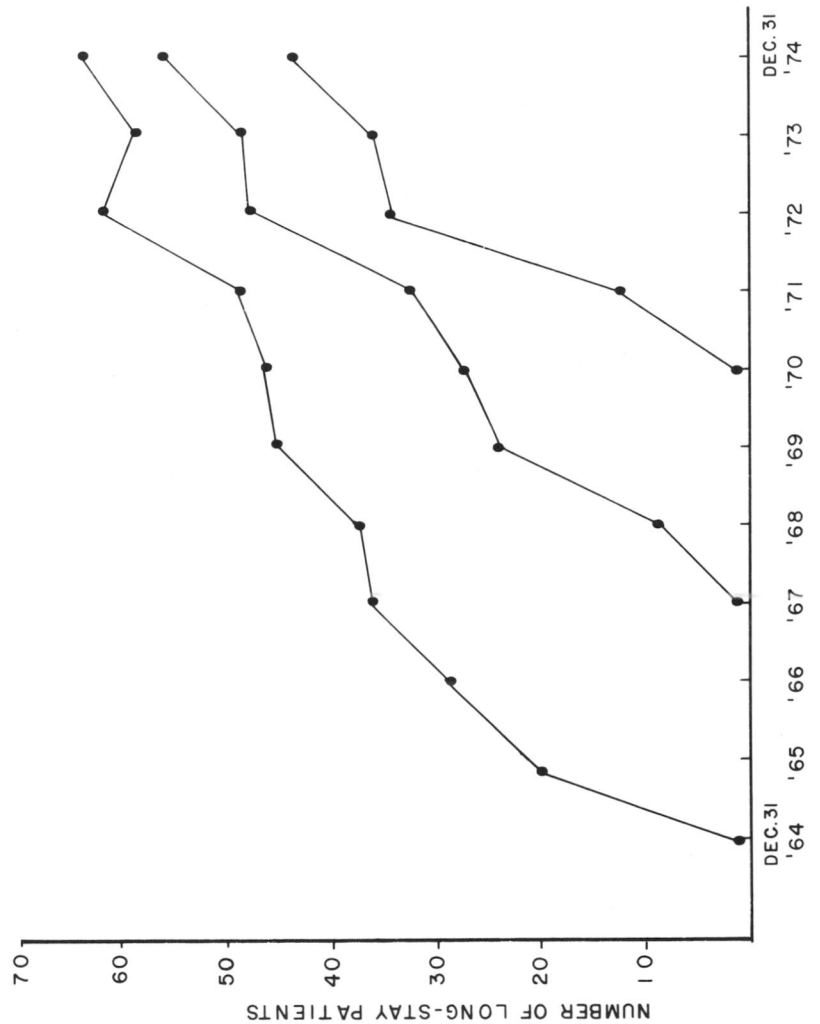

STARTING DATES

Figure 1.   Build-up of a new long-stay group in Camberwell
Hospitals, 1964-1974 (from Wing and Fryers, 1976).

the best way of investigating this question although they can provide useful pointers. Some of the more intensive work, often based on samples drawn from case-registers, carried out in the U.K. during the past 15 years, will now be reviewed. The great advantage of studies of the British services is that they can have an epidemiological basis. Nearly everyone who needs care can receive it from the national health and social services, irrespective of his or her ability to pay. In general therefore, there is less problem about service studies than there is in the U.S.A., where one is rarely certain as to what selective processes are at work.

THE OLD LONG-STAY IN MENTAL HOSPITALS

Much attention was paid to the needs of the long-stay population during the 1950's and early 1960's. Studies of institutionalism, rehabilitation and resettlement, particularly of patients suffering from schizophrenia, were reviewed in a paper read at Madison in 1964 (Wing, 1966a). It was clear from many experiments and surveys that long-stay patients were handicapped in several different ways. First, they had "intrinsic" impairments that were part of an illness. These were particularly evident in the schizophrenic syndrome of "clinical poverty" and thought disorder, and in the vulnerability to acute relapse which these patients showed. Social understimulation, characteristic of the poorer hospitals, made the clinical poverty syndrome worse, while emotionally neutral pressure from trusted staff could reduce the negative symptoms very considerably (Wing and Freudenberg, 1961; Wing and Brown, 1970). However, too eager attempts at socialization could actually precipitate relapse of symptoms that had not been experienced for many years (Wing, Bennett and Denham, 1964).

Just as important as these "intrinsic" impairments, were secondary disadvantages that accumulated as a result of the patient's illness and prolonged stay in hospital. These resulted in a deterioration in self-attitudes, in self-confidence, in social skills and in personal habits. The syndrome of institutionalism was described as the limiting case of one type of secondary impairment; at the heart of the syndrome was a gradually acquired preference for the institutional way of life, so that the individual no longer had any desire to live any other. Sometimes such a reaction could be regarded as protective and desirable, when intrinsic handicaps were severe enough to preclude any possibility of returning to ordinary life. Quite often, however, they had developed in people whose intrinsic handicaps were not insuperable or improved with the course of time. A county hospital not 100 miles from Madison provided extremely clear-cut evidence of the harmful effects of institutionalism in people labeled as schizophrenic although they would not have been regarded as such in England (Wing and Brown, 1970). It was amongst this group, and among those whose intrinsic impairments had while they were in hospital, so that the remaining handicaps were, in the main, secondary and extrinsic, that methods of social treatment directed towards the change of attitude and behavior through social pressure and example (Wing, 1960, 1966b; Wing, Bennett and Denham, 1964) were most successful.

Finally, there were the "extrinsic" disadvantages often accumulated by many long-stay patients before they were ever recognized as having schizophrenia. It is characteristic of all types of institutions that they tend to select and retain people who have poor social and vocational skills, poor social roots and little social support. This is true irrespective of diagnosis, although there is, of course, a tendency for some conditions, such as schizophrenia, to be associated with a disadvantaged "pre-morbid" personality. Correction consisted in trying to make up for these disadvantages by maximizing assets through extra education and training (Bennett and Wing, 1963).

It was the interaction of all three types of handicap that resulted in the unique condition of social disablement characteristic of each long-stay patient. Rehabilitation was seen to be a matter of setting up attainable and realistic goals, assessing the different kinds of impairment that hindered their achievement and then utilizing the knowledge gained from clinical experience and research to devise methods of decreasing handicaps, maintaining them at the lowest level possible, and increasing assets. It was recognized, for example, that phenothiazine medication was less necessary in a sheltered environment than in a stressful one, that some handicaps were permanent and that some patients living outside hospital were actually worse off than some who were resident. Moreover, even the best planned and executed programs of rehabilitation would not be able to compensate for the most severe handicaps and it had to be accepted that many patients could not be resettled outside hospital. What they needed was asylum, including not only somewhere to live and work but also space to wander about in without being in the public eye (Catterson, Bennett and Freudenberg, 1963).

In summary, by the mid-1960's, a body of knowledge and practice was accumulating that provided a sensible guide to the needs of people with long-term handicaps. Much of this knowledge was confirmed by studies of hospitals and hostels for the mentally retarded and aged (King, Raynes and Tizard, 1971; Townsend, 1962). The disadvantages of mental hospitals were well known; Belknap (1956), Dunham and Weinberg (1960), Goffman (1961) and Scheff (1964) had illustrated them in profuse and gruesome detail. Most important were geographical and social isolation, stigma or prejudiced labeling, institutionalism, pauperism, neglect and ill-treatment. Much of our knowledge about these problems and how to overcome them has come from studies of mental hospitals. What was less well understood

was that similar criticisms could be made, in certain cases, of
every other kind of protected environment, and that the principles
of prevention were the same.

In fact, at just the time that the problems of protected
environments were beginning to be understood, at least in the most
progressive hospitals (which were usually also in the vanguard of
the movement towards "community care"), the general climate of
opinion changed. There were many reasons for this but one of the
most important was over-optimism within the psychiatric profession.
It is easy now to say that the anti-psychiatry movement was responsible for a tendency to deny that handicap could be "intrinsic" in
psychiatric conditions, that it was in fact a creation of the very
institutions that claimed to treat it. In my view, the anti-psychi-
atrists took over and eagerly exploited views that were already
current in the profession, both in the U.S. and the U.K. However
that may be, it is clear that, in the early 1960's in England, the
emphasis began to shift away from the problems of chronically
handicapped people. It was assumed that, if sufficient attention
were given at the acute stage, chronic disabilities would be prevented. It was permissible for an English Minister of Health to
talk about bulldozing the mental hospitals several years before
anti-psychiatry became popular.

Since virtually no recent work has dealt with the problems of
the old long-stay, we can transfer our attention to those of the
smaller group that is still accumulating in spite of predictions
to the contrary.

THE NEW LONG-STAY IN MENTAL HOSPITALS

Mann and Sproule (1972) interviewed all the patients from the
Camberwell area, aged under 65 and not suffering from organic conditions, who had been in hospital between six months and three
years, and also their relatives. They found that nearly half were
suffering from schizophrenia and that the second most common condition was severe recurrent affective psychosis. More than one-
third still had active psychotic symptoms, such as delusions and
hallucinations. In contrast to what was found in previous studies
of long-stay patients (Wing and Brown, 1970), half of the group
expressed a wish to remain in hospital, indicating a comparatively
rapid onset of institutionalism; most probably due to the fact that
only highly selected and vulnerable people now become long-stay.
The patients' estimate of the welcome they would receive at home, if
they did leave hospital, was notably more optimistic than that of
their relatives; an observation which has been made many times.

Approximately a quarter of the 62 patients in the sample were
thought to need further treatment in hospital, with the hope that

improvement would eventually allow discharge. This proportion
became one-third if patients with a "security" problem were included;
that is, their behavior was such that there would be risk to them or
to their relatives if they were allowed outside hospital unaccom-
panied. Another quarter could be discharged to a hostel so long as
there was a fair degree of supervision. Such hostels were, however,
not available in the Camberwell area. The other patients needed
less supervised accommodation, such as group homes, or specialized
accommodation for the blind, physically disabled or mentally retarded. In a few instances they could go home.

In order to test these conclusions, a more extensive survey
was carried out (Mann and Cree, 1975, 1976). One hospital was
chosen at random from each of the fifteen regions of England and
Wales and a sample taken of all the patients who had been resident
between 12 and 36 months and were aged from 15 to 64. Four hundred
in all were interviewed. The two sexes were equally represented.
Two thirds were over 45 years of age. They were an isolated group,
less than half being visited regularly and less than one quarter
paying visits home. Most were single and those who were still
married were usually at odds with their partners or made no contact
at all. Nearly half suffered from schizophrenia. Affective psychosis and dementia made up about one third.

The views of hospital and local authority staff - doctors,
nurses and social workers - were canvassed in order to discover
why the patients had remained so long in hospital and what would
be the ideal arrangements supposing they could be made. The research team made a similar judgment on the basis of all the information available (see Table 3).

About one-third seemed to need hospital care, in the sense
that they presented disturbed behavior of the kind usually best
coped with by experienced nurses or were thought to be a danger to
themselves or others. About half were formally committed. In
most cases the diagnosis was schizophrenia and many patients still
had active symptoms of that condition. About half were thought
likely to respond to treatment and rehabilitation in due course
and then to be discharged in the usual way. The others had already
failed to respond to the full range of treatments available or they
seemed likely to relapse rapidly if discharged. For these groups,
the hospital was home as well as a place of treatment and shelter.
In spite of the fact that the architectural and social setting was
rarely domestic in scale, very few patients were enthusiastic
about the idea of leaving the hospital. This group represents 17
beds per 100,000 population but this is almost certainly an under-
estimate since no one with more than three years residence was
included.

Table 3

Judgement of research team concerning the most appropriate
accommodation for sample of new long-stay patients
aged 15-64 in mental hospitals in England and Wales, 1974

(Mann and Cree, 1976)

Accommodation required	%
Long-term in-patient	33.8
Supervised hostel	22.0
Less supervised accommodation	9.3
Unsupervised accommodation	5.3
Elderly frail	15.6
Other (multiple handicaps)	10.00
On extended leave	4.3

(N = 400)

A further quarter of the sample were thought to need supervised
residential accommodation but not necessarily in a hospital. The
commonest diagnosis was again schizophrenia but there were also
many patients with unstable affective disorders, for example frequently relapsing manic or derpessive conditions. Most were also
thought to need day care or sheltered work as well since they would
not be able to hold down a job in competition on the open market.
Many were schizophrenic patients with marked social withdrawal,
slowness, underactivity and lack of motivation. They needed to be
got up in the morning; it was important that someone should know
where they were during the day, and it would be necessary to provide
transport if they were to travel from hostel to day center. In
other words, twenty-four-hour supervision was needed, even though
the patient's time was divided between different night-time and
day-time settings.

Another 15% were thought by the research team to need less
supervised or unsupervised accommodation. They were more likely
to have had stable marriages and to have been living recently in
a family setting. Often they lived in "hostel" wards with minimal

supervision within the hospital. Yet another 16%, in spite of the upper age limit of 65, were "elderly" people with moderate or severe dementia of presenile type. The remaining 10% had a diversity of needs all of which are being met at the present time only by mental illness hospitals. Most were deaf, blind, epileptic, mentally retarded or brain damaged but had ended up in a mental hospital because they had also, at some time, had psychiatric symptoms as well. In other words, they had multiple difficulties. The mental hospital is still able to cope with such problems; very few of the alternatives are.

A final observation made in this survey is worth mentioning. There seemed to be a lack of a cohesive administrative structure, in which medical, nursing, social work and vocational skills could all be brought together to consider the problems of each individual patient who "graduates" to long-stay status, and at regular intervals thereafter, in order to make a considered judgment about his own wishes and needs and as to the best arrangements that could be made. It may, of course, turn out that the ideal arrangements non-existent. This is often the case in Britain today. Nevertheless, we shall never make progress unless the average service knows what ought to happen, even if it is not happening.

THE NEW LONG-STAY IN OTHER SHELTERED SETTINGS

It would be expected that, by now, a substantial body of research would have been built up to demonstrate the advantages that accrue when the educational, occupational, domestic and protective functions of mental hospitals are taken over by alternative agencies. In fact, such studies as these have been, in the main, descriptive rather than experimental, and are rarely epidemiological in nature, so that it is difficult to know how far the results can be generalized. Most of the English studies on hostels have been concerned with short-stay accommodation rather than with places where people with long-term handicaps are expected to make their homes.

Short-term hostels seem to be of limited value (Clark and Cooper, 1960). A national survey, including the 31 local authority hostels open in 1966, showed that all had been designed for rehabilitation purposes but the average daily occupancy was only 60%. In the 39 hostels studied by Apte (1968), out of a total of 725 places 41 per cent were occupied by people who had been resident for more than a year although only 6 of the hostels were intended to be long-stay. The three hostels described by Fletcher (1970) also contained mainly long-stay patients although two of them were called "short-stay."

The message conveyed by these studies is one of regret that
the intended short-stay hostels were not fulfilling their functions
of rehabilitation and resettlement. Mountney (1965) warned that
"transitional" hostels could become "almost a replica of the worst
aspects of old Institution life but at almost twice the cost." Apte
found that communications between hospital and local authority had
often broken down. The routine of the hostels was frequently based
upon administrative rather than therapeutic criteria. Occupational
and industrial therapy was the exception rather than the rule, there
were few organized recreational activities and many of the wardens
had "stereotyped and institutional attitudes." Some of the details
of hostel life are strongly reminiscent of those described by
Goffman (1961) as typical of "total" institutions. Apte even men-
tions that "a large number of the hostel-employed residents have
been in the home for several years and have become part of the
establishment" and comments on their similarity to "worker-patients."
Many other residents, who were working out, stayed in the hostels
long after they could have been discharged. Forty percent of the
hostels were classified as restrictive in regime and characterized
by a low expectation of responsibility in the resident (based on
scales similar to those used in Wing and Brown's study). Nearly
one-half of the residents were totally unemployed during their
stay in the hostels although employment opportunities at that time
were plentiful.

Thus in terms of social milieu and function, the hostels did
not appear to be as much superior to hospital wards as might have
been expected. They were, however, considerably smaller (on average
containing eighteen residents, though they were under-occupied) and
they were all within the area they served. They were pleasant and
home-like in appearance but Apte points out that this made discharge
more difficult. His most serious warning deserves quotation:
"Without a clarification of purpose, the half-way house could turn
into a diffuse and aimless institution, similar to the workhouse
of former years." This echoes precisely the reverse warning of
Early and Magnus (1966) who pointed out that if all its therapeutic
functions were removed, "the mental hospital will have become what
the workhouse was a century ago." Fletcher (1970) puts it like
this: "Some way must be found to avoid the development of new
chronic wards; isolated and forgotten in the middle of the community
as surely as they were at the back of the asylum".

We decided therefore to take a look at the hostel accomodation
being provided in our own area of south-east London. Three boroughs
- Lambeth, Southward and Lewisham - make up one "health services
area." The social service departments provided lists of all those
being financially supported in residential accommodation because of
mental illness. Only those aged 16-64 and who had not been suffering from mental retardation, organic conditions or addictions were

considered.   Of the 90 people meeting these criteria, 84 were living
in hostels and only six in group homes.   These 84 were living in 25
hostels, mostly provided by voluntary associations, scattered widely
over south-east and southern England.   Only 28 were living fairly
close to their former homes.   Most of the others were very far from
their home ground.   Community care clearly does not necessarily
mean local care.   However, we were agreeably impressed with the
quality of the accommodation provided.   Three-quarters of the
clients had been diagnosed as suffering from schizophrenia and
two-thirds were over 45 years of age.   They were a fairly solitary
group but most were holding down full-time jobs in open employment.
The rest were attending day centers.   Only 16 were in long-stay
hostels where outside work was not expected.   The rest were uneasily
aware that they were expected to move on, but most wanted to stay.
More than half had already been resident for over two years.

The social environment provided by these hostels seemed
reasonably non-restrictive, indeed permissive, according to our
measures.   We took a closer look at the few practices retained by
the majority of hostels that had been regarded by Apte as restrictive.   There were only five such items: staff liked to know where
residents were when they were away overnight or at weekends; residents did not have keys to their rooms; staff could enter rooms at
any time; staff called residents or checked that they were up in
the mornings; staff retained some control of medication.   On the
whole, we did not think that these restrictions were worse than
most people expect at home.   Total freedom from such constraints
is experienced only by people living quite alone.

The hostels we studied provided an environment that was socially
and economically sheltered.   Residents did not have to do their own
shopping, manage a financial budget or cope with all the problems
of running a household.   Their rent was subsidized.   They did not
have to compete for accommodation on the open market against non-
handicapped people with a much higher income.   Even so they were
often exhausted when they returned from work.   Those who lived near
relatives were able to keep up a sort of social life but in most
cases it was the family that stimulated this.   Some residents, however, did go out together (Hewett and Ryan, 1975).

Most local authorities in England do not support more places
than the three boroughs we studied, and this group was supposed to
move on to less sheltered accommodation.   This hostel group was
less handicapped than the equivalent group of new long-stay hospital
residents selected as being suitable for hostels.   The latter were
more socially withdrawn, slow and underactive and were unlikely to
be able to work in open competition.   Any provision for these
people has to be additional to, and somewhat different from, what
is already available.

Some areas in England have made a good deal of progress in setting up group homes, subsidized housing and boarding out schemes for
people with psychiatric handicaps. So far there has been no critical
evaluation of these alternatives although clinically they seem very
promising. However, it is impossible to be sure that the quality
will always be as high as in the hostels we studied. One of the
most enduring lessons of evaluative work is that the claims made on
behalf of services, like those made on behalf of treatments, can
never be taken at face value.

Very little research has been carried out on the need for daytime accommodation. Some years ago, it was established that the
sheltered factory system run by the Department of Employment, which
has 90 Remploy factories all over the country providing realistic
work for handicapped people, could be utilized by carefully selected
people discharged from psychiatric hospitals (Wing, Bennett and
Denham, 1964). There has also been some work on "enclaves" within
open industry but not enough to lay down guidelines about the numbers of places needed. The Soviet system is very much more advanced
in this kind of provision (Wing, 1974). The kind of work being
pioneered by Bennett in Camberwell will provide valuable information
as to the need for sheltered work opportunities in an urban area
(Bennett, 1976). Almost certainly it will be necessary to provide
a "Remploy" system for chronically handicapped psychiatric patients,
including the intellectually retarded, and that at least one day
center in each district should be upgraded in this way.

UNMET NEEDS FOR SHELTERED ACCOMMODATION

So far, we have been considering the needs of people who are
already receiving some form of care. Twenty years ago, when the
numbers of long-stay beds in mental hospitals was at its peak,
this could be assumed to cover most of the need. Nowadays, when
we talk about alternatives to the mental hospital, we have to
consider the state of all those who in the old days would have been
long-stay patients but now are not. Quite a lot of these people
are not in touch with services at all. Do they need to be?

Leff and Vaughn (1972) interviewed Camberwell people with
diagnoses of psychosis (mostly schizophrenia and mania) who were
either attending out-patient clinics or had been out of contact
for a year. Their medical condition was fairly well under control
but social problems (poor housing, unemployment, social isolation)
were often prominent.

Wing and her colleagues (1972; Stevens, 1972) studied a group
of patients who had been out of work for at least a year because
of psychotic conditions (mostly schizophrenia) but who had not
recently been in hospital. Rehabilitation was not very successful

but the need for sheltered residential accommodation was potentially
very high in this group, though it was not always immediately urgent.
Many were quite severely disabled, living with elderly relatives
and needing to attend day centers. However, the parents (often a
widowed mother aged 70 or more) were very worried as to what would
happen if they were no longer able to care for the patient, since
brothers or sisters were rarely keen to take on the responsibility.
The voluntary body recently formed to promote the interests and
welfare of schizophrenic people and their relatives, the National
Schizophrenia Fellowship, calls this the WIAG syndrome ("when I am
gone").

    If high quality residential accommodation were available nearby,
which the patient could begin to use while the parent was still
alive, retaining the links with home at weekends, holidays and evening visits, there might well be considerable call for it. There
were 25 such cases in the study, for an area of 170,000 people.

    Another indication of need is the number of handicapped
psychiatric patients who are found living rough or at soup kitchens
or in Reception Centers for the destitute. In one such center that
we studied, the largest in London, which happens to be situated in
Camberwell, some 8,000 men came and went during the year 1970.
Half of these were new and nearly one-quarter of them were suffering from mental illness (mostly schizophrenia). The other half
were known as "casuals," they had used the center before and were
expected to do so again. Of these, 14% were mentally ill. These
proportions take no account of alcoholism or personality disorder.
Table 4 shows the predominant impairment or problem of these 8,000
men. Clearly psychiatric problems were more important than any
other category (Tidmarsh and Wood, 1972).

    Destitute men tend, of course, to be solitary and friendless.
Those who had active schizophrenic symptoms at the time of admission to the center had usually been admitted several times previously to mental hospitals. Tracing their career back to the
first hospital admission, it was clear that nearly all had, at
that time, been living with their families. There is a strong
suspicion in England that part of the growing problem of destitution is due to the fact that mentally ill people are treated in
hospital, leave prematurely, drift gradually away from their
relatives, fail to keep jobs, and eventually are unable to support
themselves at all.

    These studies all combine to suggest that there is a greater
need for alternative forms of sheltered accommodation than is
apparent from a study of the existing services. This suggestion
is further reinforced by studies of patients who are living with
their relatives. Most of the recent scientific work has been

Table 4

Main impairment or problem of men attending the main London

center for the destitute during the course of 1970

Main impairment or problem	New Cases		Casuals	
	No.	%	No.	%
Mental illness	892	22	540	14
Alcoholism and addiction	553	14	1520	37
Personality disorder	680	16	800	19
Pathological gambling	90	2	140	4
Epilepsy	30	1	70	2
Physical illness	120	3	230	6
Old age	60	2	70	2
Migrant worker	60	2	120	3
Job problem	1145	29	420	11
Situational	370	9	90	2
Total	4000		4000	

(from: Tidmarsh and Wood, 1972)

concerned with chronic schizophrenia[1] and I will confine this brief review to that condition.

SCHIZOPHRENIA AT HOME

In view of the fact that the likelihood of someone with schizo-phrenia living at home instead of in hospital has been very greatly increased, it is surprising that few surveys have been made of the problems experienced by their relatives. A charitable society, the National Schizophrenia Fellowship, has recently been set up in the U.K., the object of which is to promote the welfare of sufferers and their families. This provided an opportunity to visit a sample

of fifty of the members at home. These were articulate and thoughtful people but quite unrepresentative, of course, because of self-
selection into the Fellowship. A comparison group of relatives of
schizophrenic patients living at home, was therefore drawn from the
Camberwell register, none of whom was a member of the Fellowship
(Creer, 1975; Creer and Wing, 1974). This group was also unrepresentative, but in the opposite direction, since they were all in
touch with services in an area where medical and social service
standards were high. Thus we can estimate upper and lower limits,
to the frequency of problems likely to be encountered, as seen
through the eyes of relatives.

Table 5 shows the frequency of various characteristics of
behavior. The commonest were those associated with the "social
poverty syndrome:" decreased social interaction, slowness, lack
of conversation, few leisure interests, self-neglect (Wing, 1961).
The most withdrawn tried to avoid all contact with other people.
One young man grabbed his cigarettes and dashed upstairs to his
room the moment the front doorbell rang. Others spent hours or
even days shut up alone in the bedroom, refusing to allow anyone
in. Some made an effort to interact with other people but found
they did not know how to go about it and became disheartened by
their failure. They had lost (or never acquired) the complex skills
needed for social interaction and could not behave in the manner
that was socially expected. Despite their avoidance of other people,
many patients craved companionship and felt deeply lonely. Often
their relatives were their only social contacts and they could be
very demanding.

Many relatives had tried to help by encouraging the patient
to join a club or to take up some other social activity but had
finally discovered, after years of trial and error, that all such
efforts were unsuccessful. A very common problem was the patient
who was unable to occupy himself during the day and had little
interest in anything, so that life was a long series of empty hours
stretching between breakfast and bedtime. Even those who were
occupied during the daytime, for example at a day center, tended
to be very lethargic in the evenings and weekends. For example,
one mother said:

"In the evenings you go into the sitting-room and it's in
darkness. You turn on the light and there he is, just
sitting there, staring in front of him. It's uncanny."

We obtained dozens of examples of this sort of behavior and
of the way that relatives had tried to cope. Some pushed too hard,
some did not push enough, some fluctuated from one extreme to
another, some found a means of response that seemed to be satisfactory for that particular family. What nearly all of them

Table 5

Behavioral characteristics of patients described
by two series of relatives

Characteristic	N.S.F. (N=50)	Camberwell (N=30)	Total No	%
Social withdrawal	38	21	59	74
Underactivity	30	15	45	56
Lack of conversation	27	16	43	54
Few leisure interests	27	13	40	50
Slowness	17	21	38	48
Overactivity	27	6	33	41
Odd ideas	22	5	27	34
Depression	19	8	27	34
Odd Behavior	22	5	27	34
Neglect of appearance	19	5	24	30
Odd postures and movements	19	1	20	25
Threats or violence	16	2	18	23
Poor mealtime behavior	10	-	10	13
Socially embarrassing behavior	5	1	6	8
Sexually unusual behavior	3	3	6	8
Suicide attempts	3	-	3	4
Incontinence	-	3	3	4

(from: Creer and Wing, 1974)

reported was that they had never received a word of useful advice from professional people, most of whom did not seem to recognize that the problem was a real and serious one.

Another major group of behavioral problems consisted of more obviously disturbed and socially embarrassing behavior. The most common example took the form of bouts of uncontrollable restlessness. A patient might pace up and down the room for long periods or round and round the table for an hour at a time. When these bursts of overactivity occurred at night they could place a great strain on the relatives' tolerance. Some patients would play the same pop record endlessly at a loud volume in the middle of the night. Others developed irrational ideas such as the man who would not go into his room because he thought there was a poisonous gas there or the woman who thought there were snakes under the bed. Yet others would sit through a meal silently laughing to themselves, or would swear out loud in public, or call on the neighbors and create a scene because of persecutory ideas.

Depression was not uncommon in the patients, particularly those who had some awareness of their condition. One young patient, in her early twenties, told her mother: "I would rather be a cripple than be like I am. I'm no use to anybody." Often a patient with a brother or sister who was married or successful in a career felt a failure by comparison. A number of patients had spoken about suicide or recently attempted it. We know from other studies that the suicide rate is greatly raised in schizophrenia (Wing L. et al, 1972).

As with social withdrawal, the relatives had tried all sorts of ways of coping with these problems, sometimes successful, often unsuccessful. Most had experienced anxiety, depression, guilt and anger by turns, and often these emotions were entirely appropriate to the situation. Many described how the unpredictability of the patient's behavior kept them "living on their nerves" or "living on the edge of a volcano." One elderly mother whose health was poor awoke each morning full of apprehension because she never knew from one day to the next how her son would behave or what mood he would be in. If she woke to hear him swearing and stamping noisily round his room she knew she was in for a bad time. Relatives frequently pointed out that those who have not lived in such a situation cannot really understand the kind of emotional state it induces. Obviously, a relationship of trust and sympathy between relative and patient facilitated the process of coping, but this was often only achieved after years of bitter experience on each side had shown the way (Stevens, 1973). By that time the patient might have left home of his or her own accord or been rejected by relatives (Brown, Bone, Dalison and Wing, 1966).

All sorts of difficulties with services were reported, even with getting help at the time of first onset, when preventive measures might perhaps have been most effective. Clearly, problems ignored are likely to multiply until the end result is a compulsory admission, which may initiate rigidly hostile attitudes in the patient. It is also traumatic for the relatives, who may feel enormously guilty at having put the patient into hospital against his will. Other specific problems mentioned included a lack of initial information, a dearth of guidance on management of medication and how to obtain various welfare benefits, a failure to consider the place of relatives in an overall plan of treatment, and scarcity of simple aftercare provision such as day centers and hostels. There was a general failure to realize that relatives are themselves important primary care agents, often with a greater awareness and experience of management problems than the professional people who are supposed to advise them.

We did not find that relatives, in general, were tetchy and complaining. On the contrary, the majority were tolerant and accepting in the face of problems that many people would find insupportable. In many cases, relatives and patients had discovered for themselves how best to limit handicaps, promote assets and achieve a life that had its pleasures and rewards as well as its disappointments. Such examples of positive coping suggest that the principles involved can be described and adapted for more general use. Moreover, many people did have some experience of successful coping. Services were not uniformly bad and everyone could think of individual professional people whose help was invaluable and specific situations in which a particular service performed its functions quickly, effectively and humanely. What was lacking was the maintenance of a uniformly high standard, with close coordination between different branches of the service.

A recent collection of essays by people who had themselves experienced schizophrenia "from within" (Wing, 1975a) opens another perspective on these problems. Inevitably, the most literate and articulate have to speak for the large majority of their fellow sufferers who find it much more difficult to express themselves. It is plain from these accounts that "sufferer" is the right word. With an effort of the imagination, it is possible to conceive what it must be like to have the experiences instead of just to read about them. Some of the authors are despairing:

"I have often felt that the mad cannot explain and the sane cannot comprehend."

"To me schizophrenia means 'living a lie'. Outwardly being cheerful, smiling, resourceful, but creeping away at night to try and lose myself deep within my being. Knowing that I will be frightened sometimes beyond what I can bear, wondering how bad it will get, how long I will be able to work, knowing that soon one way or another it must end."

Others have come to terms with their illness, learned to live with it and, in the process, learned how to avoid some of the most unpleasant experiences:

"Of course, there is a sensitivity in myself and I have to try to harden my emotions and cut myself off from potentially dangerous situations. For example, I now tend to avoid contact with people who antagonize me or whom I seem to upset. I sometimes find myself getting worked up about some topic - it might be something political or religious, or it might be the general stupidity of certain people's attitudes or behavior - and I then tell myself to cool down; to accept rather than attack. I am sure this is the right way for me to cope. At times like these, when I get worked up, I often experience a slight recurrence of delusional thoughts. I begin to notice coincidences which otherwise I should not have noticed. I might meet someone I hadn't expected to see. Then I might start testing some delusional theory. Let me see whether that car turns the corner behind me. If so, is it still there several turnings later? Then it must be following me! I now feel that I have sufficient knowledge of myself to know that this kind of thinking is dangerous. I can control my mind sufficiently to prevent such thoughts getting out of control and destroying my inner self."

Those authors who had found themselves able, through trial and error, to recognize danger and take appropriate avoiding action, were clear that they could manage without taking phenothiazines. I must emphasize, however, that this degree of insight is rare.

The question arises whether the trial and error approach used, willy-nilly, by relatives and patients, could not be improved upon; whether there is not some means of systematizing the various coping mechanisms so that both parties, separately but preferably together, could learn, if they wished to do so, what is the best way to live with schizophrenia.

Of course, the very question is anathema to some authors, who think that schizophrenia is caused by "society" in general or "the family" in particular. Theodore Lidz (1975) thinks that:

"The patient's emergence as an individual is thwarted by his subservience to the completion of a parent's life or to salvaging his parents' marriage."

"The families of schizophrenic patients fail in global ways to carry out the tasks requisite of the adequate personality development of their children."

"Their noxious influences upon the patient are not malevolent but rather the product of their own personal tragedies and egocentric orientations."

These confident conclusions are based on the study of seventeen hand-picked wealthy families. Lidz does not discuss any of the considerable body of scientific work that has tested those parts of the theory that are accessible to reason, perhaps because most of the results are negative (Hirsch and Leff, 1975).

There is, however, some work that may be of value to patients and relatives.

THE SOCIAL REACTIVITY OF SCHIZOPHRENIA

In the section on the "old long-stay", we discussed the re-activity of negative schizophrenic impairments to the social environment. One of the observations made during the course of those investigations was that too eager attempts at rehabilitation might lead to a recondescence of delusions and hallucinations that had been quiescent for years. In a subsequent study, it was found that too enthusiastic group therapy could have the same effect (Stevens, 1974). This observation may provide an important clue towards understanding what happens when a patient relapses outside hospital.

Our unit has now undertaken four studies of family factors associated with relapse in schizophrenia, each one tending to re-inforce the results of the others (Brown, Carstairs and Topping, 1958; Brown, Monck, Carstairs and Wing, 1962; Brown, Birley and Wing, 1972; Vaughn and Leff, 1976). The essence of the results is that living with a relative who is critical, hostile or emotionally over-involved is more likely to lead to a florid relapse than living with one who is uncritical and friendly or neutral in mood. Table 6 shows the result of the most recent replication, which also illustrates two other important facts. First, decreasing the amount of face-to-face contact between over-involved relative and patient has a protective effect. Second, if the patient takes phenothiazines, this also reduces the likelihood of relapse in those exposed to critical relatives, whereas in non-critical homes drugs did not seem so important.

We have shown in other studies that phenothiazine drugs do have the effect of preventing much relapse in schizophrenia (Hirsch et al, 1973; Leff and Wing, 1971). However, it is also clear that, as with all the other aspects of schizophrenia, there is an inter-action between disease and environment. In a protected setting there is less need for drugs than in a stressful one. This is true of both the hospital and the home environment (Wing, Leff and Hirsch, 1973).

The significance of the preventive effect of reduction in face-to-face contact between patient and critical relative (not with non-critical relatives), is that activities outside the home, even just attending a day center, may be sufficient to reduce the threshold of sensitivity. Patients may find their own techniques to reduce the amount of contact with an over-involved relative, such as sleeping by day and getting up at night or leaving home altogether. However, this can lead to exposure to the reverse kind of problem, a poverty of social stimulation, which leads, just as in a poor mental hospital, to an increase in negative impairments.

Table 6

A. Relationship between number of critical comments made by relatives at time of admission, medication after discharge, and relapse

No. of critical comments	% Relapse	
	Medication	No medication
High (6+)	25 (3/12)	78 (7/9)
Low (0-5)	- (0/0)	14 (1/7)

B. Relationship between number of critical comments made by relatives at time of admission, time spent in face to face contact per week, and relapse

No. of critical comments	% Relapse	
	Less than 35 hr.	More than 35 hr.
High (6+)	29 (2/7)	57 (8/14)
Low (0-5)	14 (1/7).	- (0/9)

(from: Vaughn and Leff, to be published)

We did not think that there was reasonable evidence that the parents in our studies were highly abnormal, still less that most were schizophrenic themselves. Many reacted unhelpfully to the patient but no one had shown them a more helpful reaction was possible. There is, of course, the possibility of a genetic link in some cases but many of the parents we came to know were far from the ogres they have been painted. Indeed, many provided the only hope the patients had of remaining out of hospital, and this in spite of considerable burden and stress to themselves.

Another kind of stress comes from everyday life events. Brown and Birley (1970) showed that schizophrenic patients were particularly vulnerable to events that most of us take in our stride; not just threatening and unpleasant events but virtually any major change within the patient's social life-space. They seem to have a lower threshold to stress than other people rather than responding to some specific kind of stress.

Thus we might sum up by saying that the schizophrenic patient has to walk a tight-rope, with different kinds of danger on each side. On the one hand is the danger that too much social stimulation will be experienced as an intrusion and will provoke the public expression of an abnormal thought content that might otherwise have remained private or below the patient's own experiential threshold. On the other hand, if the patient tries to avoid social stimulation, there is the danger of overdoing social withdrawal and increasing the negative impairments (Wing, 1975b).

Either of these unwanted consequences can occur in hospital settings, in hostels, day centers or at home. An understimulating social environment is most often found in old-fashioned mental hospitals. This does not mean it has to be characteristic of them or that it cannot occur elsewhere. The overstimulating social environment is most often found at home with an over-involved relative. This does not mean that all relatives are over-involved, or that a similar situation cannot occur elsewhere. As is so often the case in psychiatry, theorists tend to generalize from the particular kind of observation with which they are familiar without asking the crucial questions that would enable them to make a scientific test of their theory. Perhaps this tendency is not confined to psychiatry.

There is still a good deal more work needed on the ways the patients and relatives react to illness and chronic handicap. Some of the work concerned with social skills training and behavioral therapy may well be relevant (Argyle, 1974) particularly perhaps in relatives' and mixed patient-relatives' groups. Moreover, some of the structural features of the social environment must be taken into account. Thus social expectations of a handicapped person

living with his parents are quite different to those of a handicapped person living with a wife and family (Brown, Birley and
Wing, 1972). If professional people can approach these issues
humbly and compassionately, and not on the basis of a secret
consciousness of superiority, it might be easier to obtain the cooperation of patients and relatives and to learn from them in a
pragmatic way what the basic principles of management are. Denial
of real disability can only heighten suffering.

CONCLUSIONS CONCERNING ALTERNATIVES
TO THE MENTAL HOSPITAL

This paper has been mainly concerned with those functions of
the mental hospital that are concerned with the rehabilitation or
shelter of people with chronic psychiatric handicaps. Schizophrenia
is the acid test of any alternative services set up to take over
these functions but it is only one of the many groups of psychiatric
conditions that leads to chronic intrinsic impairments. Dementia,
organic psychoses, chronic affective disorders, obsessional neuroses,
personality disorders and chronic addictions are collectively even
more important.

The principles of rehabilitation are much the same as those
laid down in physical medicine. It is necessary to define the aims
of the patient and his social group, to assess the handicaps (intrinsic, extrinsic and secondary) that limit the achievement of
these aims and that collectively account for social disablement,
and then to devise techniques of overcoming them or compensating
for those that cannot be overcome. The principles are scientific
but their application in practice is an art.

The quality of life lived by the patient and his relatives is
the final criterion by which services must be judged. A good
hospital is better than a poor hostel or a poor family environment.
A good hostel is better than a poor hospital or a poor family environment. A good family environment is better than a poor hospital
or a poor hostel. The same may be said of daytime environments -
open employment, enclaves in ordinary commercial business, rehabilitation or sheltered workshops, or protected day centers. Universal
denunciation of any one type of setting is likely to be harmful
since it is clearly not based on rational principles of assessment,
treatment or care.

In England, the government has expressed an intention to move
away from the comprehensive mental hospital but to do so in a
gradual fashion. One of the most obvious problems is economic.
Running the alternative services is not necessarily more costly
than running mental hospitals but the initial capital cost of

creating the new environments does mean extra expense. Some saving
may be made by the use of volunteers (particularly relatives, who
often have a high motivation to help) and the training of nurses
and less qualified staff to take on important roles in the management of long-term handicap. Already community psychiatric nurses
have taken over a good deal of responsibility from psychiatrists
and others have shown that they can use simple behavior therapy.
The relations between social work and nursing services also need
complete re-thinking (CCETSW, 1974).

The possible disadvantages of protected environments have been
demonstrated mainly by studies in mental hospitals but it is now
clear that social isolation, stigma, institutionalism, pauperism,
neglect and ill-treatment can occur anywhere, in response to the
problems of handicapped people. Abolishing mental hospitals will
not abolish these evils. Hostels may be much larger than hospital
villas. Local authorities support people in nonhospital residential
accommodation far from their homes. The processes underlying the
development of "stigma" are little understood but no one who has
tried to open a small hostel for practically any category of disadvantaged person is likely to think that large mental hospitals
are the only cause of it. Like stigma, institutionalism is to
some extent inevitable with severely handicapped people who cannot
take on all the responsibilities of everyday life. Both institutionalism and stigma, however, tend to add unnecessary handicaps,
in the way of lack of self-confidence and a diminished desire to
achieve an optimally independent life, to those disabilities that
are already unavoidable. Pauperism and neglect have a similar
effect.

The inhumanities of Goffman's total institution are no more
acceptable if they occur in a respectable-looking house in a subur-
ban street than if they occur in a Victorian institution. The
same is true of exploitation and ill-treatment. A close study of
the few scandals that have occurred in British hospitals (DHSS,
1969, 1971, 1972) shows how easily they could occur in any setting
where severely handicapped and disturbed individuals are cared for
with little supervision of the staff. Small and geographically
scattered units might actually be at higher risk, because of lack
of supervision and low staff morale, than larger organizations with
strong professional traditions, good management and open communications.

The essential reasons for living in a protected environment
are nearly always social, since most psychiatric investigation and
treatment does not in itself necessitate a residential setting.
The main functions to be undertaken, apart from the obviously
medical ones, are supervision, active rehabilitation and shelter
(including long-term management). These may sometimes best be
carried out in a hospital setting. Once the acute condition has

improved but has left either residual disabilities (such as slowness and withdrawal in schizophrenia) or a vulnerability to various environmental stressors (often very clearly predictable in schizophrenia, in frequently recurring affective psychoses, and in severely disabling neuroses), a decision about discharge has to be carefully balanced, taking the patient's wishes and the social circumstances into account. If the patient is discharged too quickly the risk of relapse may be high with a consequent loss of confidence and motivation and increase of "stigma." On the other hand, if the patient stays too long he may come to appreciate the protection of the hospital too highly and fear to leave. A period of rehabilitation while still in hospital, particularly if environmental modification can also be effected during this time, may then be more beneficial than discharge to the care of some other agency (even if available). The supervision of seriously disturbed behavior is not likely to be challenged as a hospital function; at least, not by anyone who wants to take it over. This is traditionally a nursing function.

Another reason why rehabilitation as a resident may have some advantages has to do with the degree to which the patient's active, as opposed to his passive cooperation, is required. Chronic schizophrenic patients tend to be inactive. In a residential environment, it is possible to exercise certain of their motor and intellectual functions for them, since they will not usually refuse to attend a workshop if the whole group goes as part of the daily routine. If they have to catch a bus, or walk a mile or more, there has to be a certain initiative about attending and a certain ability to cope with unexpected events (what to do when the bus conductor has no change, or a policeman thinks the patient looks odd and questions him, or someone asks the way). Similarly, it is much easier to manage adverse reactions if the patient is in residence; the level of expectation, the hours of attendance and the alternative occupations available can all be manipulated so that the patient is never out of his depth and reassurance can continue when the patient is _not_ in a sheltered day setting. Above all, it is possible to keep in touch with the patient so that he can be reintroduced to the workshop as soon as it is feasible. The information available to day-unit staff is less complete since they often do not know what is going on when the patient is not in the unit and therefore cannot react immediately when something goes wrong or if the opportunity arises to advance another step. It cannot be too much emphasized how much can be lost in two or three days during which the patient does not attend a day-unit. The day-unit staff cannot, however, always be calling at the patient's home whenever his attendance lapses. Finally, there is the fact that a fairly large residential community can offer more opportunities for activation during leisure hours, a more varied social interaction and sometimes a higher standard of living.

These differences are partly responsible for the necessity, in the day-unit, always to be anticipating eventualities and always to be making sure that gaps and deficiencies in the services do not occur. A transfer to another unit, for example, is theoretically fairly simple in hospital, but may need a good deal of planning between different community agencies. The patient must be introduced to the new unit in advance. The staff there must know his level of functioning and not expect anything much higher or much lower. The date of first attendance must be absolutely clear to the patient, he must not be left at home doing nothing in between whiles, and if he does not turn up as instructed someone must immediately discover why. The staff of the new unit must know what kinds of adverse reaction could occur and be ready to deal with them. All this takes time and intelligent and coordinated planning on the part of two sets of staff. It is no wonder that it often goes wrong.

For all these reasons, clear rules, clear social structure, and a clear allocation of responsibility for decision-making seem to be particularly necessary in a day-unit. This may appear to be advocacy of a more authoritarian regime but it would be sad if it were thought that clarity of social structure was inevitably authoritarian. Maxwell Jones (1962) considers that the leadership of a therapeutic community should be charismatic but this can be one of the most uncritical and authoritarian kinds of leadership. A democratic system can operate without charisma; it allows criticism of leadership without obscuring the fact that someone must finally make decisions and take responsibility for seeing that they are carried out.

Our own government has made it quite clear that there is no intention to close a single mental hospital until the necessary alternative services are not only in existence but demonstrably working effectively (DHSS, 1975). That will take a very long time given our present financial circumstances. Meanwhile, we need to experiment with the provision of different models of sheltered care. For example, a range of units for handicapped people, occupational and residential, hospital and local authority, might be linked together functionally but scattered geographically over a convenient city area. Several adjacent houses with large gardens, perhaps situated in a residential square, might be linked to others within easy walking distance and yet others an easy bus ride away. Such a cluster of units could serve a wide range of functions for a sizable group of handicapped people, while retaining a domestic and human scale. The staff numbers would be sufficient to make communication, supervision and training feasible. Links between relatives and friends and with the sympathetic public would be simple. The use of family care, particularly on the Dutch model (Wing, 1957) and even the construction of one or two experimental

sheltered communities jointly between a hospital and a local
authority, should also be considered. Local authority day centers
also need re-evaluation. At least one in each area might be upgraded closer to the status of a Remploy factory.

When the mental hospital is in the center of its catchment
area, houses on the periphery of the site, with the front door
opening onto the public street and the back door opening on to a
private open space, would have considerable advantages.

Finally, I would emphasize the need for constant evaluative
research (Wing, 1974; Wing and Hafner, 1973). The more rational
we can be about the provision of services, as about the provision
of treatments, the less likely are we to be trapped into well-
meaning but ultimately harmful excesses such as saying that mental
illness does not "exist" or that all mental hospitals must be
abolished or that all hostels are simply backwards in the community
or that parents are the main cause of schizophrenia. Above all, I
hope that it will not come to be accepted, as Hallek (1966) and
Zwerling and Rosenbaum (1966) proposed in the last Madison symposium,
that community psychiatry is a subspecialty of psychiatry. If this
were true it would have totally failed (Rieder, 1974). Community
psychiatry is the ordinary practice of good psychiatry, in association with all the other services and professional skills that are
necessary. If the structure of services does not allow this
practice to be carried out effectively, acceptably and economically,
there is something wrong with that structure and it ought to be
changed.

Footnotes

1.   The term "schizophrenia" is used in a rather more restrictive
     way in Europe than America (Cooper et al, 1972; Wing, Cooper
     and Sartorius, 1974; WHO, 1973).

REFERENCES

Apte, R. Z. Halfway Houses. London: Bell, 1968.

Argyle, M. Explorations in the treatment of personality disorders
   and neuroses by social skills training. British Journal of
   Medical Psychology, 1974, 47, 63-72.

Belknap, I. Human problems of a state mental hospital. New York:
   McGraw Hill, 1956.

Bennett, D. The value of work in psychiatric rehabilitation.
  Soc. Psychiat., 1970, 5, 224-230.

Bennett, D. H. Alternatives to mental hospital care in Camberwell.
  To be published. University of Wisconsin Press, 1976.

Bennett, D. H. and Wing, J. K. Sheltered workshops for the
  psychiatrically handicapped. In H. Freeman and J. Farndale (Eds.),
  Trends in the mental health services. London: Pergamon Press,
  1963.

Brooke, E. M. International statistics. In J. K. Wing and
  H. Hafner (Eds.) Roots of evaluation: The epidemiological basis
  for planning psychiatric services. London: Oxford University
  Press, 1973.

Brown, G. W. and Birley, J. L. T. Social precipitants of severe
  psychiatric disorders. In E. H. Hare and J. K. Wing (Eds.),
  Psychiatric Epidemiology. London: Oxford University Press, 1970.

Brown, G. W., Birley, J. L. T. and Wing, J. K. Influence of family
  life on the course of schizophrenic disorders: a replication.
  British Journal of Psychiatry, 1972, 121, 241-258.

Brown, G. W., Bone, M., Dalison, B. and Wing, J. K. Schizophrenia
  and social care. London: Oxford University Press, 1966.

Brown, G. W., Carstairs, G. M. and Topping, G. G. Post-hospital adjustment of chronic mental patients. Lancet ii, 1958, 685.

Brown, G. W., Monck, E., Carstairs, G. M. and Wing, J. K. Influence
  of family life on the course of schizophrenic illness. British
  Journal of Prev. Soc. Med., 1962, 16, 55-68.

Catterson, A., Bennett, D. H. and Freudenberg, R. K. A survey of
  long-stay schizophrenic patients. British Journal of Psychiatry,
  1963, 109, 750.

Central Council for Education and Training in Social Work. People
  with handicaps need better trained workers. Paper No. 5.
  London: CCETSW, Clifton House, Euston Road, London. NWL 2RS,
  1974.

Clark, D. H. and Cooper, L. W. Psychiatric halfway hostel: A
  Cambridge experiment. Lancet i, 1960, 588.

Cooper, J. E., Kendell, R. E., Gurland, B. J., Sharpe, L.,
    Copeland, J. R. M. and Simon, R. Psychiatric diagnosis in
    New York and London. Maudsley Monograph No. 20, London: Oxford
    University Press, 1972.

Creer, C. Living with schizophrenia. Social Work Today, 1975,
    6, 2-7.

Creer, C. and Wing, J. K. Schizophrenia at home. National
    Schizophrenia Fellowship, 29 Victoria Road, Surbiton, Surrey
    KT6 4JT, 1974.

Department of Health and Social Security. A pilot survey of
    patients attending day hospitals. Stat. Rep. Series No. 7.
    London: H.M.S.O., 1969.

Department of Health and Social Security. Better services for the
    mentally ill. Cmnd. 6233, London: H.M.S.O., 1975.

Dunham, H. W. and Weinberg, S. K. Culture of the State Mental
    Hospital. Detroit: Wayne State University Press, 1960.

Early, D. F. and Magnus, R. V. Population trends in a mental
    hospital. British Journal of Psychiatry, 1966, 112, 595.

Fletcher, J. C. Mental health hostels: Progress and problems.
    Working Papers No. 2, Aylesbury: Buckinghamshire County Council,
    1970.

Fryers, T. Psychiatric in-patients from an urban community,
    1968-72. British Medical Journal, 1973, 2, 76-80.

Goffman, E. On the characteristics of total institutions. In
    D. R. Gressey (Ed.), The Prison. New York: Holt, Rinehart and
    Winston, 1961.

Hallek, S. L. Community psychiatry: some troubling questions.
    In L. M. Roberts, S. L. Hallek and M. B. Loeb (Eds.), Community
    Psychiatry. University of Wisconsin Press, 1966.

Hassall, C., Gath, D. and Cross, K. W. Psychiatric day-care in
    Birmingham. British Journal Prev. Soc. Med., 1962, 26, 112-120.

Hayley, A. M. The new chronic psychiatric population. British
    Journal Prev. Soc. Med., 1974, 28, 180-6.

Hewett, S. and Ryan, P. Alternatives to living in psychiatric
    hospitals - a pilot study. British Journal Hosp. Med., 1975,
    64-70.

Hewett, S. Ryan, P. and Wing, J. K. Living without the mental hospitals. Journal Soc. Policy, 1975, 4, 391-404.

Hirsch, S. R., Gaind, R., Rohde, P. D., Stevens, B. C. and Wing, J. K. Out-patient maintenance of chronic schizophrenic patients with long-acting fluphenazine: double-blind placebo trial. British Medical Journal, 1973, 1, 633-637.

Hirsch, S. H. and Leff, J. P. Abnormalities in parents of schizophrenics. London: Oxford University Press, 1975.

Jones, M. Social psychiatry in the community, in hospitals and in prisons. Springfield, Illinois: Thomas, 1962.

Joseph, K. Introduction. In R. Cawley and G. MacLachlan (Eds.), Policy for Action. Oxford University Press, 1973.

King, R. D., Raynes, N. V. and Tizard, J. Patterns of Residential Care. London: Routledge, 1971.

Leff, J. P. and Vaughn, C. Psychiatric patients in-contact and out-of-contact with services: a clinical and social assessment. In J. K. Wing and A. M. Hailey (Eds.), Evaluating a community psychiatric service. London: Oxford University Press, 1972.

Leff, J. P. and Wing, J. K. Trial of maintenance therapy in schizophrenia. British Medical Journal, 1971, 3, 599-604.

Lidz, T. The origin and treatment of schizophrenic disorders. London: Hutchinson, 1975.

Moss, G. R. and Liberman, R. P. Empirisism in psychotherapy: behavioral specification and measurement. British Journal of Psychiatry, 1975, 126, 73-80.

Mann, S. and Cree, W. New long-stay psychiatric patients: A national sample of 15 mental hospitals in England and Wales, 1972/3, 1976 (To be published).

Mann, S. and Cree, W. The "new long-stay" in mental hospitals. British Journal Hosp. Med., 1975, 56-63.

Mann, S. and Sproule, J. Reasons for a six-month stay. In J. K. Wing and A. M. Hailey (Eds.), Evaluating a community psychiatric service. London: Oxford University Press, 1972.

Mountney, G. Local authority psychiatric hostels. British Journal Psychiat. Soc. Work, 1965, 10, 20-26.

Rieder, R. O. Hospitals, patients and politics. Schizophrenia
    Bulletin, 1974, 11, 9-15.

Ryan, P. J. and Hewett, S. H. A pilot study of mental after-care
    hostels. Social work today, 1975. (To be published. November.)

Scheff, T. J. The societal reaction to deviance. Social Problems,
    1964, 2, 401.

Stevens, B. C. Dependence of schizophrenic patients on elderly
    relatives. Psychol. Med., 1972, 2, 17-32.

Stevens, B. Evaluation of rehabilitation for psychotic patients
    in the community. Acts Psychiat. Scand., 1973, 49, 169-180.

Stevens, B. C. The role of fluphenazine decanoate in lessening
    the burden of chronic schizophrenics on the community. Psychol.
    Med., 1973, 3, 141-158.

Tidmarsh, D. and Wood, S. Psychiatric aspects of destitution.
    In J. K. Wing and A. M. Hailey (Eds.), Evaluating a community
    psychiatric service. London: Oxford University Press, 1972.

Townsend, P. The last refuge. London: Routledge, 1962.

Vaughn, C. and Leff, J. P. Interaction characteristics in families
    of schizophrenic patients. (To be published.)

Wing, J. K. Family care systems in Norway and Holland. Lancet,
    1957, 2, 884.

Wing, J. K. A pilot experiment on the rehabilitation of long-
    hospitalized male schizophrenic patients. British Journal Prev.
    Soc. Med., 1960, 14, 173.

Wing, J. K. A simple and reliable sub-classification of chronic
    schizophrenia. Journal Ment. Sci., 1961, 107, 862.

Wing, J. K. Evaluating community care for schizophrenic patients
    in the U.K. In L. M. Roberts, S. L. Hallek and M. B. Loeb (Eds.),
    Community Psychiatry. Madison: University of Wisconsin Press,
    1966a.

Wing, J. K. Social and psychological changes in a rehabilitation
    unit. Soc. Psychiat., 1966b, 1, 22-28.

Wing, J. K. Psychiatry in the Soviet Union. British Medical
    Journal, 1974a, 1, 433-6.

Wing, J. K. The research worker. In G. McLachlan (Ed.), Positions, movements and directions in health services research. London: Oxford University Press, 1974b.

Wing, J. K. (Ed.) Schizophrenia from within. London: National Schizophrenia Fellowship, 29 Victoria Road, Surbiton, Surrey KT6 4JT, 1975a.

Wing, J. K. Impairments in schizophrenia: A rational basis for social treatment. In R. D. Wirt, G. Winokur and M. Roff (Eds.), Life History Research in Psychopathology Volume 4. Minneapolis: University of Minnesota Press, 1975b.

Wing, J. K., Bennett, D. H. and Denham, J. The industrial rehabilitation of long-stay schizophrenic patients. Med. Res. Council memo, No. 42, London: H.M.S.O., 1964.

Wing, J. K. and Brown, G. W. Institutionalism and schizophrenia. London: Cambridge University Press, 1970.

Wing, J. K., Cooper, J. E. and Sartorius, N. The description and classification of psychiatric symptoms: An instruction manual for the PSE and Catego system. London: Cambridge University Press, 1974.

Wing, J. K. and Freudenberg, R. K. The response of severely ill chronic schizophrenic patients to social stimulation. American Journal of Psychiatry, 1961, 118, 311.

Wing, J. K. and Fryers, T. Psychiatric services in Camberwell and Salford. Statistics from the Camberwell and Salford case-registers, 1964-1975. 1976 (To be published).

Wing, J. K. and Hafner, H. (Eds.) Roots of evaluation: The Epidemiologial basis for planning psychiatric services. London: Oxford University Press, 1973.

Wing, J. K. and Hailey, A. M. (Eds.) Evaluating a community psychiatric service: The Camberwell register 1964-1971. London: Oxford University Press, 1972.

Wing, J. K., Leff, J. P. and Hirsch, S. R. Preventive treatment of schizophrenia: some theoretical and methodological issues. In J. O. Cole, A. M. Freedman and A. J. Friedhoff (Eds.) Psychopathology and psychopharmacology. Baltimore: Johns Hopkins University Press, 1973.

Wing, L., Wing, J. K., Griffiths, D. and Stevens, B. An epidemiological and experimental evaluation of industrial rehabilitation of chronic psychotic patients in the community. In J. K. Wing and A. N. Hailey (Eds.), Evaluating a community psychiatric service. London: Oxford University Press, 1972.

World Health Organization. The international pilot study of schizophrenia. Geneva: W.H.O., 1973.

Zwerling, I. and Rosenbaum, M. Training for community psychiatry in a psychoanalytically-oriented department of psychiatry. In L. M. Roberts, S. L. Hallek and M. B. Loeb (Eds.), Community Psychiatry. Madison: University of Wisconsin Press, 1966.

THE CAMBERWELL DISTRICT PSYCHIATRIC SERVICES 1964-1974:

THE PROVISION OF ALTERNATIVES TO MENTAL HOSPITAL CARE

Douglas Bennett

The Bethlem Royal and The Maudsley Hospital

London, England

In the nineteenth century mental hospitals were conceived in hope and established by such convinced and dedicated reformers as Conolly and Dorothea Dix. More recently, in the 1950's, community psychiatry was hailed no less hopefully as an alternative and better form of care for the mentally ill. In the United States and in Great Britain, energetic attempts were made to implement the community policy and during the sixties hopes ran high. The stage seemed to be set for the successful development of community care for the mentally ill. Speakers at the Madison Symposium on Community Psychiatry in 1964 were enthusiastic and optimistic. "Whatever community psychiatry is, it has taken the profession by storm," said one speaker (Roberts, Halleck, & Loeb, 1966). But the storm seems to have blown itself out on both sides of the Atlantic. Last year in one of a series of articles on the defects of mental health services in New York State, Murray Schumach writing in the New York Times (Schumach, 1974) said that "the widely accepted theory that mental patients should be released from large institutions and placed in community facilities for rehabilitation-- a subject of bitter controversy--is now being viewed with important reservations by leading British experts who pioneered in this program." The article admitted that we in Britain still regarded the basic premises of this approach as sound, but suggested that we believed that patients should not be discharged when aftercare facilities were lacking and that many patients should never be released at all. Certainly there has been no wholesale discharge of patients from British mental hospitals and the run-down proceeds in a reasonably orderly way. But in our two countries criticism takes different forms. In Britain, psychiatrists doubt whether

psychiatric units in district general hospitals, which are supposed
to replace the mental hospitals, can cope with all patients or with
all forms of psychiatric disorder. There is much argument about
the number of beds to be provided in these hospital units and doubts
expressed about the successful financing of alternative community
services by the government and local authorities. Some psychiatrists
believe that, with the manpower available, patients will only receive
first-aid care and also doubt whether psychiatrists will find it a
satisfactory vocation to work in such services (Mental Health
Service, 1972; NAMH, 1974; & Policy for Action, 1973). They often
rationalize their fears of change with nostalgic and sentimental
talk of "some quiet refuge of trees and fields with friendly people,"
which is their idea, if not Goffman's, of an asylum (Annotation,
1973). As I understand it, the feeling in the States is that many
pay lip service to community psychiatry to secure state and federal
funds. Doubts are expressed whether the provision of community
mental health centers has reduced the admission of patients to state
hospitals. Finally, there has been criticism of the lack of provision for those mental patients discharged, perhaps hastily, from
state mental hospitals which have been closed.

Whatever the truth of all these assertions, it is clear that
doubt and criticism have replaced hope and confidence. So it is
opportune to reconsider whether the belief that it is possible to
provide alternatives to the mental hospital is mistaken, or whether
it is a sound proposition which has been misinterpreted and mis-
handled.

The early enthusiasm for extra institutional care was aroused
by the pioneer services in Amsterdam, Nottingham, Chichester,
San Mateo and elsewhere (Carse, Panton & Watt, 1958; MacMillan,
1956). However, there has been little attempt to evaluate these
services and when it has been undertaken, the results have not
always been encouraging (Brown, Bone, Dalison, & Wing, 1966). So
the question remains: is it possible to provide adequate and
effective alternatives to the mental hospital? It is obvious that
the answer must depend on the evaluation of a community service
where new methods of care are being pioneered and where, of course,
facilities for evaluation are available.

THE EVALUATION OF AN ALTERNATIVE SERVICE

It seemed that the Bethlem Royal and the Maudsley Hospitals
(which jointly constitute and compose one hospital, usually
referred to as the Joint Hospital) and the Medical Research Council
Social Psychiatry Unit, located at the Institute of Psychiatry
nearby, were well placed to undertake this task. What follows is

an account of a service which has begun to provide alternatives to
the mental hospital; describing how it was conceived, how it has
developed, what has been accomplished so far and what evaluation
shows.

The Joint Hospital is neither a district general hospital nor
a mental hospital in the usual sense of those terms. It is a
university psychiatric teaching hospital for post-graduate students,
but it is equipped to contribute the hospital element of a district
psychiatric service. The Maudsley half of the Joint Hospital is
situated in an inner London suburb. As a university teaching
hospital it has always admitted selected patients who are thought
to be of interest for teaching and research. These patients come
from any part of Britain or abroad, although most of them were
from the southeast of London. Patients who exhibited difficult
behavior or were less intelligent, or who had previously failed to
respond to treatment were not excluded, but they were less likely
to be admitted. When the potentialities of treatment were "exhausted" (Blacker, 1959) and the patients became chronic, they
were referred to the appropriate mental hospital. The Joint Hospital
took no responsibility for patients from a particular population or
catchment area and it did not admit legally committed patients.
However, it seemed that if these policies were changed, there was
no reason why it could not provide a service for a defined population, in association with the health authorities and the social
services, complemented by local voluntary organizations.

Community psychiatry had been defined by members of the Royal
Commission on the Law relating to Mental Illness and Mental
Deficiency in 1957. They described it as the increasing emphasis
on "forms of treatment and training and social services which can
be given without bringing patients into hospitals as inpatients,
or which make it possible to discharge them from the hospital
sooner than was usual in the past." (Royal Commission, 1957) In
1964, at the Joint Hospital, community psychiatry was still regarded in this way and seen principally as the treatment of the
adult mentally disordered patients as outpatients, as day patients
or in their own homes. But these views were changing. Sabshin
(1966) defined community psychiatry as involving "the utilization
of techniques, methods, and theories of social psychiatry and
other behavioral sciences to investigate and meet the mental health
needs of a functionally or geographically defined population over
a significant period of time and the feeding back of information
to modify the central body of social psychiatric and other
behavioral science knowledge." As the Joint Hospital began to
consider the possibilities of providing a district service for
teaching and research, it was Sabshin's views which informed our
practice rather than those of the Royal Commission. It was clear

that we had to offer a service to a defined population over an
indefinite period of time.

CAMBERWELL AND ITS PSYCHIATRIC SERVICES

The then borough of Camberwell, within whose borders the
Maudsley Hospital is sited, was thought to provide a very suitable
population. Its people are not a community in the sense that they
have any close historical, commercial or social links; but they
could be defined in geographical terms. This population, which
grew rapidly as a working class suburb in Victorian times, is
now in slow decline. In 1966, the population was 172,000 but it
is now perhaps 145,000. In 1965 the borough lost its administrative identity when it was merged with two other boroughs to form
the new, larger borough of Southwark. Camberwell now constitutes
the southern two-thirds of the new borough and is rather better
off than the northern third in respect of its parks, open spaces
and the quality of its housing. The old borough was a socially
stable area compared with other London boroughs. It was in the
average range for poverty and delinquency; there were less people
than average living alone in hotels and lodging houses and a
greater proportion of the population were London born. Rates for
divorce and suicide were relatively low.

The implementation of this new Camberwell psychiatric service
was imposed on a background of a rather complicated pattern of
services built up over the years (Wing, Bennett, Hailey, Isaacs &
Tidmarsh, 1972). This was fully revealed when the Camberwell
Register was established in the latter part of 1964 (Wing, 1971).
The Register is a data linkage system which collects and reports
information about all Camberwell residents, whether adults or
children, who suffer from mental illness or mental retardation and
who are in contact with the psychiatric services. Contacts with
the social services departments have been studied from time to time
but patients' contacts with family doctors are not recorded. The
Register commenced its operation with a census of all patients
with a Camberwell address and contact with the psychiatric services
as defined above on the 31st of December 1964 (Table 1). On that
day there were 559 psychiatric inpatients. These were found in a
number of traditional mental hospitals in the London area but the
majority of patients were in one mental hospital, Cane Hill Hospital. This was a large Victorian institution, fifteen miles from
the Camberwell area. The presentation will be simplified by
assuming that all the long-term inpatients were accommodated there.
So when it is said that 408 of the long-stay patients were in the
area mental hospital, what is meant is that the bulk of them were
in Cane Hill Hospital, but that some such patients were in a number
of other similar hospitals. Most of the short-stay patients--

110 out of 151--were also in this mental hospital. Only 35 short-
stay mental patients were in the Joint Hospital. A further six
patients were resident in an Emergency Admission Unit at St. Francis
Hospital. This Unit, staffed by Maudsley doctors and situated in
a geriatric hospital, provided at that time an emergency service
for the whole of London. The geriatric wards at St. Francis Hospital did not admit psychiatric patients.

Table 1

Number of Camberwell Patients in Contact with In- and

Day-Patient Services on Three Census Days

Type of Service	Number of Patients on Census Days					
	12-31-64		12-31-69		12-31-74	
Inpatients for MORE than 1 year						
Mental Hospital (Cane Hill)	406)		314)		228)	
University Clinic (Maudsley)	2)	408	7)	326	5)	246
District Treatment Unit (St. Francis)	-)		5)		13)	
Inpatients for LESS than 1 year						
Mental Hospital	110)		39)		26)	
University Clinic	35)	151	69)	163	100)	157
District Treatment Unit	6)		55)		31)	
		559		489		403
Day Patients						
Maudsley Day Hospital	14)		15)		26)	
Maudsley Rehab. Workshop	-)		9)		22)	
District Treatment Unit	-)	36	8)	86	22)	139
Local Authority Day Center	16)		46)		59)	
Private Workshops	6)		8)		10)	
TOTAL inpatients and day patients	595		575		542	

The majority of outpatients were attending the Maudsley Hospital but many also attended King's College Hospital--a general teaching hospital which had a psychiatric service. So at the end of 1964 the Joint Hospital, while seeing most of the outpatients, was making only a very modest contribution to the care of mentally ill inpatients from the Camberwell area. The Maudsley also had a day hospital which, on the census day, had 14 Camberwell patients. During the previous two years negotiations with the local authority health and mental health departments had led to the establishment of closer working links and the setting up of two day centers which, at the census, accommodated 22 Camberwell patients.

So, in 1964, Camberwell had a traditional service in which patients with recent illness and a good prognosis were admitted to a university psychiatric hospital while those who needed readmission or were chronically disabled went to the traditional mental hospital. During 1965 and 1966, the development of the service was slowed by local government change, by changes in the local hospital organization, by administrative delay and by the usual reluctance for change among individuals and institutions. During this time, however, decisions were made about the policies to be followed and the changes which should be made to provide a useful service. It must be made clear that in line with British practice, the Camberwell service did not aim to provide primary psychiatric care. This is usually given by the family doctors in the area (Shepherd, Cooper, Brown & Kalton, 1966). Nor was it intended to concentrate services on the discharged long-stay patients from the mental hospitals. Of course, when we came across such patients we accepted their care. But we did not intend to uproot the long-stay patients in Cane Hill or the other mental hospitals and try to resettle them in the community. At the same time we would do all we could to assist the resettlement of individual patients who had some chance of managing outside the mental hospital.

PSYCHIATRY IN THE BRITISH HEALTH SERVICE

Before describing the aims of our service it is necessary to say a few words about the British scene, and place our service in its social and political context (Bennett, 1972). At the end of the last war it was accepted that it was a proper function of government to ward off stress and strain, not only amongst the poor, but amongst all classes of our society. Sir William Beveridge's plan to combat the evils of want, disease, ignorance, squalor and idleness was implemented in a series of enactments which led to what we now call the Welfare State. In an attempt to deal with disease, the National Health Service was established as one limb of this body. In this service, psychiatrists, like other doctors, were salaried. The service brought all the hospitals, whether general or mental, formerly managed by local bodies, under the same regional and national direction. Everyone is eligible for treatment, without additional payment, in both psychiatric and physical hospitals. But the difference in the quality of care given to the mentally disordered and the physically ill and the difference in terms under which people were eligible for treatment in these two services was so great that quite soon the whole question of legal commitment was referred to a Royal Commission (Royal Commission, 1957). Their inquiry and recommendations led to a new Mental Health Act which was passed by Parliament in 1959. This Act made it possible for the mentally ill person who could accept the role of patient to be admitted to a hospital without the formality of commitment. Committal when needed was rare and today less than 17% of all admissions to our psychiatric hospitals are compulsory. In 1971 the Social Services Act placed all social workers under the management of the social service departments of the local authorities. This development grew out of the appreciation by social workers and government that the existing social services were responsible only for certain types of social problems. It was felt that human need could not be categorized in such an arbitrary fashion, so it was decreed that social workers should give up such former specialties as mental health, child care and social welfare, and merge these into departments which would provide a unified family service. While some people regret the disappearance of the former mental health and psychiatric social workers, the new departments provide a useful social counterpoise to the medically oriented psychiatric service. So when we plan alternatives to the mental hospital we have a National Health Service which finances our hospitals, our family doctors' service and our community service from the same source. On the other hand, the administrative discontinuity between health and social services makes some necessary teamwork difficult.

AIMS OF THE CAMBERWELL PSYCHIATRIC SERVICE

In setting up the service our aims were pragmatic rather than utopian. No one knew what form the service should take or what provision would be required. Such evaluations as were available indicated that alternative care might be less satisfactory than mental hospital care (Brown, Bone, Dalison, Wing, 1966). But it was thought possible to eliminate some of the errors of the mental hospital system as these had been shown to increase the disablement of schizophrenic patients (Wing & Brown, 1970). So our approach was informed by Karl Popper's principles of "piecemeal social engineering" and "negative utilitarianism" which suggests that relief of suffering has priority over the promotion of happiness (Popper, 1945). In other words, we sought to eradicate, in a

piecemeal fashion, those features of the former services which
caused distress or disablement to patients, rather than to promote
"mental health." We had a general strategy but we depended on the
Camberwell Register to give us a clear perspective of what was, or
was not, being done for which patients and where this was happening.
Of course, the Register could not tell us what we should do nor
how we should do it. But when we had made our decisions and our
piecemeal changes, information from the Register showed what the
effects had been. We were anxious to provide a service alternative
to the mental hospital for the mental hospital's traditional
patients. There is no doubt that in the process we recruited
patients who would never have sought the services of a mental hospital. But our prime concern has been those patients who cannot,
or will not, function independently in society. We also recognized that we had to continue to protect society from the severely
socially deviant or dangerously disordered patients. This care
requires new forms of accommodation and these will be described
below. But accommodation is not enough. Community psychiatry is
not just a matter of where treatment is given or by whom. We
need to consider new ways of doing things. Although there was no
wish to interfere with the freedom of choice of patients or their
doctors, it seemed reasonable that the Camberwell service should
be rationalized so that patients could receive treatment nearer
their own homes. The advantages of this were not just geographical
although this emphasis is important in the development of day care.
One of our aims was to care, not for the defined patient alone but
for a population over a significant period of time. One has to be
aware of those who contribute to the patient's illness or who are
put at risk by it. Our approach may be pragmatic, but we try to
use the facts gained by social psychiatry and the behavioral
sciences in recent years and are very aware of the ways in which
the social environment in the home and the hostel, as well as in
the hospital, can influence the mental state of patients as well
as the course of their psychiatric disorders (Wing, 1971). Some
doctors seem to think that, with the disappearance of the mental
hospital, psychiatric disabilities too will go away. Most doctors
involved in the Camberwell district services have always believed
that however good the treatment given, in some patients mental
illness would progress to persisting disability; so rehabilitation
has always been given a relatively high priority in our plans.
When we speak of rehabilitation we do not think of it as a time-
limited once-for-all process of refurbishment. It is not like this
for most psychiatric inpatients; for them, it is a continually
repeated process of readaptation to changing demands for role
performance in a continually changing social environment. Many
of our patients become ill and are readmitted when their fragile
social adaptation breaks down. For others, of course, it is a
recurrence of illness that shatters their adjustment. In either

case, admission to hospital for "treatment" and discharge from hospital after "cure" is often totally inappropriate if nothing is done to support the patient in the community or to facilitate his adjustment. This has been shown in physical illness by Ferguson and MacPhail (1954) while in 1920, Varrier-Jones recognized that the failure to do this with tuberculous patients led to a process of discharge and readmission which in psychiatry today we know only too well as the "revolving door." Varrier-Jones called it "a game of cat and mouse," and saw it as a cruel game, too (Woodhead & Varrier-Jones, 1920).

Our final principle might be called "the use of the minimal institutional dose" or the support of "the maximum role performance." This means that we look very carefully at all demands for a haven and asylum and ask what the patient would gain from it, compared with what he would lose in terms of his social role or his coping capacity. Similarly, placement of disabled persons in any social environment or in any service should be seen in these terms. It is only too easy to move a mental hospital ward nearer to the High Street and call it a hostel. This is not community psychiatric practice as envisaged in Sabshin's definition.

IMPLEMENTATION OF THE CAMBERWELL SERVICE

We had to ask ourselves how these aims were to be implemented. To date most British pioneers of alternative services have worked in county boroughs which have a compact population of about 250,000 (Carse, Panton & Watt, 1958; MacMillan, 1956). Such a borough was the responsibility of one local authority, and had unified health and social provision, including one mental hospital responsible for that area alone. When developing new community services, these hospital psychiatrists still retained responsibility for their same catchment area and their present and former patients. In our situation none of the hospitals was responsible for the Camberwell area alone. All admitted patients from other areas. Further, we were planning to move provision from a mental hospital which, as we have seen, was doing the bulk of the inpatient work, to other hospitals and services nearer the catchment area. If our plan was going to work we had not only to understand what was happening in all parts of the service; we also had to have some responsibility in each part. To achieve this the author, who is on the staff of the Bethlem and Maudsley Hospital, and a psychiatric colleague, Dr. Anthony Isaacs, who was at that time on the staff of the mental hospital, were given staff appointments in all the major units serving Camberwell patients. Thus, I received an honorary appointment in the Joint Hospital, while we both received honorary appointments at King's College Hospital and St. Francis

Hospital.   We were both members of the Southwark Medical Officer of
Health's psychiatric advisory committee.   Some of the social workers
who worked with us were jointly appointed with the Borough of Southwark and the Maudsley and St. Francis Hospitals.   These arrangements,
made in 1967, gave us the opportunity, with the active cooperation
of many hospital psychiatrists, social workers and family doctors,
to redirect patients away from the mental hospital and into other
services when possible.   Although other contemporaneous changes
played their part, the effect of this activity can be seen in
Table 1, where census data are recorded, and in Table 2, which
shows changes in the number of admissions to the various hospitals
between 1964 and 1974.   The exercise required some tact and patience
and a willingness to be on call at nights and at weekends, if we
were to prevent and correct the inevitable misunderstandings and
misdirections, as well as problems of over- and under-referral.
Doctors are jealous of their prerogative of admission, and they
are not very willing to check patients' addresses from street lists.

        Although we doubted that the mental hospital could survive
in the long run, we avoided any anti-institutional over-reaction,
for we both had responsibility in each hospital and in most parts
of the service.   We could not dispose of patients, we could only
refer them to ourselves in another setting.   Even so, we frequently
had to resist the wish of staff, in one or other unit, to dispose
of some particular patient to a ward or bed for which we were
responsible.   When transfer did take place it gave us the opportunity to see how patients who might be difficult in one setting
prospered in another.   So while we were quite clear that we hoped
to phase out the traditional mental hospital, we recognized, as
members of its staff, that it would be with us for some time to
come.   We had to consider the steps to be taken in moving care,
based on the mental hospital, to a system centered on other units
and other services.   In many cases this had led to patients being
discharged from hospital before other forms of care were available.
This had resulted in public resentment and outcry, for local
authorities had not always been willing to provide alternatives
until forced to do so by the discharge of patients.   It was not our
policy to concentrate on the discharge of patients from the mental
hospital, but instead to provide services which gave them the help
they needed without admission.   At first this community provision
was incomplete and patients slipped through the coarse mesh of our
"alternative net" into the mental hospital.   The mental hospital
remains as a back-up service and will do so until it is no longer
needed.   This is less hazardous than discharge for disabled long-
stay patients.   If discharge is to be successful, patients need
long periods of rehabilitation before they can adapt to a more
independent life outside hospital.   Further, experience had shown
that new provision was rarely there when one needed it.   It did
not always materialize, or it was delayed, or it did not arrive in

Table 2

Camberwell Admissions to Hospital Year by Year

	1965	1966	1967	1968	1969	1970	1971	1972	1973	1974
Cane Hill	345	330	297	187	155	96	63	72	49	47
St. Francis	103	98	128	266	251	259	230	209	176	154
Maudsley/Bethlem	197	187	238	331	373	410	398	467	410	487
KCH, Guys	6	8	17	5	56	44	65	86	59	44
Other mental hospitals	79	49	44	33	31	45	56	46	70	35
St. Francis geriatric unit	-	-	-	-	-	11	26	12	18	12
TOTAL	730	672	724	822	866	865	838	892	782	779

the planned order. As a psychiatrist, one may have some control
over hospital planning, but one has little or no say when community
organizations are involved. Doctors and patients need community
services, but they have to use existing services until new provision
is made.

Fortunately, in Camberwell there was no headlong rush of
patients from the mental hospital. At times we were anxious lest
those responsible for the mental hospital should ask us to accept
the care of a large number of discharged chronic patients; but it
never happened. So there was only a slow but continuing drift of
patients away from the mental hospital and we were able to pursue
our policy of progressively reducing admissions there. At first
we provided district care for the less difficult and less disabled
patients. Slowly, everyone, patients, staff, families and not
least ourselves, began to adjust to the new way of doing things,
and we were able to increase admissions to the Maudsley and
St. Francis Hospitals. But other changes were needed too. First,
the Emergency Admission Unit at St. Francis was closed for some
months. It was reopened as a District Psychiatric Treatment Unit
for Camberwell patients with recurrent, or chronically disabling,
psychiatric conditions who would have a relatively short stay.
Then it was agreed that the number of patients admitted to the
Cane Hill mental hospital should be progressively reduced. After
1970, admissions were limited to not more than 45 in one year. As
we shall see later, most of these were of elderly patients suffering
from organic mental syndromes. Then a new Vocational Resettlement
Unit was opened to provide the later pre-settlement stages of
rehabilitation for disabled patients. The earlier stages of rehabilitation were undertaken in the wards of the Maudsley from which
patients proceeded to the day hospital and then on to the Vocational
Resettlement Unit which was situated next door (Bennett, 1972).
This unit provides facilities usually associated with a government
Employment Rehabilitation Center. It offers disabled psychiatric
patients preparation and practice in paid clerical, manual and
machine work in a 38-hour week. The effects of these changes can
be seen if one compares the disposition of patients between
December 1964 and December 1969 (Tables 1 and 2). While the
pattern of admission had been altered, the census data show that
there were now a few long-stay patients at the St. Francis district
treatment unit and at the Maudsley. We were moving slowly, for a
sudden change was not only likely to produce a backlash from the
community but also from the university teaching hospital. Fears
were certainly expressed that, if the Joint Hospital were involved
in a service providing an alternative to the mental hospital,
chronic patients would replace those needed for teaching and research
and these activities would suffer accordingly. However, persuasion
within the hospital, alterations in the health services and changes

in government policy, together with the passage of time, led to an acceptance of the change. By 1970 the Board of Governors of the hospital accepted responsibility for providing a hospital service for mental illness for the adult population of Camberwell. During the same year it also decided that the Joint Hospital would accept patients committed on compulsory orders. These decisions reversed long established practice. The Joint Hospital had never had a catchment area and the freedom to admit any suitable patient, regardless of his domicile, was considered to be an essential prerequisite for the maintenance of high standards of teaching and research. To encourage patients to seek early treatment the Maudsley, from the time it opened, had never accepted committed patients. Any patient who required compulsory treatment had always been referred to the St. Francis Emergency Admission Unit. These policy changes increased Camberwell admissions to the Joint Hospital, reduced admissions to Cane Hill mental hospital still further, and began to change the function of the St. Francis District Treatment Unit.

Patients had been redirected from the traditional mental hospital. Table 2 shows that over the 10-year period, admissions to the mental hospital have been reduced, although the total number of short-stay patients (less than one year) resident on census days remains the same (Table 1). This seems to confirm the view that there is little difficulty in moving the care of short-stay patients from the mental hospital to a district psychiatric unit. But we have to ask how the service is helping the chronic disabled long-stay patients. For these patients offer the most searching test for any service which claims to be a satisfactory alternative to the mental hospital. It will be seen in Table 1 that over the 10 years, 1964-1974, there has been a significant decrease in the number of long-stay patients, due largely to a reduction in the number of "old" long-stay patients   (Table 3). These are the patients who, in our terminology, already had an uninterrupted hospital stay of more than one year at the time of the initial Register census in 1964. It can be seen that their numbers had suffered slow attrition and this has occurred more by death than by discharge. Most of the 150 patients who now remain are not suitable for resettlement because of their age, or their disability. We anticipate they will live out the rest of their lives in the mental hospital. This, then, is a suitable point to introduce two further principles of our alternative service: to decentralize care and to treat people where "they ought to belong." For example, we believe that most of the "old" long-stay patients belong in the mental hospital. If not exactly a home, it has been their residence for long years. They have grown accustomed to it and often attached to some other patients and members of staff. It would be no great kindness to uproot them now. It is possible to illustrate further

Table 3

Patients in Hospital One Year or More on

December 31 (Each Year)

Census Date	Original "Old" Long-Stay Group	"New" Long-Stay	Total
December 1964	408	--	408
December 1965	369	36	405
December 1966	330	57	387
December 1967	295	72	367
December 1968	275	69	344
December 1969	250	76	326
December 1970	232	74	306
December 1971	208	74	282
December 1972	193	91	284
December 1973	167	95	262
December 1974	150	96	246

our aims, and our way of implementing them through a discussion of the "new" long-stay hospital patients. While a number of "old" long-stay patients in the mental hospital has been decreasing, a number of "new" long-stay patients has accumulated (Table 3). They are the patients who demonstrate the limits of our treatment and rehabilitation and show that psychiatric disability is not due to "institutionalization" alone. They show that while there may be alternatives to the mental hospital, there is at present, for them, no alternative to some form of hospital care. We have seen that the "old" long-stay patients who remain in hospital have had

more than a year's continuous hospital stay <u>before</u> December 31,
1964.   These "new" long-stay patients have had more than a year's
continuous hospital stay since December 31, 1964, and are still in
residence.   They are not all those who have stayed in hospital a
year in that period.   They are not a fixed or static group.   Members
are continually leaving hospital while new members are being added
to their number.   After the initial rise in 1965 and 1966, their
number reached a plateau.   This seemed to be constant (Table 3).
But between 1972 and 1974 the number of these patients has risen
again.   A very few are patients who, because of physical illness,
have been transferred from the mental hospital to a general hospital for treatment for a period greater than 30 days.   On transfer
they are discharged from the mental hospital but when they recover
physically they are readmitted as "new" patients.   One year later
they become "new" long-stay patients.   While this practice is
correct according to the Register's rules, it inflates the numbers
of "new" long-stay patients by the inclusion of those patients
whose "old" long-stay has been interrupted.   This does not account
for the whole of the increase; nor does it affect the total of
long-stay patients.   But it may mean that for planning purposes,
the number of the "old" long-stay group should be slightly higher
and the number of "new" long-stay patients rather lower.

     This group of patients has been carefully studied and reported
by Dr. Anthea Hailey (1971, 1973 & 1974), Dr. Sheila Mann (1972 &
1975),   and Professor John Wing.   More recently, with the assistance
of Dr. Lorna Wing and Miss Jane Hurry, I looked at those who had
become "new" long-stay since December 31, 1970:   that is all those
patients admitted between December 31, 1970, and December 31, 1974,
who stayed more than a year and were still in residence on the
latter date.   Their numbers naturally are less than the "new"
long-stay patients remaining since December 1964.   But this smaller
population is representative of those for whom the Joint Hospital
assumed responsibility in 1970 and for whom it will have to provide
inpatient care.   They cannot be resettled in work or life for they
are too disabled, and are too antisocial or lack skill or sufficient
community support.   A few are dangerous to others and need secure
provision.

     The needs of the 65 patients who make up this "new" long-stay
group are varied.   Thirty-four of them are aged over 65 and are
disabled by senile dementia.   All 34 are in the mental hospital and
all but four of them are women.   Their numbers may seem large.   Even
so, Wing and Hailey have shown (1972) that the number of elderly
Camberwell patients admitted with organic dementia who have a long
stay has reduced over the years.   In 1964, twenty-five patients
admitted suffering from dementia stayed a year, in 1966 fifteen
patients, in 1968 twelve patients and in 1970 only nine patients

had a year's stay. This may have been due to the increasing
attention paid to the care of such patients in the community,
with excellent back-up services provided by the social services.
The St. Francis geriatric hospital has a day hospital which accepts
many of these patients if they have associated physical disorder,
while volunteers have established other day centers and luncheon
clubs. Geriatricians look after many patients with organic
dementia for Copeland (1975) has shown that 28% of a sample of
Camberwell patients in the geriatric section of St. Francis
Hospital have this diagnosis. A unit developed at St. Francis in
1971 to decide whether a particular patient was the responsibility
of the geriatrician or the psychiatrist, has greatly improved
communication and cooperation between the specialties. It is now
a firm plan to site a unit for the elderly mentally infirm patients
with organic dementia in the geriatric section of St. Francis
Hospital--for that is where we think these patients should belong.

     Of the other 31 "new" long-stay patients, 16 (11 men and 5
women) are suffering from schizophrenia or its residual disabilities.
Their disabilities vary greatly in type and in severity. Five can
be said to be very disabled. In spite of all treatment they remain
deluded and hallucinated. They cannot look after themselves and
need nursing supervision because of their slowness, their tendency
to self-neglect, or because they wander or cause social nuisance.
Two constantly irritate other patients by stealing cigarettes.
One has caused annoyance by exposing himself and another has been
accused of interfering with a small girl. They need supervision
and limited security. A further six are less seriously ill and
might in time improve or manage in a protected environment outside
the hospital. Another two patients are in Broadmoor, the only high
security hospital in England and Wales for so-called "criminal
lunatics." One further patient has been discharged from Broadmoor
and is making a rather precarious adjustment in the mental hospital.
Two women, although they were newly admitted to a year's hospital
stay during this period, were over 60 and had already spent many
years in a mental hospital. They had tried to live with relatives
or in hostels but could not manage. Their social disposition was
really with the "old" long-stay patient group in the mental hospital.
There are 15 other patients, most with vulnerable personalities,
who were experiencing, or had experienced, considerable social
stress and who exhibit rather atypical affective symptoms. Only
one of these patients who suffers from pathological jealousy had
been in Broadmoor. Ten of these patients are at present in the
mental hospital (including the two patients over 60 years of age
who are really long-stay). The rest are now in the district
psychiatric units as illustrated in the 1974 census data in
Table 1. This is not necessarily their final disposition for "new"
long-stay patients are continually being discharged as facilities

for after-care and day care are extended.   At the same time we are planning new forms of hospital provision.

FUTURE PLANS

A decision has been made to experiment with two new units which will be provided on the Maudsley Hospital campus.

The New Chronic Unit

It has been found that when chronic patients with schizophrenia are treated in the Joint Hospital, they become very isolated; for while other patients come and go, they remain. Special provision is needed, therefore, for those new patients who will be in hospital for more than three or four years. Of course, they need medical and nursing supervision in a ward, but since they will have to stay for such a period, they are entitled to comfort and privacy rather than the "pathological togetherness" of ward life in a mental hospital. It was decided to put them in a house and this has led to some confusion. Some have queried whether it is really a hostel. It is not. It is a "ward in a house." This ward will accommodate about 15 long-stay patients who require this type of care and we hope it will open in April 1976.

The District Services Center

Some people believe that the worst result of mental hospital stay was not "institutionalization," but that admission constituted a "final disposal" for many patients. There is some evidence for this. Donovan and Wilson (1971) found that if mentally infirm old people were admitted to the unit for elderly people with both physical and psychiatric disabilities, they were more likely to be discharged than if they were admitted to the mental hospital. So for the less disabled "new" long-stay patients we shall try to keep their options for treatment and social placement open, by caring for them in the same facilities as the short-stay patients. It has been assumed by the government that the treatment of all mentally disordered patients will be centered on psychiatric units in district general hospitals. This is questioned, since it seems doubtful whether such units can deal either with aggressive, anti-social and immature personalities, or with patients with the chronic disabilities of schizophrenia. Even if the present district general hospital units are limited in this way because of their setting, design or facilities, there is no reason why they could not be redesigned. So an attempt is being made to design a unit

which will not only meet the needs of acutely disturbed patients
but those "new" long-stay patients who need rehabilitation. It
will be built on the Maudsley Hospital site and will combine and
replace the present functions of the District Psychiatric Treatment Unit at St. Francis Hospital and the Day Hospital at the
Maudsley. It will accommodate 70 day patients and a further 42
inpatients. The purpose of the building is to enable patients to
be treated, rehabilitated and cared for by the same hospital team,
whether they are outpatients, daypatients or inpatients. For there
is no longer a clear-cut distinction between the needs of patients
who are in hospital, attending as daypatients or outpatients or
being supported while living at home. A person is no longer ill
and in hospital or well and out of hospital. At any moment in
time a patient must be treated in the most appropriate situation,
according to his behavior, his capabilities and his family's
ability to cope with him. Yet, at present, the care given by the
hospital service is often fragmented between male and female wards,
the day hospital, outpatient and other departments. Nor is it
integrated with the help provided by community resources. Inef-
ficient care is inevitable. In the new building there will be no
wards. It will be used as a day hospital with beds and will be
designed to remove some impediments to continuous personal care,
effective teamwork and continuity between medical and social work
with the patient and his family. This District Services Center
is expected to open early in 1978.

Hospital Unit for the Elderly Mentally Infirm

It has already been indicated that we are planning wards in
the St. Francis Geriatric Unit for these patients, as soon as the
patients from the Psychiatric Treatment Unit have moved into the
new District Services Center.

ALTERNATIVE PATTERNS OF CARE

Of course the success of an alternative service does not
depend on new buildings alone. The critical task is the care of
both the "old" and the "new" long-stay patients. Experience
shows that many staff find it difficult to accept the care of
patients who do not show rapid and significant improvement. There
is a natural tendency to separate curable from incurable and
desirable for undesirable patients. This would not matter so much
if it did not lead to the less seriously ill being treated by the
most highly trained staff while the most disabled are left to
those less trained. The movement of patients from the mental hospital could make this situation worse, for a time. It is natural

that recoverable patients are likely to be treated outside the
hospital but this inevitably leads to a greater concentration
of the less desirable and less treatable patients in the institution. Our new facilities are designed to counteract that tendency,
but success depends largely on staff attitudes. Every now and
again through the years since 1963, one has looked at some particularly difficult patient with a seemingly hopeless problem and
longed for, or even accepted, the easy solution of mental hospital
admission. But when there is no substitute to district service care,
and no escape from responsibility it concentrates the mind and one
gets to work. When chronic patients are viewed from a distance
they are often seen as a sad and faceless crowd. But when one
reconstructs their individual histories and becomes familiar
with them as disabled people, it is possible to think of useful
and even ingenious approaches to their difficulties. Morale and
staff competence are always necessary but, when there is no mental
hospital admission, they are essential. For the mental hospital
has always buttressed society and its own staff against many of
the anxieties which we all experience when dealing with explosive
emotions, unpredictable behavior and other frightening or dis-
tressing situations. It is not possible to develop the point
fully here but it is not unimportant. Symptoms of this anxiety
can be seen in the present day concern in Britain about secure
provision in psychiatric hospitals. Without the mental hospital
we have to find new ways of containing staff anxiety as well as
to develop new systems of social control.

SECURITY

The secure containment and care of patients who are dangerous
or cause distress to the public has always been an essential part
of the mental hospital's function. We accept this responsibility
in the Camberwell service, although it is not too easy to fulfill
our obligation at present. For at the same time as staff, and
particularly nursing staff, are beginning to reject these functions,
the courts and the public are anxious to hand the care of aggressive
or antisocial people to psychiatrists. As a result, difficult or
aggressive patients who are not accepted by the hospitals accumulate
in prisons or in Broadmoor. The government's solution is to construct regional medium-security units in association with psychiatric hospitals. One cannot say whether this is a sound idea.
But only four of our "new" long-stay patients had, at some time,
needed a high degree of security. Two continue to need this.
The other two, although they cause some anxiety from time to time,
are at present managed without it. These were not the only patients
who had been in Broadmoor. Two other "new" long-stay ex-Broadmoor
patients have been successfully discharged during the four-year

period of the study and are at present being followed up in the
community. A few other patients need only a very limited degree
of security. About eight might require the occasional hindrance
of a locked door, depending on the number of staff on duty, the
time of day and the design of the unit. One has to accept that
while the open door is best for most patients, a small proportion
will need some slight physical check on their freedom, at least
for a time.

COMMUNITY RESOURCES

Up to this point we have concentrated on hospital aspects
of the Camberwell district service. But there are other services
outside the hospital which are themselves alternatives to mental
hospital care. They can also influence the part hospital services
play. These services have differing functions for both the individual and for society, and if they are to be used effectively these
differences must be understood. Some services are relatively
controlling, some are more supportive and some are a mixture of
the two. They all help to maintain social integration and social
order. Clients approach these services with difficulties which
have been classified by Cumming (1968) as transition states, role
failures, and contingencies. We all encounter those problems of
adjustment, which are included under the heading of transition
states, such as marital misunderstandings, bereavement and lone-
liness in old age; some are transient and resolve themselves with
time. Contingent problems depend largely on the organization of
our society and its defects and include such difficulties as
insufficient income and temporary unemployment. Their correction
usually depends on concrete resources. Role failure stems in
part from within the individual. Under this heading Cumming includes the problems of those who are unable to get along with
others, or hold a job, or are deviant or dangerous.

Camberwell, like all communities, has a large number of
agencies, charities, clubs, welfare organizations, public assistance offices, doctors and hospitals, lawyers and policemen, clergy-
men and churches, which all help people with such problems. Some
deal mainly with contingencies; others with role failures or
transitional states. Some with a mixture of all three. We are
naturally interested in the supportive and controlling services
for those who have role failure which is due to mental disorder.
For, in general, it is these community services, rather than those
which deal with contingent problems or transitional states, which
prevent recruitment of the psychiatric hospital's "new" long-stay
patients. They are the services which reduce the mesh of the net
through which the patient would otherwise slip into the mental
hospital.

Our National Association of Mental Health recently ran a campaign which urged that the disabled mentally ill should be given "a job to do and a place to live." It is their incapacity to play many of the roles of everyday life which has combined with the contingencies of housing and employment to bring some of the psychiatrically disabled into mental hospitals and keep them there. Only local authorities or private charities have the resources to meet these concrete needs in our district. First the local authorities have developed day centers for the psychiatrically disabled as well as for the subnormal and the elderly with senile dementia. Many of those who at present attend these centers have been assessed in the hospital rehabilitation services, where it has been decided that they are too disabled to be capable of either open or sheltered employment. In a day center they are occupied but they do not receive treatment as in a day hospital. The importance of occupation for patients with schizophrenia has been demonstrated by Wing and Brown in their well-known studies. Occupation was the only factor in the patients' social environment which could be correlated with a reduction in primary disability (Wing & Brown, 1970). Regular attendance at a day center also reduces the amount of time which a patient with schizophrenia spends with his family, and the consequent risk of relapse and readmission to a mental hospital (Brown, Birley & Wing, 1972). Of course, only about 38% of those attending day hospitals, centers and workshops, suffer from schizophrenia. What is more important is that the growth in day care population parallels the reduction in long-stay hospital inpatients. Further, 44% have a stay of one year or more (Table 4) (Hailey, 1974).

These figures are very similar to those of Cross and his colleagues in Birmingham who found that 40% of their day care patients had a long stay and 36% suffered from schizophrenia. There were less patients with senile psychosis in day centers in Camberwell than in Birmingham (Cross, Hassall, & Gath, 1972; Hassall, Gath, & Cross, 1972). So, many patients, who might have become long-stay inpatients, are now in long-term day care. They are better off because they do not have to accept a deviant role which cannot be reversed (Erikson, 1962). Instead they are able to obtain help as disabled persons while still retaining other roles in society (Erikson, 1957).

Sheltered employment for the psychiatrically and physically disabled patient is provided by Remploy Limited--a government sponsored agency. A number of patients from our service are employed by this organization. But to extend these facilities, a voluntary body, the Camberwell Rehabilitation Association Limited, has been established. Its aim is to "enable the psychiatrically and physically disabled to become economically independent through paid employment." The first project of this organization has been

Table 4

Camberwell Residents Attending Day Hospitals,

Day Centers or Workshops for One Year or More.

Day Patients	Census Date										
	Dec. 1965	Dec. 1966	Dec. 1967	Dec. 1968	Dec. 1969	Dec. 1970	Dec. 1971	Dec. 1972	Dec. 1973	Dec. 1974	
Original Group	18	11	11	10	5	4	4	4	3	3	
"New" Long-Stay	--	5	21	15	33	39	46	48	49	59	
Total	18	16	32	25	38	43	50	52	52	62	

the establishment of a sheltered workshop which will eventually
employ 20 or more disabled workers. This follows the present
trend in vocational rehabilitation by offering sheltered work,
which is subsidized, to both the physically and psychiatrically
disabled. While in our community there are many hostels, boarding houses and other forms of accommodation, we know that patients
with "role failure" have great difficulty in finding somewhere
to live. In London and some other great cities, such patients have
to fall back on rather sordid rooms in Reception Centers and common
lodging houses. In other parts of the country local authorities
offer hostel living to some of the mentally ill. This has not
happened in Camberwell although the Borough of Southwark has two
hostels for the mentally retarded. The only special accommodation
for the adult mentally ill has been provided by two charitable
Housing Associations. One is a Catholic Housing Association
sponsored by the St. Vincent de Paul organization. It is supervised by resident staff and accommodates about twenty extremely
disabled women in two houses. The Windsor Walk Housing Association
was established about three years ago on the initiative of staff
on the Joint Hospital. It rents 17 bedsitting rooms in two houses.
There are no resident staff but a manageress visits the houses two
or three times a week and when necessary can be contacted by the
men and women residents. This Association, which is subsidized
by the local authority, is purchasing another house for a hostel
which will have more staff supervision. Studies undertaken in the
area had shown that while 19 patients who had been in hospital
between six months and three years required "comparatively unsupervised" hostel accommodation, seven required a hostel with supervision (Mann & Sproule, 1972).

CONCLUSION

The Register figures show the changing pattern of care in
Camberwell. The numbers of patients who stay in hospital less
than one year are unchanged, but the majority are now treated in
the district hospitals. Admissions to the mental hospital have
been considerably reduced, as to a lesser extent have the numbers
of long-stay patients in residence on census days. The overall
admission figures have remained approximately the same and the
increase in Maudsley admissions almost equals the decrease in
Cane Hill admissions. The census figures show a reduction of
"old" long-stay inpatients and an increase in "new" long-stay
patients and long staying day care patients. So it seems that
as far as hospital services are concerned, we have transferred
the care of patients from the mental hospital to the district
services rather than reduced the numbers needing hospital care.
On the other hand the numbers of long-stay mental hospital

residents are being steadily, if slowly, diminished. While these
figures demonstrate the slow, but progressive, move from the
mental hospital to alternative forms of care, they do not tell us
whether these alternatives offer better or worse care for the
patient then the mental hospital. This would require a study of
a group of patients drawn from the whole sample along the lines
described by Brown, et. al (1966). The mental hospital is no
longer the only service for the mentally ill. It is still a part
of the service but it is no longer at the center. This is not surprising, for it is difficult to believe that today a vigorous,
innovative, community-centered service could be run from a Victorian
institution which has come to house aged and forgotten people. With
a changing service come changing aims, for patients and staff. One
is not even seeking the closure or abolition of the mental hospital
unless it is replaced and thus rendered obsolete. For while the
site and the nature of treatment and care have changed, we are still
caring for a like number of patients with similar disabilities. If
there is no mental hospital many psychiatric patients will still
need some form of hospital care.

    What is apparent from this account is the slow pace of change.
Doubtless this could and will be speeded up in some communities,
but one must doubt whether it will ever be very rapid. For although
one talks of social engineering, it must be remembered that one is
not dealing with inanimate objects, but with human beings who have
vested interests, and who answer back. Perhaps it is this slowness
of change which has dulled the optimism and stirred up the doubts
about community psychiatry; or it may be that in the absence of
feedback from a Register, people have despaired when they have not
been able to see and recognize what is really taking place. Yet
our experience, and the figures, seem to show that we are beginning
to provide a pattern of service which is an effective alternative
to the mental hospital. In Camberwell we have not achieved this
fully yet but the possibility seems to be within our grasp.

REFERENCES

Annotation. Back to the "bin." Lancet, 1, pp. 527-528, 1973.

Bennett, D. H. Principles underlying a new rehabilitation workshop
    in Evaluating a Community Psychiatric Service, pp. 275-282.
    Wing, J. K. & Hailey, A. M. (Eds.) London: Oxford Univ. Press,
    1972.

Bennett, D. H. Community mental health services in Britain.
    Amer. J. Psychiat., 130, pp. 1065-1070, 1973.

Bennett, D. H., Birley, J. L. T., Hailey, A. M., & Wing, J. K.
   Non-residential services for the mentally ill, pp. 141-158,
   in Evaluating a Community Psychiatric Service. Wing, J. K.,
   & Hailey, A. M. (Eds.) London: Oxford Univ. Press, 1972.

Blacker, C. P. Mentally infirm people over sixty-five. Published
   by Board of Governors, The Bethlem Royal and the Maudsley
   Hospital, London, 1959.

Brown, G. W., Birley, J. L. T., & Wing, J. K. The influence of
   family life on the course of schizophrenic illness. Brit. J.
   Psychiat., 121, pp. 241-258, 1972.

Brown, G. W., Bone, M., Dalison, B., & Wing, J. K. Schizophrenia
   and social care. Maudsley Monograph No. 17, 1966. London:
   Oxford Univ. Press.

Carse, J., Panton, N. E., & Watt, A. A district mental health
   service. The Worthing experiment. Lancet, 1, pp. 39-41, 1958.

Copeland, J. R. M., Kelleher, M. J., Kellett, J. M., Barron, G.,
   Cowan, D. W., & Gourlay, A. J. Evaluation of a psychogeriatric
   service: the distinction between psychogeriatric and geriatric
   patients. Brit. J. Psychiat., 126, pp. 20-21, 1975.

Cross, K. W., Hassall, C., & Gath, D. Psychiatric day care. The
   new chronic population? Brit. J. Prev. Soc. Med., 26, pp. 199-
   204, 1972.

Cumming, E. Systems of social regulation. New York: Atherton
   Press, 1968.

Donovan, J. F., William, I. E. I., & Wilson, T. S. A fully
   integrated psychogeriatric service. Chapter 10 in Recent
   Developments in Psycho-geriatrics. Kay, D. W. K. & Walk, A.
   (Eds.), 1971.

Erikson, K. T. Patient role and social uncertainty--a dilemma of
   the mentally ill. Psychiatry, 20, pp. 263-274, 1957.

Erikson, K. T. Notes on the sociology of deviance. Social Problems,
   9, pp. 307-314, 1962.

Ferguson, T., & MacPhail, A. N. Hospital and community. London:
   Oxford Univ. Press, 1954.

Hailey, A. M. Long-stay psychiatric inpatients: a study based
   on the Camberwell Register. Psychol. Med., 1, pp. 128-142, 1971.

Hailey, A. M. The chronic mental hospital population: a six-year
    follow-up study. Brit. J. Prev. Soc. Med., 27, pp. 255-260,
    1973.

Hailey, A. M. The new chronic psychiatric population. Brit. J.
    Prev. Soc. Med., 28, pp. 180-186, 1974.

Hassall, C., Gath, D., & Cross, K. W. Psychiatric day-care in
    Birmingham. Brit. J. Prev. Soc. Med., 26, pp. 112-120, 1972.

MacMillan, D. An integrated mental health service. Lancet, 11,
    pp. 1094-1095, 1956.

Mann, S., & Cree, W. The "new long-stay" in mental hospital.
    Brit. J. Hos. Med., 14, pp. 56-63, 1975.

Mann, S., & Sproule, J. Reasons for a six-months stay, pp. 41-76,
    in Evaluating a Community Psychiatric Service. Wing, J. K. &
    Hailey, A. M. (Eds.) London: Oxford Univ. Press, 1972.

The Mental Health Service after Unification. Report of the Tri-
    partite Committee of the Royal College of Psychiatrists, the
    Society of Medical Officers of Health, and the British Medical
    Association. London: B.M.A., 1972.

National Association for Mental Health. Co-ordination or chaos?
    The rundown of psychiatric hospitals. N.A.M.H. MIND Report
    No. 13, 1974.

Policy for Action. A symposium on the planning of a comprehensive
    district psychiatric service. Cawley, R. H., & McLachlan, G.
    (Eds.), 1973.

Popper, K. R. The open society and its enemies. London: Routledge
    & Kegan Paul, 1945.

Roberts, L. M., Halleck, S. L., & Loeb, M. B. (Eds.). Community
    Psychiatry. Madison: Univ. of Wisconsin Press, 1966.

Royal Commission on the law relating to mental illness and mental
    deficiency. London: H.M.S.O. Command No. 169, 1957.

Sabshin, M. Theoretical models in community and social psychiatry.
    In Community Psychiatry, pp. 15-30. Roberts, L. M., Halleck,
    S. L., & Loeb, M. B. (Eds.) Madison: Univ. of Wisconsin Press,
    1966.

Schumach, M. Shift in mental-hospital theory. New York Times,
    Aug. 20, 1974.

Shepherd, M., Cooper, B., Brown, A. C., & Kalton, G. W. Psychiatric illness in general practice. London: Oxford Univ. Press, 1966.

Wing, J. K. Social psychiatry. Brit. J. Hos. Med., 5, pp. 153-156, 1971.

Wing, J. K. The Camberwell Register and the development of evaluative research. In Evaluating a Community Psychiatric Service: The Camberwell Register, pp. 3-9, 1964-1971. Wing, J. K., & Hailey, A. M. (Eds.) London: Oxford Univ. Press, 1972.

Wing, J. K., Bennett, D. H., Hailey, A. M., Isaacs, A. D., & Tidmarsh, D. Camberwell and its services before 1964. In Evaluating a Community Psychiatric Service: The Camberwell Register, 1964-1971, pp. 41-76. Wing, J. K., & Hailey, A. M. (Eds.) London: Oxford Univ. Press, 1972.

Wing, J. K., & Brown, G. W. Institutionalism and schizophrenia. London: Cambridge Univ. Press, 1970.

Wing, J. K., & Hailey, A. M. Evaluating a community psychiatric service: The Camberwell Register 1964-1971. London: Oxford Univ. Press, 1972.

Woodhead, G. S., & Varrier-Jones, P. C. Industrial colonies and village settlements for the consumptive. London: Cambridge Univ. Press, 1920.

Part V

PLANNING AND IMPLEMENTING

MODELS FOR CHANGE

THE DEVELOPMENT, EVALUATION, AND DIFFUSION OF

REHABILITATIVE PROGRAMS: A SOCIAL CHANGE PROCESS

George Fairweather

Michigan State University

East Lansing, Michigan

The central theme of this conference concerns alternatives to mental hospital treatment. Taking the title literally, it means to me that different treatment programs have been found which are considered more beneficial to patients than the treatment afforded in the contemporary mental hospital. Secondly, the title implies that such alternatives are available to the mental health professionals in our society. The undergirding for this entire process, quite obviously, is the process of change because alternatives to mental hospital programs are not possible unless there is a change in the social organization of not only the mental hospital but of mental health organizations generally. Therefore, I would like to concentrate my remarks upon the process of how such change can be achieved. In the course of the discussion I will describe the contemporary "lodge society" which was developed as an alternative to the mental hospital and evaluated by myself and several colleagues over a span of many years.

There are essentially two processes involved in creating change in social organizations. The first process is the creation of new models and, from a scientific point of view, these models have to be demonstrated to be valid alternatives to the existing social practice, in this case the mental hospital. To put it differently, no new model can, in the long run, be considered a viable alternative to the mental hospital unless its outcomes have been shown to be demonstrably more beneficial. The second process is the process of the dissemination of such beneficial models. Here again, we enter an area of ignorance since little experimental work has been done in implementation processes. Here, I am differentiating between surveys, participant observations, and other forms of data

If we could create problem solving groups of patients who could take care of one another and we could then move them into the community as groups, perhaps they could care for one another there, at least for a period of time which would permit them to stabilize themselves in a new community role. Thus patients' recidivism could be reduced while making a more adequate adjustment. But this, in turn, raised the question of how such groups could be created. This question eventually led to a second five year experiment in which a small group program was created in a hospital ward and contrasted with a ward which maintained the typical supervisory staff and subordinate patients roles (Fairweather, 1964). This work-only situation was, as you will recall, as equally effective in the hospital setting as any other commonly used program as shown in the previous study. The purpose of this small group study was to attempt to understand the parameters of problem solving groups and to answer such questions as: Could such groups be created? If so, what type of leadership would they need? What would the composition be? What kind of communication patterns would develop? What type of reward systems were essential? and so on. The experiment was instituted and again it had a follow-up period.

Very briefly, the findings from this study showed that small groups of problem solving patients could in fact be formed, even though the membership was mainly chronically hospitalized patients. However, in order that problem solving could be obtained and cohesiveness or a sense of belongingness fostered several variables had to be operative. A few selected ones were:

1.   The groups had to function autonomously without staff members present because the mere presence of staff members in a group reduced patient participation and willingness to assume responsibility for their own conduct. So staff roles were changed. Staff members were used to feed-back information about group performance to the group itself but they did not meet with the group or interfere in any way with group decision-making except to reward them for valid and valuable group decisions.

2.   A meaningful reward system had to be established to reinforce motives and responsible group decisions. This was accomplished by sanctioning group control over money and time out of the hospital for visits and trial employment.

3.   Communication processes between staff and the small groups had to be developed that did not result in advocating what the group action should be since the groups had to establish their own problem solving norms.

4.   Heterogenity of group composition was found to be essential. A distribution of social activity and degree of impairment among the group members was necessary or it could not function well. Thus if all chronic and inactive

persons were assigned to a group, it could not function
adequately. Groups needed to function as a team. When
one member could not function well another had to be able
and willing to assume his role.

This program resulted in a very high morale by both patients
and staff contrasted with the work-only condition. Thus by contrast
with the control ward the morale of the small group ward was very
high, staff morale was high, social behaviors were much improved,
social perceptions were much more realistic, and so on. Alas, however, when the follow-up period occurred and members of the small
group program returned to the community - individual homes, hotels,
or whatever - the recidivism rate between this program and its
control was essentially the same, and approximately the same return
rate was found in this study as was found in the previous five year
study. But there was one encouraging note in this experiment and
that was that a high correlation was established between the sup-
portiveness of the community situation to which the discharged
patient went and the degree of his community adjustmental success.
The more accepting and supportive the community situation, the
longer the ex-patient would remain there. Putting this finding together with the now known parameters of small group functioning
among chronic and hospitalized neurotic patients the next five year
experiment was begun (Fairweather, et al, 1969).

This experiment involved the development of a discharged
patient-run small society which was organized around the principles
of the small group operation discovered in the hospital setting.
The experiment involved the following two treatment models. One
model included the small group program in the hospital where persons
went to traditional community settings and received whatever treatment was prescribed there. It was, in fact, the experimental program
in the previous study. The innovative model involved the hospital
small group program linked directly with the establishment of an
autonomous society in the community. In this model patients went
directly from the hospital small group program to their autonomous
society. Staff roles in that society were all consultative except
for the transition period which occurred over several months. During
that time members from the research team helped the ex-patient group
establish the autonomous society along the lines of the small groups
developed in the hospital setting. Once it was obvious that the
lodge members had behaviorally shown that they could, in fact, operate the small society the staff members gradually withdrew to play
only consultative roles to the lodge members. Eventually the lodge
society became self-supporting with no dependence at all upon the
research or hospital staffs.

The lodge society contrasted with the control program showed
a highly significant reduction in recidivism over a four year span;
a much higher employment record; and an equal amount of job

satisfaction and personal enhancement. Furthermore, the initial
cost per person in the lodge program was only 1/3 of the cost for
the control patients, many of whom remained hospitalized for extensive periods of time; eventually the lodge became self-supporting
with no cost to society at all. The lodge members showed that they
could develop their own business having created a janitorial and
gardening service that eventually became quite monetarily successful.
They set up a governing body and demonstrated that they were indeed
capable of operating a small society as well as taking care of their
own members. By any outcome criteria one wished to use this was a
successful treatment program.

But for those of you unfamiliar, and I doubt there are any here,
with the hierarchial and bureaucratic nature of mental health organizations generally and the stagnation of their organizational structure, it should be easy to guess that even though an overwhelming
amount of scientific evidence had been created to show the advantage
of the lodge society, few mental hospitals were willing to accept
it. The reason clearly was that to accept it demanded rather extensive social role and status changes among professional people. They
had to become problem solvers and had in fact, in the final analysis,
to become consultants rather than supervisors and, indirectly, to
phase themselves out of the patients' society in order to give first-
class citizenship to ex-mental patients. It was this role that was
so difficult for professionals to accept. It was therefore decided
that another five year research effort to disseminate the new model,
which the experimentors felt they had an obligation to do because of
its demonstrated value to mental health hospitals, throughout the
nation would be attempted so that the researchers could explore the
parameters of change itself (Fairweather, Sanders and Tornatzky,
1974). The basic general questions now became: How does one
approach organizations about change? How does one persuade them to
change? How does the process from verbalness to actual action get
implemented? and How does the diffusion of a program occur after
it has been established? To accomplish this a nationwide dissemination experiment was planned and carried out over another five year
time span. This rather complex experiment took place in three
phases.

  1.   The first phase involved an attempt to get volunteers
        who were interested in establishing a lodge society from
        among all mental hospitals in the United States. The
        sample here was comprised of all 255 mental hospitals in
        the country except 8 who were eliminated from the sample
        by random draw. Different conditions of persuasion were
        explored including active to inactive persuasion methods
        which involved written methods, workshops like this one,
        and demonstration programs.
  2.   Another question explored was whether it would make any
        difference if the persons contacted in the institutions

held a high or low social status level there. Thus in
some hospitals superintendents were contacted, in others
the chief of psychiatry or psychology, and in still
others social workers and nurses.
3. Rural and urban hospitals were contrasted for change as
well as federal and state hospitals.

When the list of hospitals was obtained they were matched on
background information and assigned to an active (social action
consultant) or inactive (written condition) for the actual activation of the lodge. The narrative written condition was a manual
which described in great detail every step necessary to create the
lodge society from planning through actual establishment of a work
situation in the community. The social action consultant condition
consisted of giving the same information to the interested implementation group through actual face-to-face consultation rather than
through written material. The attempt here was to discover the
degree to which social change agents were actually essential in
implementing a new social model. Finally, two years after all experimental attempts at dissemination of the lodge society had ended,
a follow-up was made of all 255 mental hospitals to find out the
degree to which unsolicited diffusion occurred.

As you might imagine there were many findings from these inter-
related studies but I shall report only a few of the most significant.
First, it might be important to report some major variables that were
found not to make any difference in determining whether or not a
hospital was willing to change its practices by adopting the lodge
society.
1. First, the amount of money that the hospital had available
was unrelated to change.
2. Geographical area of the hospital was unrelated to change.
3. Federal and state hospitals change at approximately the
same rates.
Some of the variables that were related to change and, in fact,
often were responsible for it were the following:
1. Demonstration programs were significantly more valuable
in leading to change than were written programs or workshops.
2. In every case where change occurred a small group of
individuals within the hospital banded together and
attempted to establish the lodge usually as a result of
their small group ward experiences because of the group
cohesiveness created in the demonstration program.
3. Hospitals with better communication processes between
administrators and staff; superintendents who had had
greater geographic mobility and career moves but who were
not necessarily higher status individuals; hospitals in
which delegation of decision-making from top officials to

staff members had been created, were all positively related to the social change process.
4.   Finally, and this cannot be overemphasized, a change
      agent working with the hospital change group was abso-
      lutely essential to the creation of a lodge society.

Before I shift gears to the more general problem of creating
needed continuous social change in order to correct current outmoded
social systems, I would like to point out that the process of dis-
seminating any innovation, in fact any social innovation, is an
extremely time consuming and difficult process that takes place
over a period of years and that requires continuous attention,
action, and evaluation, if it is to be achieved.

At the outset of this paper I tried to show that alternatives
to hospital treatment programs essentially involved the adoption of
new programs to replace the mental hospital. Basically, this is a
social change process. There are, I believe, two parameters essential for social change in mental hospitals and for that matter, for
social problems everywhere. They involve the creation and the dissemination of social models found to be beneficial through actual
scientific experiments. It is only through actual experiments that
the value of a new innovation and the routes for dissemination can
be determined. Thus society needs, in the mental health area as
well as other human problem areas, to establish what I have called
elsewhere "Centers for Experimental Innovation". It seems absolutely
essential that such centers be established to work directly with the
social administrators in the society and the problem population in
a cooperative effort to create continuously new and innovative models
and to implement them when the usual programs developed and used by
society are not solving the problem for which such programs have
been designed as solutions.

If experimental centers that continuously innovate and evaluate
new social programs and diffuse them through experimental techniques
are to be established, it will require a major investment on the
part of local, state and federal governments. Further, it would
mean that scientific techniques would need to be integrated directly
into the social policy making process. Thus, rather than making
decisions about new programs in mental health, for example, through
the avenue of expert knowledge held by any one "expert" or through
political and economic processes acceptable to the various mental
health power groups, it would require that new programs be attempted
that were different than normative programs and that such programs
would be evaluated to determine their effectiveness. As you can see,
this would also require a continuous training process because new
programs with demonstrated effectiveness would probably require, as
the lodge did, new roles for mental health personnel. They would
have to be trained to play these new roles. This would, of course,
go against the grain of almost all <u>traditional</u> training programs in

the mental health area because they have accepted certain types of
training as basic to the promotion of their professional group
which are designed to inculcate their trainees into the belief
systems and accepted behaviors espoused by that particular professional group. For example, many contemporary training programs
in the field of mental health educate individuals only in testing
techniques and psychotherapeutic techniques that have been around
for half a century now without any demonstrable benefit occurring
to those who participate in them through actual comparative experiments. And worse, these programs do not train individuals to innovate new programs nor even to place a high value on evaluating the
outcomes of programs. What I am trying to pinpoint here is that
the willingness on the part of mental health professionals to
create a center which could be used to continuously invent new
treatment models, and disseminate them through experimental techniques so that in the future ineffective treatment and dissemination
processes could be eliminated and replaced by new, more effective
processes, is an essential element in determining whether or not
they will be created. Such change processes would require a degree
of flexibility not generally associated with mental health professionals and their training programs. It would also require that
people at least be willing to question their basic assumptions
about the "causes and cures" of mental illness itself.

Assuming, however, that this barrier of resistance to change
could be overcome and a sufficient number of persons in the mental
health area were interested in establishing centers for the purpose
of program innovation and evaluation, what would the necessary
ingredients for such a center be. In my judgment there are at
least seven essential ingredients. They are:

1.   Democratic organization;
2.   Freedom of inquiry;
3.   Longevity;
4.   Operational control of treatment programs;
5.   Dissemination ability;
6.   Training opportunities; and
7.   A multidisciplinary orientation.

Let us briefly examine each of these necessary ingredients in
turn. First and foremost in American society it is necessary that
such an organization be democratic. To accomplish this the concerned representatives of three primary groups need to be involved
in planning new social treatment models as well as in the experimental aspects of diffusing them. They are the mental health
administrators, the patient population, and the researchers themselves. Any program that hopes to be successful must be acceptable
to all ghree groups as an alternative to contemporary practice before it should be placed in operation in an actual setting for
evaluation. Such a process maintains the contribution of the three

groups involved and gives the persons who plan the programs as well
as those who will be the participants an active voice in what the
program will be. In addition, it permits the scientists who have
an interest in the problem to make a substantial contribution to
the planning process itself. Thus, any new social treatment
innovation is a result of the combined decision-making process of
these three groups.

The second aspect that would be necessary for such a center
as an operating principle would be freedom of inquiry. When the
three groups mentioned above decide upon the possible value of a
particular treatment evaluation it is essential that they arrange
to create the new treatment model without undue pressure from outside, including various mental health power groups that might oppose
the program for selfish reasons even prior to its evaluation. It is
very often the case that mental health organizations become "captives"
of various professional groups so that the possibility of innovation
is very limited. From this perspective the researchers should be
able to attempt to view any treatment program as not sacrosanct so
that its benefit or lack of beneficial outcomes could be evaluated
without bias.

Another important characteristic of such a research center
would be the need for longevity. The past studies that we have
reviewed show that the solution to problems like those of mental
illness and probably the solution to most human social problems are
a gradual process requiring successive approximations to problem
solution. It is highly unlikely that any single research would
reveal immediately the solution to a particular problem. Furthermore, when new treatments are created they will have to be implanted
in the appropriate setting and actually carried out in order that
they can be evaluated and this takes time. Persons within the
research centers would thus need to be funded for long periods of
time so that the problem solving experimental approach could be
established and maintained.

Such treatment evaluation and evaluation of social programs
generally occurs without the researchers having any control over
the program that they are attempting to evaluate. For example,
often researchers are called in to evaluate a particular mental
health program without any voice in what program is established or
how it ought to be carried out. Furthermore, most service programs
operate without a knowledge of the need for the experimental control
required for actual evaluation and hence it is not possible to
evaluate most of them in a regular service context. It is therefore essential that new programs be established so that sufficient
operational control lies in the hands of the researchers so that
they can carry out the new treatment plans in a research context.
Without such control treatment programs cannot be evaluated. They

can only be monitored, viewed, guessed about, and the like, but they cannot be experimentally evaluated.

A research center of the type I envision would also have to have a dissemination capability. As shown in the research about the lodge society there were few ready takers for the lodge even after a great deal of scientific information had been amassed to show its benefits. This, of course, is understandable because most persons who have studied the process of the diffusion of innovations, in whatever field they may have occurred, have found that unless there is a strong effort to "sell" the new innovation to other persons who can use it there is little likelihood that the new innovation will become a constructive force in the society. What this means is that simply creating and evaluating a new program does not insure that it will be widely used by others regardless of how successful the research shows it actually is. The diffusion effort is therefore an essential part of any social change process and is central to the experimental center for social innovation visualized here.

Such a center could and should provide training opportunities for mental health personnel who will need to be trained for the new roles found through continuous innovative treatment experiments. In addition, the center should provide training for a new generation of socially conscious scientists who themselves should not only participate in the research endeavors of the center but become advocates for more scientifically valid humanitarian programs. It is just such training that the center could provide since it is rarely, if ever, available in univeristy settings or in other field settings.

Finally, any such program should be multidisciplinary in nature. It is important to understand that dealing with problems of mental illness at its broadest social level is not the province of any particular discipline. This is the case because programs designed for the mentally iss are political, economic, psychological, medical, legal, sociological, and religious to name a few of the involved disciplinary areas. In order to design adequate treatment programs, therefore, the approach to them must include variables from all of the concerned disciplines that have been historically considered separate areas of investigation.

The next question one might ask is where such centers could be located since very clearly they will need to have organizational support. Let us briefly review some of the responsibilities such a center would have and try to discover what the assets and liabilities of such organizations might be. First of all, let us look closely at a university setting.

A university would seem to have all the necessary ingredients. It would promote freedom of inquiry. It would have the training

facilities and a number of people who have worked historically on
social problems from different perspectives. However, there are
many disadvantages to a university setting. First of all, univer-
sities rarely have been willing to make a commitment to community
activities and often have a negative attitude toward "applied"
contrasted with "basic" scientific endeavors. While, to me at least,
this is a shibboleth with social status connotations, the perceptions
still exist in the university setting. Furthermore, individual
departments in their constant search for political and economic
power often prevent a multidisciplinary researcy effort because of
their disciplinary chauvanism. But the biggest drawback to univer-
sities as a location for the center is that they rarely control the
field settings where such researches would have to be carried out.
For this reason they would not be an entirely appropriate place for
the organizational location of such research centers.

We might then ask what about mental health governmental agencies.
They often have control of field settings and do in fact administer
both research and service programs. However, here again there are
additional drawbacks not the least of which is that very often governmental organizations in the health area severely limit freedom of
inquiry and thus the possible innovations that might develop. This
often occurs because these governmental organizations have adopted
a particular social policy which they demand that their subordinate
groups implement. Furthermore, there may be short-term longevity
because funding frequently changes for projects as the administrators
of the organizations change. Again the drawbacks for the location
of the centers for experimental innovation seem to outweigh their
positive advantages.

Another place such centers could be established would be in
the private economic sector of the society. Examples of this location can be found in the current work of the drug industry and the
contracting for some human service programs by various industries.
While it would appear that many of the necessary ingredients could
be found in the private sector such as freedom of inquiry, a multidisciplinary approach, and the like, there appear several disadvantages to locating a center for experimental social innovation
for mental health treatment programs in the private sector. Foremost among them is their lack of control over service organizations.
Even if they could create their own service programs there is the
further problem that most private research groups become dependent
on governmental funding to supply the capital for their research
investment. Thus they often become "captives" of the government
and in actuality become advocates for the governmental programs
rather than experimenters investigating their validity.

Generally then, it appears that centers for experimental social
innovation will have to be set up relatively independently but with

some joint relationship with existing organizations so that they can accomplish their mission without becoming subject to the political and economic pressures that would inevitably limit their creativeness. Given the need to incorporate the seven properties of an adequate center mentioned earlier, a location that would seem to be most appropriate would be one "in between" the university and the government. From the university side, freedom of inquiry could be maintained through academic appointments but the independence of the center from interfering academic practices would permit it to bring together scientists from separate disciplines who could focus their attention upon treatment problems in a multidisciplinary fashion without violating the separate discipline norms of the university. In addition, the linkage with the university could provide a training group - it could provide professional trainees for the center where training activities would be going on in both service and research aspects of treatment. From the governmental side one could obtain access to service programs as well as to mechanisms for the diffusion of innovations once they have been found. A separate funding of such an organization through university channels would provide the independence of the organization from political domination by legislators and government administrators.

In order to "pay their way" the researchers could engage in some selected researches requested by the government while reserving time and funds for innovative research solely at their discretion. This would provide a needed service to the government - evaluating their existing social programs - but would permit the scientists, social programmers and problem population, to plan and carry out new treatment programs that they believe would improve treatment service. This research team - scientists, administrators, representatives of the problem population - could also undertake implementation experiments like those done with the lodge society. Thus the center could provide an evaluative and innovative arm for social policy.

I have attempted in this paper to mention what appears to me to be some of the essential characteristics needed to innovate alternatives to the mental hospital and to implement them. First of all, it seemed important to recognize that alternatives to any program, if they are to have any substantive meaning, require social change. The two necessary processes of social change are innovation and innovation dissemination. However, without adequate scientific evaluation the benefit of any innovation and the manner in which it might be diffused will remain unknown. It is therefore necessary to launch an experimental effort, a constant and continuing experimental effort, in both treatment innovation and diffusion. This can probably best be accomplished through the creation of centers for social innovation which would be located in organizational space somewhere between the university and governmental agencies. The centers would serve as a focal point to bring together administrators

of mental health programs, persons directly interested in the treatment process, including both staff and patients, and a group of
interested and concerned scientists. Together this group can plan
innovation and carry out the needed research provided the support
of both the university community and the governmental organization
permits the longitudinal research effort needed. Without such an
effort it seems very clear to me that alternatives to mental
hospitals will continue to be rarely used by society even when they
are found and evaluated. And in this context mental health treatment programs will continue to depend upon what treatment programs
are available to mental patients which are often a function of the
political and economic power of certain groups as well as the
theoretical biases of the mental health organizations and their
spokesmen. This process of treatment program adoption will, in my
judgment, inevitably lead to bureaucratic stagnation and rigidity
as now seems to be the case in many mental hospitals. But this
need not be the case. New programs exist and more will be found
that can replace the patients' lowly social position with first-
class citizenship in this society. To accomplish this requires
continuous social change in which experimentation is a key element.

REFERENCES

Fairweather, G.W., Simon, R., Gebbhard, M.E., Wingarten, E.,
   Holland, J.L., Sanders, R., Stone, G.B., and Reahl, J.E.
   Relative effectiveness of psychotherapeutic programs: A
   multicriteria comparison of four programs for three different
   patient groups. Psychology Monographs, American Psychological
   Association, 1960, 74(5, 492).

Fairweather, G.W. (Ed.) Social Psychology in Treating Mental
   Illness: An Experimental Approach. New York: John Wiley
   and Sons, 1964.

Fairweather, G.W., Sanders, D.H., Maynard, H., and Cressler, D.L.
   Community Life for the Mentally Ill: An Alternative to
   Institutional Care. Aldine Publishing Company, 1969.

Fairweather, G.W., Sanders, D.H., and Tornatzky, L.G. Creating
   Change in Mental Health Organizations. Pergamon Press, 1974.

Fairweather, G.W. Social Change: The Challenge to Survival.
   New Jersey: General Learning Press, 1972.

Jones, M. The Therapeutic Community: A New Treatment Method in
   Psychiatry. New York: Basic Books, 1953.

ALTERNATIVES TO MENTAL HOSPITAL TREATMENT:

A SOCIOLOGICAL PERSPECTIVE

David Mechanic

University of Wisconsin

Madison, Wisconsin

As the papers in this volume indicate, there has been an
impressive growth of attention devoted to the management of
psychotic disorders in the community as compared with hospital
contexts. The encouragement for this emphasis has come from
various quarters: changes in philosophical and administrative
attitudes concerning the retention of the mentally ill in mental
hospitals, altered funding patterns, and the growth of a vigorous
civil liberties movement on behalf of the mentally ill (Golann
and Fremouw, 1976). The development and refinement of drug therapy
for psychotic conditions, which alleviated the most blatant and
bizarre manifestations of the psychoses, gave the hospital, the
community, and the families of the mentally ill increased confidence that this displacement of responsibility was feasible and
productive (Mechanic, 1969). While this social movement was to
some extent encouraged and supported by research on the rehabilitative process, the fact was and still remains that we have
only the most crude understanding of the social forces in the
community that help contain psychotic behavior and help maintain
the psychotic at a reasonable level of social functioning.

While there have been an impressive number of community
demonstrations of the feasibility of alternatives to hospitalization, and some evidence of atrocities when responsibility for
maintaining an adequate system of services was not exercised, much
of our experience has been gained through trial and error and not
through any sophisticated theory of intervention. While a body of
research did develop, documenting the erosive influences of

custodial dependency and inactivity, much of our more positive
evidence of the ability to successfully contain psychotic behavior
in the community came from a large number of demonstration programs,
carried out in different communities, that developed ad hoc explanations to account for the results achieved. Much of the research
reported in this book stems from the good sense and wisdom of
clinicians concerned with community care rather than from any
consistent theoretical framework or sophisticated understanding
of basic processes.

As we look to the future, we would do well to strive more
vigorously for a systematic perspective that more clearly poses
the research and evaluation issues that must be dealt with if
community care alternatives to hospitalization are to develop more
focused and targeted interventions to deal with the great variety
of problems that continue to persist. These problems are obvious
at the level of individual functioning of the psychotic patient,
at the level of the community and the social and social psychological processes affecting the provision of services and their outcomes, and at the more global social and political level as it
affects the definitions and care of the mentally ill. I shall
address each of these issues in turn.

INDIVIDUAL FUNCTIONING

At the level of individual functioning we still have a great
deal to learn about the range of intervening variables that play
an important part in the progression of mental illness. These
intervening variables may characterize the person: his biological
constitution, his individual capacities, his values, life orientations, and coping devices. Or they may be characteristic of the
larger social environment as typified by the degree of stress,
stimulation, or noxious agents to which he is exposed, the social
assaults that characterize his life situation, and the network of
social supports available to him. In thinking about problems of
studying adaptation, I have found it useful to consider five types
of deficiencies affecting the disruption of effective behavior.
This classification may be a useful way to organize our thinking
about the intervening variables that require more study, and they
might possibly be useful in designing services for psychotic
patients.

1. A major impediment to effective social functioning is the
lack of material resources necessary to sustain the person or social
group. While the link between poverty and illness is certainly not
direct, the lack of material resources contributes to the problems
of adaptation among vulnerable persons and increases the probability

of disorganized behavior. Brenner (1973), for example, has found
that economic recessions are followed by increased admissions to
mental hospitals, and he makes a reasonable case that these correlations are not easily explained simply as a result of changing
definitions of disorder under changing economic conditions.

At the most primitive level, the adequacy of nutrition and
shelter is central. Inadequate nutrition, in particular, has been
linked to a general vulnerability and increased mortality resulting
from disease, and affects both social and intellectual development.
In reference specifically to psychotic patients, there are continuing indications of gross deficiencies in the material environment
necessary for a minimal standard of living quality. As communities
have mounted political pressures to resist board and care facilities,
halfway houses, and outpatient facilities, mental health departments
have often followed the line of least resistance, locating such
facilities in the most ecologically disorganized areas of the city.
Patients in such areas suffer high risk of victimization and may
further be exposed to the anomie and hopelessness that frequently
pervade these environments.

2.   Lack of Appropriate Skills. The adequacy of any social
group or of individuals depends on the effectiveness of cultural
preparation and the availability of problem-solving tools necessary
to deal with their environments. What may be an ordinary situation
to those with skills or otherwise adequate cultural preparation is
a crisis for those who lack them. As care for psychotic patients
has increasingly been provided in community contexts, it has become
more apparent how frequently such patients lack basic skills
essential for everyday living. While the problem of the psychoses
extends well beyond inadequacies of skills and cultural preparation,
the absence of these skills, or their erosion due to the chronic
course of the illness, very much exacerbates the problems of such
patients in the community. It makes it more difficult for them to
find and maintain employment, to establish functional interpersonal
relationships, to enjoy adequate living quarters, and to avoid
difficulties with the authorities. Moreover, the dependency of
the chronic psychotic patient means that these patients are likely
to have continuing contacts with official bureaucracies, and skills
in handling these become important for their satisfactory community
adjustment. Some interesting efforts have been initiated to assist
chronic schizophrenics in improving everyday skills on the assump-
tion that these contribute not only to more adequate social functioning, but also help avoid repeated rehospitalizations. While the
evidence is not all in, there are indications that this approach
facilitates more effective community performance, at least in the
short run.

Speaking more generally, there is a growing body of evidence suggesting that the movement of population from one environment to another, such as from rural to industrial life and from country to city, is associated with a higher prevalence of disease of a variety of kinds (Dubos, 1959). Perhaps the group least fitted for major social and cultural change, but subjected to it as a matter of course, are chronic psychotic patients who increasingly reside in unfamiliar settings with limited social supports. Although we still lack definite evidence to suggest that providing simple skills contributes to a more favorable course in the progression of psychosis, it would seem prudent to give this area greater emphasis than at present.

3. <u>Lack of Adequate Defenses</u>. Man's ability to engage in effective behavior depends not only on constitution and past preparation, but also on psychological capacities to deal with signals of danger and hopelessness that hamper continued coping efforts. Cultural and personal devices must be available to the person to contain and control feelings that hamper long-term adaptations and to facilitate continued attention to ordinary activities rather than to flight. It is well established that schizophrenic patients have difficulties in dealing with intense personal relationships, for whatever reason, and patients with a vulnerability to depression appear to be unusually susceptible to situations in which they suffer a sense of loss.

Building stronger personal defenses is perhaps the most difficult aspect of improving adaptation, yet this is the area where traditional psychiatry and psychoanalysis have devoted their greatest emphasis. We have no good evidence that we can successfully alter the defensive processes of psychotic patients even when great effort is devoted to this task. Perhaps a more indirect and effective route is through building social supports. Here an analogy from the accident field is instructive. Health education programs have thus far found it relatively futile to alter significantly the incidence of automobile accidents through attempts to modify driving behavior. But we know that technological and legal aspects, such as seat belts, highway construction, auto design, and speed limits, have very significant effects on the occurrence of injuries and fatalities (Haddon, Suchman, and Klein, 1964). If there is a technological side to the treatment of the psychoses it lies in how we socially organize the provision and monitoring of drug use and the efforts we make to develop viable networks of services and social support.

4. <u>Lack of Adequate Social Supports</u>. It is a truism that men are interdependent, and successful functioning depends on the material assistance and emotional support we receive from our

fellows. The absence of such supports makes people vulnerable to
interpersonal and environmental assaults and a variety of other
adversities (Cobb, 1976; Cassel, 1976). Often the knowledge itself that help is accessible gives people the confidence to cope.
But during times of difficulty we depend very heavily on the
assistance and moral support of others. Psychotic patients in the
community are particularly vulnerable because supports are frequently unavailable. First, such patients often have difficulty
in close relationships with others. Second, over the course of
time their bizarre behavior and life difficulties have often
resulted in the alienation of family and significant others. Third,
such patients often fail to maintain contact with services unless
the pattern of services is well organized and aggressive. In short,
chronic psychotics are not only very likely to lack such supports,
but they also are least likely to effectively seek them out. Although psychoactive drugs are important in the community maintenance of chronic psychotic patients, these patients often fail
to maintain their drug therapy and often stop using drugs when
their social functioning and psychological state are most tenuous.
Without well-organized and aggressive services such patients are
often lost in the community and eventually end up in difficulty.
Thus far we have had severe problems in developing and maintaining
well-organized patterns of supportive care.

    5.   Sustained Motivation. Social adaptation depends on a
continuing willingness to remain engaged and on a commitment to
ongoing social activities. While withdrawal is a natural and
often an effective means of reducing a sense of threat in the
short run, it becomes highly maladaptive in a social sense if it
persists as a continuing pattern. As people deal with problems
by withdrawing, their skills and social contacts tend to erode; and
they eventually come to develop a sense of hopelessness.

    One of the things we have learned very well in the care of
the psychotic patient is that withdrawal and inactivity lead to
an erosion of the patient's capacity to continue or to regain
important social roles (Wing & Brown, 1970). The specific
activity of the patient seems less important than that he remain
actively involved, in contact with other people, and constrained
to some degree by social expectations. While we have a difficult
time unraveling cause from effect, it seems clear that for such
patients structure that involves some demands, without overtaxing
their ability to conform, contributes to a higher level of social
functioning.

    In short, I believe that these five areas of inquiry and
programming at the level of individual functioning--material resources, skills, defenses, social supports, and sustained motiva-
tion--provide a perspective that makes explicit some of the

challenges we face. I now turn to a consideration of factors
affecting the provision of services and their outcomes.

SOCIAL AND SOCIAL-PSYCHOLOGICAL FACTORS

AFFECTING THE PROVISION OF SERVICES AND THEIR OUTCOMES

It is well-known that the factors contributing to mental disorders may be different from those leading to social intervention
and care or cooperation with treatment programs. The referral of
mental patients to services depends on the nature of their manifest symptoms, subcultural tolerance for deviant behavior, and
the degree of disturbance caused by the patient in a particular
social context (Mechanic, 1968). Similarly, there are wide varia-
tions in the extent to which patients or significant others will
cooperate with community efforts to assist them. Such problems
may be particularly acute in the case of chronic alcoholism, drug
addiction, and schizophrenia.

While it is important to understand the social and cultural
characteristics that lead patients and their families to resist
definitions of disorder and treatment efforts, it is even more
crucial for psychiatric services to be aware of how their own
patterns of organization may hinder accessibility and effective use
of assistance. First, it is necessary to establish that the treatment program itself is one that a reasonable man or woman could
wish to take advantage of. Unfortunately, much of the care available for patients with mental impairments could not pass this
rather simple test, and one of the contributions of community care
innovations is that they offered alternatives to the rather dreary
care available in most mental hospitals.

At a more conceptual level, we have learned that health
delivery systems, even when they involve no financial barriers to
care, erect a variety of other social and psychological barriers
that keep certain patients out of their systems or induce a lack
of continued participation and cooperation. There is a wide variety
of ways in which services come to be rationed: by the resources
provided to deal with a given patient load, and the limitation of
these resources; by the location of sites of care, and the difficulties involved for patients and their families in reaching such
locations; by creating social distance between providers and
patients by overprofessionalization and other barriers to communication; by waiting time to obtain services and other noneconomic
costs that divert those who particularly have ambivalence about
using services to begin with; and by the stigmatization of patients
and their families (Mechanic, 1976).

The organization of effective community care in contrast to hospital programs requires a major shift from more traditional bureaucratic perspectives to more organic organizational concepts. While even the most traditional and hierarchical mental hospital organization had to be attuned to some extent to its larger social and political environment, its programs were relatively insulated and separated from community visibility and pressures; and such organizations maintained their own bureaucratic cultures. Although there has been in recent years considerable innovation in staff roles in many of these institutions, the fact is that such hospitals continued to retain relatively rigid professional role structures, and each of the relevant professional groups staked out its own territory and professional routine. The rather marked shift to treatment of psychiatric patients in community voluntary hospitals also followed this bureaucratic emphasis. Indeed, these hospitals are so wedded to the traditional medical model that the psychiatric units tend in their organization to resemble the typical medical services in which different psychiatrists, responsible for varying patients, pass through during the day to make rounds but take little responsibility for the milieu or for dealing with patients' secondary disabilities.

In contrast, effective community care must be exceedingly sensitive to its environment and give attention to such varied concerns as community acceptance, the employment market, the integrity of the welfare and social services system, housing availability, and relationships with police and other social agencies (Mechanic, 1973). Professionals involved in the administration of such programs must be on the scene, their ears to the ground, away from the usual insulation, security, and lack of realism of the professional office. Putting it somewhat differently, the professional in the community care context is a facilitator, coordinator, and integrator. He must become tolerant of more fluid roles and relationships, and be able to work on a more equal basis with a wide range of other mental health professionals as well as with community participants. In this context he is no longer afforded the protection of his medical status or his medical mystique.

Speaking in the lingo of the organizational theorist, there is a variety of reasons explaining why classical models of organizational functioning cannot fit the provision of human services at the community level: the goals are too many and varied and often intangible; the technologies available are not clearly specified and often uncertain; the environment in which programs must operate is unpredictable and changing; the requirements for action in any particular case cannot be unconditionally specified; and the professionals themselves tend to be cosmopolitans with value systems that lead them to reject, subvert, and

manipulate traditional bureaucratic rules and structures. In
contrast, an organic model of organizational functioning is more
attuned to the realities of community care. The name of the game
is coordination, and individuals must engage in definition and
redefinition of tasks as they relate to others also involved in
programming. Responsibilities are fluid and somewhat open-ended,
and the task above all requires commitment that goes beyond the
application of any particular technical function. Professionals
in this context become brokers who must negotiate among varying
interests and agencies, and effectiveness resides in the ability
to get things done, and not in a traditional authority structure,
special degrees, or the mask of medical competence.

     In my judgment, the most difficult tasks in any community
treatment program are instilling and maintaining a sense of
commitment and momentum among program personnel. All of the
experiments reported in this volume, although exciting on their
own terms, have yet to demonstrate that these programs can maintain
their early momentum over long periods of time or communicate their
enthusiasm to others. Yet the conditions they treat are chronic
and difficult, and often intractable, and require effective and
aggressive services over the long range. In the early stages of
any new program there is a sense of excitement and innovation.
Both personnel and patients feel that something new is being
attempted and accomplished. The energy that comes from such
involvement is a very powerful treatment force, but it is difficult to maintain over the long haul. People get tired; they seek
to regularize their work patterns; they desire to control the
uncertainties and unpredictabilities in their environment. Thus
they tend to push toward the bureaucratization of roles and the
clear-cut definition of responsibilities and turfs; and they become
smug about their own failures, less sensitive to the problems of
their clients, and less committed to the jobs that have to be done.

     I am not aware of any organizational system that has been able
to deal effectively with the problem. The Chinese experiment involves collective mobilization, social disruption, and professional
reeducation as a means of dealing with natural tendencies toward
bureaucratization; but, of course, we would like to find somewhat
less profound methods of maintaining commitment to social goals.
There are some techniques that are available for encouraging
commitment--some less disruptive than others. Perhaps the most
typical way in our own society is by recruitment and turnover of
personnel. This brings to the organization people who are fresh,
enthusiastic, and who have new concepts. In the health services
area, however, continuity is essential, and the costs of professional turnover beyond some point may well exceed the benefits.
The most viable alternative, in my view, is to maintain a sense

of participatory democracy among program personnel. Personnel must
be allowed to modify programs from time to time, not so much because the changes themselves will be an improvement, but because
participants will feel more enthusiastic about and more committed
to programs that they helped formulate and in which they have a
stake.

If we have learned nothing else in recent years, we have
learned that community care for chronic mental patients, without
sustained efforts of follow-up and support, is an invitation to
a new type of erosion of human potential, except now it occurs in
a community and not in a custodial institution. With the shift
to community care we have also learned to what extent professionals
can be a disservice to patients under the guise of treatment when
they engage in excessive restrictions and foster dependency. We
must remain vigilant to the fact that care that encourages
dependency rather than incentives to cope can be exceedingly
detrimental. Similarly, focusing on life difficulties and symptoms in contrast to potential assets and strengths may reinforce
an illness behavior pattern which reduces coping effectiveness.
Mental health professionals must never forget that chronicity of
illness is one of the few widely and recognized reasons for failing to meet social responsibilities. While mental patients obviously have major handicaps that require persistent and sympathetic
professional efforts, the mental health professional must be alert
to the possibility that he may be reinforcing ineffective behavior.

The language of social behavior, of course, has moral as well
as scientific import. Our language implies a vocabulary of motives,
and how we characterize the problems of patients has an impact on
their future motives and efforts. One of the major advances of
community care has been an increasing tendency to move away from
deterministic models of social functioning and to encourage
patients to utilize their potential capacities. We must continue
to move in this direction but with empathy and avoidance of a
crass and cynical behaviorism. The effectiveness of community
care will depend on how well we can avoid iatrogenic disabilities
without abandoning a humanitarian perspective. The ability to do
this depends in large part on forces beyond the control of mental
health professionals. It depends on the social and political
context of community care, an issue to which I now turn.

THE SOCIAL AND POLITICAL CONTEXT OF COMMUNITY CARE

One of the major difficulties in organizing community environments for the care of the mentally ill is the lack of predictability
of the social and political climate. Part of the problem also resides in the fact that we have not yet learned how to successfully

balance, or even measure, the social costs for the community
against the advantages and ideologies of community care. Despite
much rhetoric there is continuing difficulty in maintaining a
supportive network of mental health services: in part because of
funding problems and the lack of stability in funding patterns;
in part because of the difficulty in continuing a sense of innovation and momentum in the care of chronic patients, which is a frustrating task (and a problem I have already discussed); in part
because of the difficulties of the reactions and pressures of
communities that accept the idea of community care, but in other
people's communities; and in part because we often just do not
know what we are doing or how to do it.

Anyone involved in serious programming has to be sensitive to
the tremendous gap between the enunciation of goals and their implementation. It is one thing to assert a right to treatment; it
is quite another to get legislatures to appropriate the funds or
to build the network of services required to implement the right.
We can talk about less restrictive alternatives and spin legal
theories, but it's to no avail if we lack choices in levels or
patterns of care. We can theorize about the constructive role of
appropriate work in the rehabilitation of mental patients, and
its contribution to the sense of dignity and self-esteem of the
patient, but we have an uphill battle when ten percent of the labor
force is unemployed, and employers face a buyer's market.

As we have moved a larger proportion of patients into community care contexts, we have come face to face with massive resistance of politicians, communities, and neighborhoods. No one
really has adequate information to assess the extent to which
the problems receiving considerable publicity in New York and
California were characteristic of the nation as a whole, but it
is evident that in most areas of the country there has been
inadequate development of networks of appropriate services consistent with the prevalent rhetoric. A recent inquiry in California,
examining the social functioning of patients in board and care
facilities throughout the state, found that the best predictor of
their levels of integration was the degree of community acceptance
of the facility (Segal and Aviram, 1977). Mental health officials,
instead of making efforts to develop an appropriate community
climate, often follow the line of least resistance, locating
patients in areas that already suffer from disorganization and
anomie. Moreover, there is ample indication that a growing number
of patients, previously managed within the mental health system,
are being processed through the criminal justice system, being
charged with minor and vague violations to justify their removal
from the community.

If we have learned anything from the history of attempts to desegregate schools and busing, we have learned how difficult it is to translate what we believe to be just and reasonable into workable plans. Certainly, mental health officials must give attention to the concentration of mental patients being relocated in the community, if for no other reason than obvious political desire to avoid a community backlash. While the courts have not sustained the right of a community to pass ordinances to restrict the residence of mental patients, it is hard to believe that a community that wishes to do so can be a very healthy place to carry out programs of community integration. Even the most cursory review of the history of mental health law, I believe, would support the proposition that no matter how wise the courts or how passionate the beliefs of public interest lawyers who have come to the defense of the mentally ill, the development of effective and just solutions depends on the larger context of care and the quality of program alternatives that exist. No legal theory or social ideology, no matter how forceful, can substitute for the willingness of the community to provide the resources for adequate care or for the availability of knowledgeable and committed personnel who are willing to struggle with the frustrating problems involved in providing continuing care on a long-term basis for chronic patients.

I think the studies reviewed in this volume indicate that we have learned a good deal in the past two decades about the community management of chronic mental disorders. We have learned that, whatever the biological or genetic characteristics of these conditions may be, they can be exacerbated or contained by the manner in which the patients are defined and managed and by the social climate of treatment. We have learned to locate many of the sources of "institutionalism" and factors promoting secondary disabilities. We are making progress in moving from the prevalent concept that a standard therapy fits all mental illness to more careful description and more targeted interventions. We have become more sophisticated about the character of mental disorders and more aware of the labeling process while at the same time avoiding both a glib disease perspective and a crude labeling approach. Perhaps most important of all we have learned how much there is yet to know, and how difficult it is to implement the things we do know. These understandings are the basis of more serious and effective programs of community care in the future.

REFERENCES

Brenner, H. H. Mental illness and the economy. Cambridge: Harvard University Press, 1973.

Cassel, J.   The contribution of the social environment to host
    resistance. American Journal of Epidemiology, 104:107-123,
    1976.

Cobb, S.   Social support as a moderator of life stress. Psycho-
    somatic Medicine, 38:300-314, Sept.-Oct., 1976.

Dubos, R. Mirage of health. New York: Harper, 1959.

Golann, S., and Fremouw, W. J. (Eds.). The right to treatment for
    mental patients. New York: Irvington, 1976.

Haddon, W. Jr., Suchman, E. A., and Klein, D. (Eds.). Accident
    research: methods and approaches. New York: Harper and Row,
    1964.

Mechanic, D. Medical sociology: a selective view. New York:
    The Free Press, 1968.

Mechanic, D. Mental health and social policy. Englewood Cliffs,
    N. J.: Prentice-Hall, 1969.

Mechanic, D. The sociology of organizations, in Saul Feldman (Ed.),
    The Administration of Mental Health Services. Springfield, Ill.:
    Charles C. Thomas, 1973.

Mechanic, D. The growth of bureaucratic medicine. New York:
    Wiley-Interscience, 1976.

Miller, K. S. Managing madness: the case against civil commitment.
    New York: Free Press, 1976.

Segal, S. P., and Aviram, U. The mentally ill in community-based
    sheltered care: a study of community care and social integration.
    New York: Wiley-Interscience, 1977.

Wing, J. K., and Brown, G. W. Institutionalism and schizophrenia.
    Cambridge: Cambridge University Press, 1970.

LIST OF CONTRIBUTORS

Robert E. Allen, M.D., Assistant Professor, Department of Psychiatry, University of Southern California School of Medicine, Los Angeles, California, 90033.

John H. Beard, M.S.W., Executive Director, Fountain House, 425 W. 47th St., New York, New York, 10036.

Douglas Bennett, F.R.C., Psych., Consultant Psychiatrist, The Bethlem Royal and the Maudsley Hospital, London, England.

David L. Chambers, LL.B., Professor of Law, University of Michigan Law School, Ann Arbor, Michigan, 48104.

Jonathan O. Cole, M.D., Director of Clinical Research, Boston State Hospital, Boston, Massachusetts, 02124.

George Fairweather, Ph.D., Professor of Psychology, Michigan State University, Department of Psychology, East Lansing Michigan, 48824.

George Gardos, M.D., Director of Institute of Research & Rehabilitation, Boston State Hospital, Boston, Massachusetts, 02124.

Robert J. Kleiner, Ph.D., Professor of Sociology, Department of Sociology, Temple University, Philadelphia, Pennsylvania, 19122.

Donald G. Langsley, M.D., Professor and Chairman, Department of Psychiatry, Cincinnati Medical Center, Cincinnati, Ohio, 45267.

David Mechanic, Ph.D., John Bascom Professor of Sociology, Department of Sociology, University of Wisconsin, Madison, Wisconsin, 53706.

Werner M. Mendel, M.D., Professor of Psychiatry, University of Southern California School of Medicine, Los Angeles, California, 90033.

Alma Z. Menn, A.C.S.W., Soteria Project Director, Mental Research
   Institute, Palo Alto, California, 94301.

Loren R. Mosher, M.D., Chief, Center for Studies of Schizophrenia,
   Clinical Research Branch, NIMH Alcohol, Drug Abuse and Mental
   Health Administration, 5600 Fishers Lane, Rockville, Maryland,
   20852.

Michael Nelson, M.D., Clinical Tutor, Department of Psychiatry,
   Massachusetts General Hospital, Boston, Massachusetts, 02114.

Paul R. Polak, M.D., Executive Director, Southwest Denver Mental
   Health Services, Denver, Colorado, 80219.

Leonard I. Stein, M.D., Professor, Department of Psychiatry,
   University of Wisconsin, Madison, Wisconsin, 53706.

Mary Ann Test, Ph.D., Director of Research and Psychology, Mendota
   Mental Health Institute, Madison, Wisconsin 53704.

Bernard Weinman, Ph.D., Director of Research, Philadelphia State
   Hospital, Philadelphia, Pennsylvania, 19114.

John K. Wing, Ph.D., M.D., Professor of Social Psychiatry,
   Institute of Psychiatry, DeCrespigny Park, London, England.

Richard M. Yarvis, M.D., Clinical Director, Division of Mental
   Health, Sacramento Medical Center, Sacramento, California, 95817.